CHINA IN TURMOIL

CHINA IN TURMOIL

Eye-witness, 1924–1948

G. H. GOMPERTZ

LONDON
J. M. DENT & SONS LTD

Made in Great Britain
at the
Aldine Press · Letchworth · Herts
for
J. M. DENT & SONS LTD
Aldine House · Bedford Street · London
First published 1967

CONTENTS

ILLUSTRATIONS

ILLUSTRATIONS

Between pages 98 and 99

ACKNOWLEDGMENTS

CHRONOLOGICALLY my first indebtedness is to the then Miss Barbara Ward, whose keen interest in such writing as I had done during internment encouraged me when I met her in 1947.

Many other friends helped me greatly, but none more so than Mr Alan J. Watson, now, at twenty-five, a B.B.C. 2 commentator and with several books to his credit.

I should also like to record my thanks to the librarians of the Colonial Office and the Royal Commonwealth Society, the Research Department of Surrey County Library's headquarters at Esher, with special mention of their Mr Heissig; also Messrs Matheson & Co. Ltd of Lombard Street, access to whose files of the now defunct *North China Daily News* has been an invaluable corrective to a memory which has sometimes faltered after so many years. To the *Illustrated London News* for permission to reproduce their own artist's picture of the Wanhsien incident. To the National Maritime Museum at Greenwich for factual details of the British gunboats which comprised the Yangtsze Flotilla. Captain A. R. Williamson, O.B.E., D.S.C., R.N.R., also merits very special mention. His personal experiences at the Wanhsien battle, in which he played a notable part; his unrivalled knowledge of the hazards of navigation and of bandits on the upper Yangtsze river—these have been invaluable. If my account of the Wanhsien incident is too tersely matter-of-fact, it is because I have found it hard to divorce myself from the detached and terse phraseology of his own account of the affair. Also to all those friends whose names or actions I have taken in vain throughout the book and to the many writers on China into whose books I have dipped for factual corroboration.

Finally to Mrs Josephine Frazier, whose skilful and indefatigable evening labours, after her normal daily occupations, enabled all my manuscripts to be expertly prepared for publication, and to Mrs Sheila Chennell who, at an earlier stage, was good enough to 'practise her typing' upon a lot of my preliminary work.

My thanks are also due to Miss Heather Williams for drafting the maps.

G. H. G.

INTRODUCTION

This book attempts to portray the life of the expatriate communities in Hongkong and on the coast and rivers of China during the first half of the century, with special emphasis upon the second quarter. All this is woven into the pattern of contemporary events, for the politics of the time decided the fate of expatriate endeavour in the Far East.

These are my justifications for making the attempt: my roots are in Hongkong. I was born there and my father was there for between twenty-five and thirty years as Colonial Service Cadet, Magistrate, Puisne Judge of the Supreme Court and, on a number of occasions, Acting Chief Justice for long periods. After leaving Hongkong in early childhood for education in England, I returned in February 1924 in the service of Jardine, Matheson & Co. Ltd, general merchants. This combination of colonial service background with my own commercial career of over twenty-four years in Hongkong, China and other Far Eastern countries helped me to see the panorama of events of the time, great and small, in better perspective than, I feel, I could otherwise have achieved.

After introductory chapters in which I endeavour to sketch in the historical background, I have tried to bring to life as a consecutive and, to me, fascinating story those years from the early twenties to the late forties, when so much of moment occurred. Inevitably this is a largely personal account of experiences of myself, friends and associates in the many happenings there.

Chiang Kai Shek was the first successful challenger to the rights of the white man in perpetuity to what the early traders and adventurers had won for him. Chiang, who had only accepted Communist help because no other power would support him, expelled the Russians in the late twenties. But they had left behind a hard core of dedicated Chinese Communists and, though Chiang had the outward supreme power, Communism seethed in vast areas which he lacked the forces to control or to govern sufficiently well to discourage its growth. But to Japan, with her dreams of world domination, a China united, organized and modernized on her doorstep was unbearable to contemplate. It mattered not to her whether Chiang Kai Shek or Mao Tse Tung became supreme. She could tolerate neither, so in 1931 began her war with China which, from 1937, accelerated in tempo until it finally merged into the great world conflict in 1941.

But many of the expatriates, with all their faults, had much in them of the stuff of the adventurers of olden times. They had their moments of luxurious living, but they also lived amidst dangers—whether from anti-foreign mobs organized against them, or from the many well-armed bandits who infested the countrysides, or from the constant internal wars which racked China at that time. There were also great cataclysms of nature such as typhoons and floods, whose victims were numbered in millions, and, in the end, the ruthless little Japanese. Through all this time they successfully pursued their varied callings and maintained family and social life.

We should not be ashamed of our former Empire; our Commonwealth is having its difficulties, but a Commonwealth is what our Empire has become. Can France say the same of Vietnam, Algeria and Morocco? The difference surely stems from the manner in which the territories were administered in the days of empire. Our forebears were human and had human weaknesses, but there must have been in them a fundamental integrity which is in short supply today.

In war life can be exciting, can be grim, can be desperately forlorn. For our China communities war in some form was always at hand. Sometimes, like the great cyclonic typhoons, it hung about interminably in the offing, only to sheer off and disperse itself when least expected. Sometimes, when least expected, it struck. Today, throughout Asia, Africa and elsewhere, the world is reaping the harvest sown by Chiang Kai Shek in the twenties. History repeats itself. Is it chance that a keen historian, who had learnt much from past behaviour and misbehaviour patterns of mankind, was able to lead us and to conduct and win the greatest war of all time? If we can see the recent past in perspective, will not this equip us better to cope with our future?

The period of which I write had its moments of bitterness and squalor, moments of greatness and of glamour, moments of splendour, moments of farcical comedy. Sometimes, as befits life, these moments were mixed inextricably. For years I have longed passionately to record something of some of the great but unknown men and women whom I was privileged to meet and know during my years in the Far East. If I have in any measure succeeded, I shall be very happy.

Belmont School,
Dorking.

G. H. GOMPERTZ.

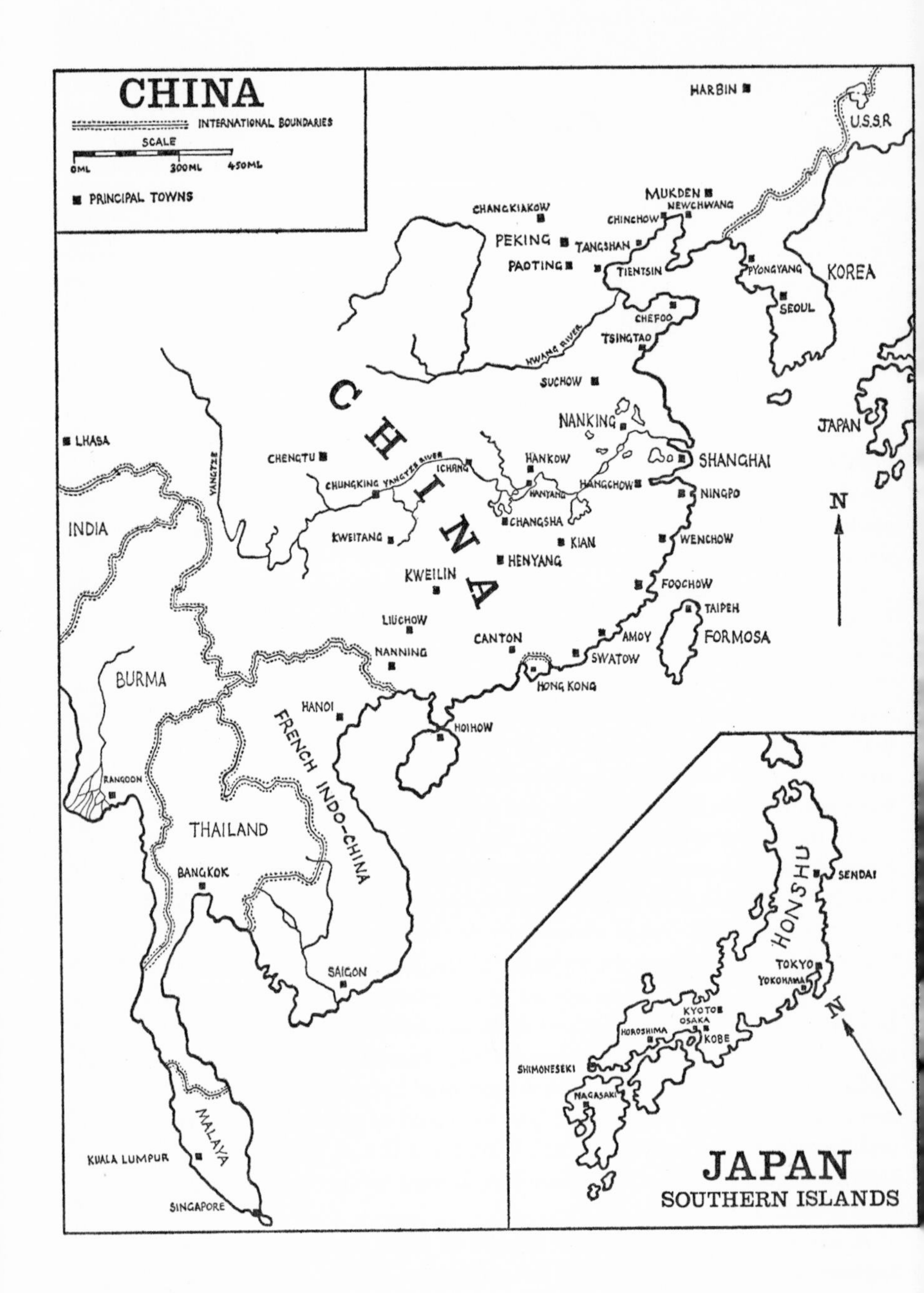
CHINA
INTERNATIONAL BOUNDARIES
SCALE
0ML
300ML
450ML
PRINCIPAL TOWNS
HARBIN
U.S.S.R
MUKDEN
NEWCHWANG
CHANGKIAKOW
CHINCHOW
PEKING
TANGSHAN
PAOTING
TIENTSIN
PYONGYANG
KOREA
SEOUL
CHEFOO
TSINGTAO
HWANG RIVER
SUCHOW
CHINA
NANKING
JAPAN
LHASA
CHENGTU
HANKOW
SHANGHAI
YANGTZE
ICHANG
CHUNGKING
YANGTZE RIVER
HANYANG
HANGCHOW
NINGPO
CHANGSHA
N
INDIA
KWEITANG
KIAN
WENCHOW
HENYANG
KWEILIN
FOOCHOW
TAIPEH
LIUCHOW
AMOY
FORMOSA
CANTON
NANNING
SWATOW
BURMA
HONG KONG
HANOI
FRENCH INDO-CHINA
HOIHOW
RANGOON
THAILAND
BANGKOK
HONSHU
SENDAI
SAIGON
TOKYO
YOKOHAMA
N
KYOTO
OSAKA
HOROSHIMA
KOBE
SHIMONESEKI
NAGASAKI
MALAYA
KUALA LUMPUR
JAPAN
SOUTHERN ISLANDS
SINGAPORE

Part One

CHAPTER ONE
EUROPE IN CHINA

WITH about a third of the twentieth century still to run, one of its most notable trends so far has been the accelerated emergence of under-developed peoples and the corresponding diminution of the influence among them of the hitherto dominant expatriate westerners in their midst.

Perhaps the beginning of it all was in the successful defiance of Imperial Russia by the upstart Japan at the turn of the century. Perhaps there was something of it in the Boer War. But the whole sequence has been something not unlike a series of earth tremors. Once the first starts, who can tell where the next tremor will come? It was in China that these really began and it was in China that the first of the great shocks occurred which have reverberated since, through India, Ceylon, Burma, Indonesia, Malaya, Egypt and Africa as a whole.

For the first time the perpetuity of the rights which the adventurous early traders had established was questioned and challenged. Did the benefits which their early exploitation had brought to the less developed countries justify the virtual sovereignty of the descendants of the old traders for ever? Perhaps the influence of the beginnings of Socialism in the capitalist countries had spread to the under-developed nations. But in earlier days merchant adventurers had risked alone and won or lost alone. Now national governments had become involved and the trading outpost or foreign settler was sponsored by a powerful government with an interest in the *status quo*. One field of great changes was undoubtedly China between World Wars I and II and, when we consider subsequent developments elsewhere, it must surely be regarded as their breeding ground.

A closer examination of some aspects of what occurred in China between the two wars may thus be of interest. Firstly, both for its effects on world trends elsewhere and for its undoubted influence on Japan's emergence as a world power. Secondly, because, in some twenty-five years, an old and long established way of life for British and other largely Western expatriates gradually diminished until it was gone for ever.

Much has been written, and often, of the early dealings of the British with the Chinese people. I do not propose anything more than a rough historical and geographical backcloth which, with the aid of a few sketch-maps for reference, may make the picture of events between the wars more readily comprehensible. Subsequent chapters will be devoted to the happenings of those years in the setting of the social and economic life of the day, with liberal illustration by factual anecdote.

The first direct sea communication with Asia appears to have been established by the Portuguese in the early years of the sixteenth century and, to those who are under the impression that the British were almost the first and certainly the foremost, it is interesting to note that it was in December 1770 that Captain Cook anchored off Batavia to refit on his way home from his first Pacific voyage.

Batavia, already long established by the Dutch, was a very unhealthy port for white people, but was a most necessary adjunct to the growing trade between the East India Company's domain and the China Sea. From about November to March the whole of the western Pacific and the China Seas are dominated by the prevailing north-east monsoon gales, against which it was impossible for sailing ships to make headway to the China Coast from the south. Ships which were too late in the year would therefore be compelled to spend the winter at Batavia and resume their northbound voyage in the spring.

Meanwhile opium had long been cultivated in China for its medicinal properties, and the poppy is indeed indigenous. But the practice of opium smoking appears to have been introduced to China from Formosa in the seventh century, and not by the oft-accused British. So fast did this practice develop that, by the eighteenth century (about 1729), the Imperial Court of China was forced to issue edicts against its use or importation. Thenceforth both its cultivation and its importation were forbidden; but the demand for it was maintained, and Peking and the power of the throne were a thousand miles away from Canton, with communications slow and precarious. The carriage of opium in its own ships was likewise forbidden by the East India Company, whose rule in India was absolute. But 'Country Born' was a name given to

Eurasians in India and 'Country Ships' were vessels of a wide range of mixed national ownerships that were also licensed to trade.

It is odd, but true, that a powerful contributor to the growth of the India-China opium trade was the immense growth of tea drinking in England. It was the 'Country Ships' that carried the opium. The tea trade had grown to such great proportions that it became necessary to find a merchandise which would be acceptable in return. For a time much of Britain's intake of tea from China was paid for in bullion: Lancashire cottons and Yorkshire woollens were offered but not accepted in any great quantities. Opium, on the other hand, was in big demand and was a substitute very popular on both sides.

The 'Government' of the East India Company was, at this time, looking for a market for the opium so widely grown in that country. In Canton local officials also were finding that the smuggling of opium, now that it was contraband, was most profitable to them in bribes. Now and again, to keep the confidence of their distant Government in Peking, a seizure would be made and a convenient scapegoat found in the shape of some foreigner who had, perhaps, been over slow or parsimonious in his hand-out. Trouble was bound to come, and it did. So British men-of-war came to protect or avenge their nationals and soon blew to pieces any antiquated pretences at forts which were supposed to stop them. The foreign devils should have known that it was not the thing to attack a fort which did have big guns in it, even if powder or shot were lacking and the garrison untrained in their effective use.

But the 'face' of local officials and indeed of the Chinese throne was easily saved. The British traders sought nothing but the chance to trade freely and in safety, and that was easily arranged. In the neighbourhood of any big city on coast or river, where they wished to trade, they were allotted a piece of waste ground, a 'Concession', to their Government, and upon this they were allowed to build their trading posts, or 'factories', as they were called in the early days. In these Concessions their own police might function and their own laws prevail, but the sites were usually most unsuitable, often swampy and fever-ridden, or arid and rocky waste lands. It did not take long for enterprise and determination to convert these unpromising satellites into fine modern cities which threw into relief the squalor and filth of the Chinese parent cities beside them, from which foreign settlers were excluded.

Much was made in later times of the imperialism which denied to the Chinese the right to own property or share in the administration of these well-laid-out settlements: this was the basis of the propaganda which finally compelled their surrender to China in the twenties. It cannot be denied that, in the right *milieu*, Chinese industry and capacity for self-government are equal to those of any race in the world. In Malaya, and indeed throughout the Commonwealth and elsewhere, the Chinese who came originally as cheap labour have, in time, infiltrated the whole body politic and shown themselves capable of being admirable citizens and administrators. But the self-satisfied isolation of the old Chinese Empire through so many centuries, under conditions of intense medievalism, had produced a vast mass, something akin to the prehistoric monster, unfit for survival in a modern world. A long tradition of bribery and corruption had saturated the officialdom of the whole nation. A business man would rather die than face failure to keep his bond, and a Chinese Shylock would have found himself with more human meat than he could deal with. But, from court intrigue downwards, the official classes were for centuries utterly rotten and, if there were an occasional would-be honest official at court with sufficient power to get his way, he could do little over so vast and almost roadless a subcontinent. Reference books of a few years ago give the area of China as about 3,380,000 square miles. Today they include Manchuria, Inner Mongolia, Tibet and Sinkiang, which bring the total area to 4,135,000 square miles, which may be compared with a Europe, when measured to the Ural Mountains and Caspian Sea, of about 3,800,000. This immensity, when coupled with the total absence of an honest class amongst the people from which to draw his subordinate administrators, makes it easy to understand the causes of Chiang Kai Shek's downfall in the years that followed the Second World War.

It is probable that the many and various ancestors of the present-day Chinese come from many different centres at many different times: from the north, from the south and from the west by way of the Tarim River basin. The Tarim, little known except to expert geographers, has a length of about a thousand miles, stretching through Sinkiang so far as to run to the north-east of Kashmir and the Karakoram Mountains. Their true home, from wherever they came, seems to have been the lower basin of the Hwang Ho, or Yellow River, but racially and culturally they came to dominate the whole of the original eighteen provinces and, to some extent, Japan.

As might be expected in so vast a territory, comprising so many extremes of climate and of geographical and physical terrain, Chinese differ greatly in type, physique and character. Into their stock have been absorbed the aboriginal inhabitants as well as the continuous succeeding waves of invaders, mostly from the north. One stock, the Hakkas (meaning 'guests' or 'sojourners'), are to this day a tough, independent, almost nomadic race with their own dialect. Some writers have called them the Highlanders of China, and indeed the immensely varied stocks from which the British of today have sprung offer some sort of comparison in miniature with the origins of the Chinese.

The whole basis of the Chinese way of life was the close-knit and highly organized family. The head of a family was responsible for his whole household and dependants, and this pattern was visible throughout the entire social structure via the subordinate official to the great father and mother of all his people, the Emperor himself, responsible only to heaven—and very directly to heaven.

With all the good which this system effected it also resulted in an intense degree of nepotism, which must have been one of the root causes of official corruption. John Galsworthy wrote a splendid play on the subject of 'loyalties'. Which came first, loyalty to family or to state? The answer to this is plainly seen in the fact that no official might hold office in his own province.

Despite the hold of the three principal religions, Confucianism, Taoism and Buddhism, ancestor worship remained probably the great common factor. The advent of Communism brought what can best be described as a fourth faith into the pattern, and it was soon apparent that this could not, in its very nature, tolerate ancestor worship, with an emphasis on the family as so inherent a part of its cult. As ancestor worship involved the worship of spirits, the dead remained part of a household and a third son remained a third son, even if both his elder brothers were dead. With all this, of course, went much superstition, and initiation of any enterprise required 'feng-shui' (literally 'wind-water') which can be roughly translated as 'luck' or, in pidgin English, 'Good Joss'.

A recent lady visitor to Hongkong told me of a large mansion, newly completed there by a very wealthy family. It was empty, and would remain so. Someone had slipped up and the first sod dug or the first stone laid had been at a moment unpropitious to the good spirits.

In such an event none of the usual firing of crackers and bangers and clangings of brass cymbals, which always accompany the formal opening of any new premises or the beginning of a new year, would be of any avail. They might frighten away the evil spirits but could not wipe out the slight upon the good ones.

Another religion which is widely followed in the north-west and south-west is Islam.

Christianity, of course, has its place here and there, but the Chinese, superstition aside, is an intensely practical person.

What is Christianity? He will ask you this and point out that, even if he accepts one main division between Roman Catholics and the others, these others are represented by a dozen warring Protestant sects competing with one another as well as with the Roman Catholics like commercial travellers touting the superiority of their own brands. Such 'travellers' are often, despite the minuteness of the white communities, scarcely on speaking terms. So the practical Chinese will join whichever seems to him to be the best club. This one will teach his useless female children skill in embroidery and drawn work; that one will teach his sons the arts of modern languages and business know-how. And so on. Of course there were many sincere and devoted converts, but their loyalty in times of peril could well be no more than that of the Chinese employee who had found at long last a stable and remunerative form of existence with his foreign masters and would risk his life, if necessary, to preserve it. Since the Communists have come to power this no longer applies, yet many Chinese have remained Christians at personal sacrifice and even peril. This is, I believe, an established fact, but what we do not know is how many of the other age-long beliefs which are inimical to the Communist creed are still nurtured by the Chinese people in secret. In the long run, will Communism mould China much more than China moulds her Communists?

In its oldest meaning, the term 'expatriate' denotes one who 'abandons his own country for another', without perhaps quite the odium that attaches to the term 'renegade'. To the vast majority of the people of whom this book seeks to tell, neither term strictly applies.

The Portuguese, it is true, became largely assimilated into their new background in settlements such as Macao, on the fringe of the Canton River delta. They intermarried with the Chinese and with other oriental races and acquired much of the local way of life. But they held firmly to their Roman Catholic faith and to the land of their origin—Portugal. In Hongkong there were many of them who were proud to acquire British nationality, but they still looked upon themselves as essentially Portuguese, however many racial admixtures their own family stock might contain.

The white British had, naturally, followed their usual pattern. Seamen and merchant adventurers and traders brought, in course of time, others in their train: bankers, lawyers, surveyors, engineers, doctors, missionary clergy and others of many vocations. But whilst the British in imperial Hongkong, and in the little British Concessions throughout China, were to some extent under the eye of the home government, dwellers in Shanghai, once it had become an International Settlement in 1863, were subject to no such close and embarrassing surveillance. But it was a long way for fugitives to come, so there were few Shanghai white Britons in this category. From the Americas and, after the revolution of 1917, from Russia, there were ever-increasing numbers of people who were there because they could not be anywhere else—abandoned by, rather than abandoning, their homelands. No stigma necessarily attached to such genuine expatriates as the Russians, nor to their successors in the thirties, the unfortunate refugees from the Nazis in Europe. But amongst them and from elsewhere were fugitives from past unhappinesses or from enemies such as the police in their countries of origin. The only record of numbers which I have been able to trace dates from 1935, and comprises Japanese 30 per cent, British and Russians 16 per cent each, U.S.A. 5½ per cent, French 4 per cent, Germans 2½ per cent and combined other nationals 25 per cent out of a total of some 68,000 at that time. These figures are approximate and I do not know whether, for example, Sikhs or Malays or Hongkong born Portuguese Eurasians were counted as British.

Originally Shanghai had been founded in 1854 as two Concessions, one British and one French, but, before the coalition with the U.S.A., which came into being as the International Settlement in 1863, the French had withdrawn in the previous year from any form of amalgamation. Was there always this chip-on-the-shoulder nationalistic aloofness in their make-up? Is it a legacy of Napoleonic times? Indeed, faced with contemporary Gaullist policies in Europe and Africa, one cannot but be struck by the essential consistency of French attitudes.

At the same time as the foreign Concessions were founded in Shanghai, a number of other Treaty Ports came into being: such as Hankow, on the Yangtsze, and Tientsin, the port for Peking in the north, and Shameen, a little island in mid river at Canton, with their minute Concessions which gave virtual sovereignty to the concessionaire powers over their tiny acreages—in Hankow, only eighty-five acres overall. In others, both on the coast and along the Yangtsze and its tributary, the Siang, shipping and trading firms established themselves under the eyes of the various foreign consuls, without their settlements becoming quite the tight little foreign islands that they developed into in the larger ports.

From all these, representatives of the great oil, tobacco and chemical companies travelled far and wide in the interior, promoting sales, and numerous missionaries of many denominations established their outposts.

It was not very long after the development of the power of steam in the Western world that railways were introduced into China. These were to be paid for by means of foreign loans, and how great a part, if any, of these were ultimately paid for in full I do not know, but their financing was based upon loans secured by customs revenues and by a salt monopoly, known as the Salt Gabelle.

A very fine service, the Chinese Maritime Customs, was created, whose administrators and officers were largely British and which provided the coastguards, the charting of channels, harbours and navigable rivers and many other auxiliary services, besides the usual checking of the movements of goods and shipping. Among these services was the perpetual war on dope smuggling which they tried to keep within bounds. In later years arms smuggling was another large enterprise.

Steam brought also a vast increase in foreign shipping, and a network of steamship lines soon spread along coasts and up navigable rivers. The romantic tea clippers of the great days of sail had been superseded well before the twentieth century opened. Instead of being loaded into the big sailing ships at Pagoda Anchorage, nearly twenty miles from Foochow, home of the China tea trade, tea was carried in coasters to the great ports of Hongkong or Shanghai and thence by liners of the P. & O., Blue Funnel (Alfred Holt) and other lines. At this time therefore British and others began to develop shipping fleets for the coastal trade, and before long steamers under the British flag were sailing also on the rivers: up the Min River to Foochow some twenty miles; up the narrow Pei-Ho to Tientsin, also a short run; up to Canton about eighty miles.

CHAPTER TWO

THE YANGTSZE

UP THE vast Yangtsze, however, it was over six hundred miles to Hankow—a voyage of over two days. Some ships on this regular run, in later years, were above 3,000 tons gross and there was one of over 4,000 tons. At Hankow there was transhipment into smaller ships for the 'Middle River' area, which included the Yangtsze River to Ichang at the foot of the Gorges, and the tributary Siang River and the Tung Ting Lakes which served the large city of Changsha to the south. Beyond Changsha only shallow-draught tugs and lighters operated throughout the lakes and waterways of the region, but at Ichang there was transhipment in later years into small, powerful, specially designed ships which breasted the wild rapids on the way to Chungking, another four days away to the west and about 1,250 miles from the sea.

Chungking, lying astride the now narrower but still torrential river, nestles on the lower slopes of the mountains on either side. Even the Japanese invaders never managed to penetrate so far, and Chiang Kai Shek maintained his capital and war-time headquarters there. For local transport in Chungking, one common alternative to footing it was the Szechwan mountain pony, a hardy little breed that, almost literally, charged up and down stone steps and paths with their burdens. The Dutch courage which elected for this means of getting home after a good party seldom lasted the journey.

The return journey from Chungking to Ichang by ship was usually done in about two days and was rather like sitting a runaway Szechwan pony on a downhill mountain path. Great cliffs towered on each side above the turgid, coffee-coloured torrent which, when in spate, often attained a speed of about 10 knots. But it was not so much speed of current as sheer weight of water which impeded navigation. Going up it by powered vessel provided the unusual experience of literally going uphill while afloat and, at times, it was all that the ship could do to maintain half to one knot against it, while the whole hull shuddered under the constant blows of the torrent. Of the 350-odd miles from Ichang to their final port, Chungking, the upper Yangtsze steamers had over 120 miles to negotiate before they were clear of the Great Gorges. Within four miles of leaving Ichang the ship would enter the first Gorge, about sixteen miles long, and a succession of five of these, with intervals of ordinary hilly country in between, had to be overcome in the first 120-odd miles.

The navigation of these Gorges involved a tricky and hazardous procedure. As anyone will know who has watched a mountain torrent in spate, the full force of the current seldom follows one line for long and, out of it, flotsam, if one may use the term, will swirl round in an eddy and be carried momentarily upstream along one bank or the other. Navigation of the rapids was possible only in daylight, and master and pilot had to know the appropriate upward eddies. This involved crossing and recrossing the main force of the torrent, and the captain was content to be making one knot over the ground at these stages. These conditions applied only in late spring, summer and early autumn. In winter even the Gorges were emasculated and the stretches of relatively open water between them placid and serene. There was also a steady and invariable breeze blowing strongly upriver and, in the days before steam and even since, Chinese sailing junks would make their way up. But when they came to rapids—and the Great Wushan Gorge is twenty-five miles long—it was another story. It is not easy nowadays to believe that these Chinese sailing craft used to make their way up the rapids with little power beyond that of hundreds of coolies, with vast, though primitive, tow-ropes, staggering and clutching their way along narrow catwalks hewn out of the solid rocks of the cliffs above. A slip, a lurch of the vessel and a man could plunge to certain death. His swollen corpse might be infesting Ichang harbour a day or two later.

Some idea of the fantastic character of these Gorges may be gleaned from the difference between summer and winter water levels. At Hankow, on the lower river, the variation amounts to some 40–50 feet, the latter being exceptionally high. But, at the entrance to the Great Wushan Gorge, the greatest difference I have heard recorded in any twelve months between winter and summer levels is, believe it or not, 212 feet. An overnight rise or fall of 20–30 feet is not uncommon, and these have sometimes been as much as around 40 feet. Thus, if a master should run his ship aground at dusk, she might, if firmly wedged, be completely submerged by daylight. On the other hand, she might find herself perched high and dry on a pinnacle of rock with the river running many feet below. Shades of Baron Münchausen!

About half way between Ichang and Chungking lies the riverside port of Wanhsien, a local centre of authority if not always of government as we understand it, some sixty or seventy miles beyond the last great Gorge. Here, in the early autumn of 1926, was fought one of the most dramatic naval actions in which the British Navy has ever engaged. The story of this battle will be told in a later chapter.

At one time, before the advent of nylon, much of the world's bristles for brushes of all sorts came from China's pig population and the mid to upper Yangtsze area supplied a good deal of this. Another staple product was wood oil, which for many years provided the base for most paints and varnishes. This oil was derived from the tung nut and was produced at source as a substance not dissimilar from dirty black treacle and shipped down to Hankow in large tub-shaped bamboo baskets lined with paper. There it was refined by steaming to a colour rather darker than golden syrup and stored in great steel tanks with a capacity of hundreds of gallons, prior to being pumped direct into deep tanks in ocean-going liners for transport to Europe and America.

Another product of those times was an extremely coarse strong silk material, immeasurably more so than the world-known Shantung silk. This originated in the Kiating district near Chungking, and was much used by well-to-do Chinese and by Europeans who had heard of it.

Changsha, lying south of the Middle Yangtsze basin, is a centre chiefly of coal, including a good anthracite type, antimony, lead and other metals. It is also an important railway depot on the Canton–Hankow Railway.

To Hankow, the highest port accessible on the Yangtsze to ocean-going liners, came all these and many other types of produce, either for processing in local factories or for transhipment.

Some good quality teas were found in this region, and the principal buyers in Hankow before World War I were Russian merchants in whose factories the tea was pressed, after a dehydrating process known as firing, into solid bricks for export to Imperial Russia. Other products included hides; gall nuts from which one of the basic ingredients of ink was extracted; a rather moderate grade of cotton; China grass, a fibrous substance actually processed from a type of bark; tobacco, which was widely grown, largely from seed imported from Virginia, and supplied the raw material for a number of British and American owned tobacco and cigarette factories. Eggs were also processed in large quantities as well as game frozen for export, such as pheasant, duck, partridge, etc.

It would be tedious to enumerate all commercial activities over so vast a field as China, but the random listing from memory of some of the industries of the middle and upper Yangtsze basin may give some slight idea of the diversities of the whole country's trade.

Shanghai, which lies about eight miles up the River Whangpoo, a tributary flowing from the south into the actual estuary of the Yangtsze, was, and still is, a vast city. The width of the Whangpoo at Shanghai can be very roughly compared to the Thames at points to which ocean-going ships penetrate. Shanghai's origins were similar to those of the other 'Treaty' Ports, but it had developed differently. Its main function lay in its ready, all the year round access to large liners of 15,000–20,000 tons, whereas Hankow, which could comfortably accommodate ships of over 10,000 tons gross in the high water season from about May to October, was cut off from all but shallow-draught river shipping for the rest of the year. All the largest industries therefore—cold storage plants, egg processing factories, cotton and woollen mills, silk filatures, shipbuilding and engineering works, soap, paint and chemical works, cigarette factories, furniture factories and so on—were biggest and most numerous in Shanghai.

As described earlier, the whole metropolis of adjoining foreign Concessions and areas of influence had soon become too interdependent and unwieldy to be administered by separate national authorities in each. They were therefore merged in 1863 into one large International Settlement from which only one power, France, aloof and go-it-alone then as now, remained apart. Thus, though the Shanghai Municipal Council was largely executively staffed and run by the British, it also comprised American, Japanese and other nationals. Council members were duly elected by the ratepayers but, as the majority of the large industries were British owned or controlled, the main burden of the rates was borne by British interests with understandable results. In the early summer of 1941, with Japan in almost entire military control of the surrounding countryside, feelings ran high amongst the large Japanese minority in the Settlement. When the annual meeting of rate-payers was held in the big stand of the Shanghai Race Club a fanatical little Japanese rushed up the steps and fired a small revolver at point-blank range into the body of the British chairman, W. J. Keswick,[1] who was head of the big Jardine, Matheson interests there. But even at such short range the attack was ineffective and the bullet went round Keswick's ribs without even breaking one. For 'Tony' Keswick the incident was not without its fortunate side, as it was deemed advisable for him to leave Shanghai for the time being, and he therefore escaped the internment which was to be the lot of his fellow nationals after the start of the Pacific war in the following December.

It is interesting that the lay-out of many great cities seems to tend towards east ends of like character. Shanghai's Yangtszepoo, where the Japanese had held their main area of influence and trade, comprised the eastern parts of the city and was a district of wharves, godowns (or warehouses) and factories. The officering of the section of the police force concerned with this area was largely Japanese, who were better qualified linguistically to deal with the numerous Japanese and their wide commercial interests. This was to have its effects, both in the Sino-Japanese War, which reached its full intensity in 1937, and in the subsequent opening of the Pacific war against the Allies in December 1941, after Pearl Harbor.

At the other extreme of this vast city's water-front lay the French Concession, separated only from the International Settlement by the Avenue Édouard Sept and with Nantao, the water-front area of the Chinese city, beyond it. On the water-front, or Bund, as it was called, was erected at the corner of Avenue Édouard VII an impressive cenotaph after World War I.

The river curves sharply here and the eye could scan almost the whole water-front: to the left, downriver towards the estuary, past the august portals of the adjacent Shanghai Club to the customs house and the great banks and merchant offices, then round another sweep of the river to the wharves and mills of Yangtszepoo. A hundred or two yards before one lay the British and other naval buoys in midstream and, beyond, the Pootung district on the far bank, chock-a-block with wharves, godowns, factories and shipyards. One block of these godowns, normally used for tobacco storage, was to be the home in 1943 of the Pootung Civil Assembly Centre, as the Japanese called it, where about 1,200 British, Americans and Dutch were to be interned for about two and a half years.

It was from the British naval buoy, little more than a stone's throw

[1] Not J. H. Keswick, his younger brother, as is given by Brig. Davidson-Houston's excellent book *Yellow Creek*.

from the Shanghai Club, that the doughty skipper of the tiny gunboat H.M.S. *Peterel* elected to fight it out one night in December 1941 when challenged to surrender by the massive, if antiquated, Japanese heavy cruiser *Idzumo*, berthed at Yangtszepoo. More of this incident will be told later in its proper context.

From the cenotaph, the Avenue Édouard VII stretched away at one's back towards the limits of the International Settlement and French Concession some three to five miles away. Beyond again lay areas of influence and some measure of control in which an observatory, staffed by Catholic fathers, various recreational clubs, a small aerodrome and the country houses of some top business brass were to be found.

In the French Concession the rule of law was French and the police consisted largely of Annamites or, as we say today, Vietnamese, under French officers. Thus the competent armed robber, kidnapper or smash and grab man had only to get half way across this road and the International Settlement police could no longer pursue him. Of course the reverse applied equally. The farther boundary of the French Concession marched likewise with the confines of the Chinese city beyond, and the difficulties of the authorities concerned with law and order can be imagined. Kidnapping of wealthy Chinese was one of the favourite pastimes of the seething underworld, and it was rather normal than otherwise to see groups of alert police, all in bullet-proof waistcoats, with fingers on triggers of drawn automatics, and with some of their number under cover behind some convenient wall, at certain key crossings throughout the Settlement and French town. Of course escape into Chinese territory was escape beyond recall, though I remember a one-time police commissioner telling me of a way out of this difficulty. As in all big cities, there were many underworld rackets in Shanghai. On some the police stamped with utter ruthlessness; on others, when perhaps only technical infringements of the law were involved, even the commissioner himself was content to turn a blind eye for reasons of his own, as long as matters were kept within bounds. Such rackets were often profitable side lines of some of the really big gangsters who were known to the police and whose machinations spread far into the interior of China. To such a gangster the commissioner might allow information to leak that life was not worth living in the police force, since some particularly nasty criminal had vanished into the interior. So foul was the commissioner's mood, the tale would run, that there had been mutterings about a clean up of a certain well-known and tolerated rackets in the International Settlement itself. Just lately, the commissioner told me, he had tried this very gambit and the man he so badly wanted had, somehow, been traced by the big men and persuaded back to Shanghai where, with an anonymous tip-off, he had soon been in police hands.

Another obstacle to police work was that procedure required the written assent of any particular foreign national's own consul before action could be taken against him in the 'mixed court'. Many of the very minor nationalities, however small their local trade, felt the need of an accredited representative on the spot. There was no need, of course, for such a person to be of the nationality represented, and in small communities British, French or U.S. consuls, for example, might often care for the interests of each other's or other nations' interests. But in the swarming ant-heap that was Shanghai, the better established consuls had no free time to handle a miscellaneous string of nationalities in addition to their own. So the governments of, say, Ruritania, Utopia and Erewhon often had a very mixed lot of local consuls—bar tenders or musicians in sleazy night spots, for example. Such gentry inevitably had a close working camaraderie of their own, and by the time the police had caught up with an offender's consul he might no longer be the consul concerned. New papers had by then been issued by another consul, changing the offender's nationality overnight. And so it went on.

CHAPTER THREE

NORTH CHINA

ANOTHER large 'Treaty Port' which rivalled Hankow in importance was Tientsin. Tientsin lies on a comparatively small river, the Peiho, only a few miles from its mouth, upon the Gulf of Peichili in north China. From Tientsin there was direct rail communication with Peking and thence to Hankow. There was also a railway running direct northwards to the junction with the Trans-Siberian Railway and its associate Chinese Eastern Railway, with terminal ports at Vladivostok and Dairen. The Peiho is too narrow and twisty for navigation by coasters bigger than up to 2,000–3,000 tons gross at most, but tugs and lighters served the larger vessels which lay off Taku Bar at its mouth.

It was from Taku and Tientsin that the International Relief Force had got through to Peking at the beginning of the century when the Boxer Rising had culminated in the siege of the foreign legations there. A legacy of this occurrence was a standing garrison in Tientsin from which a Legation Guard was drawn for many years. This garrison, which included, in battalion strength, British, American, French, Italian and Japanese troops, ensured a peaceful atmosphere for some time. When the troubles began, which accompanied the emergence of Chiang Kai Shek in 1925, this garrison was hurriedly reinstated and all was peace until the Japanese themselves became the provokers of tension when Sino-Japanese relations began to deteriorate in the early to mid thirties.

Here therefore all the powers (except the Germans who forfeited theirs after World War I) maintained their separate little Concessions side by side long after all had been surrendered in Hankow in the late twenties. The climate of Tientsin is as utterly dry as that of the Yangtsze Valley is utterly humid, and, in general, yields quite a different type of produce, although tobacco is widely grown here as in the Yangtsze basin.

As a pipe smoker I remember, when stationed in Tientsin, discovering that the local tobacco was very tolerable to smoke and very tolerant of one's pocket. But to open the large paper packet upon purchase was to see the contents crumble to fine dust before one's eyes. The unopened packet had to be dunked in a bucket of water and held below surface until bubbling ceased. It could then be opened up and spread on newspaper to dry to the proper degree for smoking and for storage in air-tight tins.

I once went, at short notice, from Tientsin to Hankow (in circumstances which will be narrated later), and a package of Tientsin tobacco was dispatched by post after me. When I picked up the package on its arrival I could feel and hear that it was not crackling dry—so I opened it. Sure enough, it had absorbed enough humidity *en route* to be ready for smoking.

Farther to the north again lie Chinwangtao and Newchwang. The former's principal *raison d'être* was the nearby great British-controlled Kailan mines which were a plenteous source of coal. Between Tientsin and Chinwangtao, and served by the railway, was a pleasant beach resort of huts and shacks at Peitaiho, which could be reached in the early morning by overnight train from Tientsin, and became a popular week-end spot in the summer.

A little farther north lies Newchwang, at the extreme northern end of this almost land-locked gulf. It is frequently ice-bound for much of the winter, and ice yachting was a popular pastime among the small foreign community.

The southward jutting piece of land which encloses the Yellow Sea, of which this gulf is the north-western arm, is the Korean Peninsula with the Sea of Japan beyond it to the East. To the north-west of Korea lies Manchuria, home of the Manchus, whose imperial dynasty ruled China for so long. But although Manchuria has a long eastern frontier, North Korea and Soviet Russia meet on the coast of the Sea of Japan, thus boxing in Manchuria, whose only access to the sea is elsewhere, through Dairen and Newchwang into the Yellow Sea.

From Dairen and Newchwang the railway continues north through Mukden and Harbin to join the Trans-Siberian Railway some five hundred miles west of its terminal port of Vladivostok.

In the days before the First World War a traveller from England could travel overland to the Far East via Berlin, Moscow and

Vladivostok, whence ship was taken to the China Coast. As there were no world-wide air lines, the saving in time was valuable—two or three weeks to Hongkong from London, as against five weeks by sea all the way or four weeks by rail to Marseilles and thence by ship. The comparative openness of the Sea of Japan renders Vladivostok pretty well ice free, but in the sheltered Gulf of Peichili icing over of the sea occurs even as far south as Taku Bar at the mouth of Tientsin's River Peiho, although it is comparatively rare there.

Farther south, on the Great Shantung Peninsula, lies the small trading port of Chefoo, and a few miles south of this lies Weihaiwei, the summer anchorage of the British Navy in the Far East for many years, and just round the corner, and sheltered by the peninsula from the northerly gales, Kiaochow and Tsingtao where the German Navy held sway until driven out for the Allies by the Japanese in World War I.

Shantung silk is probably the best known of the products of this area, but there was also export of walnuts and groundnuts and, in the days when straw was a fashionable material for hats for both sexes, strawbraid. There were also processing factories for eggs and game and a brewery or two.

C

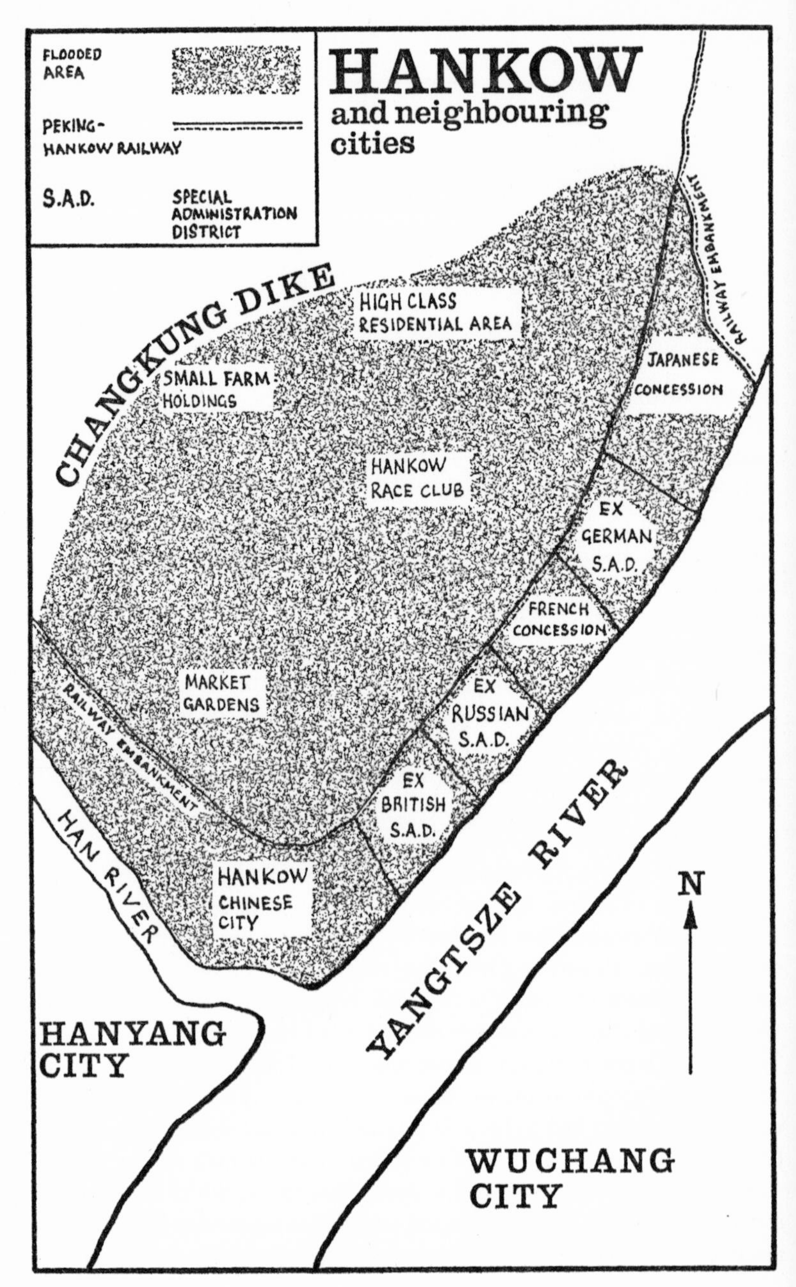

FLOODED AREA
PEKING-HANKOW RAILWAY
S.A.D.
SPECIAL ADMINISTRATION DISTRICT
HANKOW
and neighbouring cities
CHANGKUNG DIKE
HIGH CLASS RESIDENTIAL AREA
SMALL FARM HOLDINGS
RAILWAY EMBANKMENT
JAPANESE CONCESSION
HANKOW RACE CLUB
EX GERMAN S.A.D.
FRENCH CONCESSION
MARKET GARDENS
EX RUSSIAN S.A.D.
RAILWAY EMBANKMENT
EX BRITISH S.A.D.
HAN RIVER
HANKOW CHINESE CITY
YANGTSZE RIVER
N
HANYANG CITY
WUCHANG CITY

CHAPTER FOUR

SOUTH CHINA

ALTHOUGH the westward windings of the Yangtsze River place many of its cities geographically south of Shanghai, it is with coast ports south of the Yangtsze estuary that we now deal.

In Chekiang, first province to the south, lies Hangchow, one of the most beautifully situated cities in China, on a lily-strewn lake among wooded hills. But it has no proper access to the sea, and depends for its communications on a railway from Shanghai, which continues on to Ningpo on the coast. Ningpo is a shallow-draught port and is served by steamers of the river boat type, which make their way down from Shanghai in the shelter of the many islands along the coast. Already the influence of warmer climate is noticeable in the characteristics of the population. The robust, almost Nordic, types of the northern provinces supplied most of the recruits for the foreign-controlled police forces. Chekiang province is more noted for bankers and statesmen. Chiang Kai Shek is himself a native of Ningpo.

The next province to the south is Fukien and, although one passes by ship near to the border port of Wenchow which lies a few miles up a small river estuary, few foreign flag ships normally called there. My own only visit there was a brief one, made in a very small cockroach-infested Chinese coaster. I have never forgotten the scuttling sound which echoed through the tiny cabin when I first opened its door in Shanghai. I went hurriedly ashore again and bought a large tin of a lethal-looking reddish brown powder at a nearby chemist's. It was most effective but had to be well brushed from the sheets after it had done its work to avoid some of its effects on the human skin.

The real port of note in this region is Foochow, which lies on the estuary of the Min River and is the traditional monarch of the China tea trade. Foochow lies in a cluster of green-clad hills some twenty miles from Pagoda Anchorage where the great tea clippers used to anchor and its white community were predominantly tea experts. These specialists were always regarded as being somewhat apart from their fellow men, as might be experts in vintage ports or in the blending of whisky. So there was always something of an artists' quarter atmosphere about the place and, if all the little white communities tended to develop their own social characteristics, Foochow somehow managed to be more so, to be different.

And so down the coast to Amoy and then Swatow, smallish but important Treaty Ports with the climate and the inhabitants becoming progressively more eastern Mediterranean, and on to Hongkong.

As it exists today the Crown Colony of Hongkong is really a cluster of islands, mountainous in character and of varying sizes, together with a small wedge of mainland territory opposite it, lying at the north-east rim of the Canton River estuary.

Although the British occupation of Hongkong came about as a result of incidents similar to those which gave rise to the foreign Concessions in China proper, the whole position was very different. When first contemptuously ceded to the British in 1842 as trading post, harbour and depot, the main island of Hongkong was a bleak and barren rock mass, with little vegetation. But skilful afforestation over the years has now densely wooded much of the great mountainsides, and the one-time exiguous foreshore was extended by pulling down rocks and dredging up harbour mud. On this reclaimed land now stands the capital city of Victoria, with its mass of modern skyscrapers.

In 1896 a piece of the mainland opposite, together with some adjacent islands of various sizes, was leased to Britain on a ninety-nine year lease. The lay-out is perhaps best described by comparing Hongkong to the Isle of Wight in relation to Portsmouth, with the plain on which Portsmouth lies leased to Britain, including an area extending some fifteen-odd miles beyond the Portsdown Hills. But the Kowloon Hills rise to about 2,000 feet, and the distance between Victoria and the mainland city of Kowloon opposite is far less than between Portsmouth and the Isle of Wight, and narrow passes between islands and mainland mountains make of the resultant harbour a safe anchorage in any weather, except for the cyclonic storms known in those seas as typhoons. In typhoons no anchorage is safe. There is one exception to this: the special typhoon anchorages. Immensely strong moles, built out from the shore in outlying parts of Hongkong harbour, are curved to form semicircular enclosures. Into these, when warning signals are hoisted, all sailing craft within harbour limits are hustled by fussy little sheepdogs of tugs and packed and jammed into a solid immovable mass.

Hongkong is also more mountainous than the Isle of Wight, with a rocky backbone of hills of which the highest, the Peak, is 1,825 feet. Beyond the 2,000-foot hills which enclose the Kowloon plain stands Taimoshan, farther inland in the leased New Territories, which tops 3,000 feet. I will not be more precise with its exact altitude, as a young amateur pilot of my acquaintance once found that his altimeter disagreed with the textbooks and he only just managed to pull back his joystick in time to avoid hitting the top of the mountain. Poor John Potter; in December 1941 he was one of those who went up in his aged plane to try to harm the attacking Japanese aircraft in some way, although death was a certainty.

Hongkong, then, developed apace in British hands, and well-planned roads, albeit designed for Victorian traffic requirements, soon encircled the island. But the Peak, with its many lovely mountainside sites for Europeans to live, was not open to motor traffic until the middle twenties. Every stick, every stone, used to be carried up by Chinese coolies, male and female. That the women looked old and haggard by early middle age was not surprising, but the men fared little better. It is a commentary on conditions of life in China proper at that time that so many came swarming into the colony, grateful for the chance to work. Not many years before World War I a young British magistrate had two Chinese boatwomen, mother and daughter, brought up before him. They were owners and crew of a sampan, one of the small harbour boats that ply for hire between shore and ships at anchor. Like London taxi men, it is a condition of their licence to ply that they do not refuse any reasonable fare, nor charge more than the legal tariff. A zealous young Chinese constable had noticed this craft and some rather disgruntled sailors being rejected as fares, when they were in a hurry to rejoin their ship before she sailed. He had reported it, and here they all were. The older woman was voluble. The charge was ridiculous. She was a sampan owner, well known and respected. Never would she have done such a thing without good reason. She had plenty of witnesses, if they were needed, to testify that the harbour was rather squally that day, and the water choppy—so much so that she could not quite manage the boat by herself when it was loaded. And then, as luck would have it, along came these sailors, just as her daughter was having a baby. But, and here again she could produce witnesses if needed, more fares came along a little later, after her daughter had finished the job in hand, and they were accepted. But then, of course, her daughter was ready to take an oar by then. . . . Case dismissed.

The first male baby born on the Peak was the brother of P. G. Wodehouse, the famous novelist, and was duly named Peveril by parents who obviously had in mind the works of Sir Walter Scott. His father was at that time a magistrate in Hongkong, though not the magistrate of the sampan story. First access to the upper levels of the Peak on any appreciable scale was by a well-built rope railway known as the Peak Tram, with some three or four stops at suitably spaced levels on the way up.

From the various upper level tram stops, people went to their houses along well-built but narrow roads, on foot or by two-coolie ricksha. Where the roads were too steep for rickshas, even with two coolies, chairs were available at about the same fare. These large bamboo armchair contraptions, with two long poles protruding several feet fore and aft, were carried on the shoulders of sturdy coolies and, in wet weather, could be curtained so effectively that the fussiest beauty could travel unscathed in her best party dress and hair-do. Front porches were so designed that chairs could be brought under cover for the passenger to step straight in dry shod from his front door. This led on one occasion to a much loved senior government official arriving at a formal evening reception at Government House in full regalia and, as he thought, immaculate in every detail. It was His Excellency the Governor who, as he shook hands, remarked: 'You look splendid tonight, old chap. I specially like your scarlet felt slippers. . . .'

It should be understood that the Hongkong community was very different from others of the China ports. Here flew, and still flies, the Union Jack: in Shanghai the foreign quarter comprised the International Settlement, which was an amalgamation of various foreign 'Concessions', and the French Concession. Though the Chinese population of Hongkong is vast, all are on British soil or, if living afloat, in British waters and under the British rule of law. The floating population has always been virtually uncountable. Until the last war Hongkong was an important naval base, with an efficient little dockyard, overshadowed only, once it was completed, by the ill-fated Singapore base. It was also an important Army Command headquarters. The mixed strata of the white community differed therefore in character from those of the purely trading communities of the Treaty Ports.

Again, in India, in the old days, Government and Service personnel, infected perhaps by the caste system of the country, were inclined to look upon themselves as of classes apart. The British business man, until he became too important to be ignored, was rather contemptuously classified as the 'Box Wallah', a term of the origin of which I must admit ignorance. I believe that similar attitudes obtained in parts of Africa, but I have no real information in this respect. In Hongkong it was different. Although there was a high enough proportion of civil and fighting services personnel to ensure a rather aloof British insularity towards white people of other nationalities, who had not the good fortune to be born British, commercial interests were much to the fore. The Legislative and Executive Councils, which administered the whole community under the chairmanship of the Governor, included representatives of merchants and bankers, some of whom were Chinese or Parsees. The difficulties have been mentioned of assessing numbers of population, of whom many were Chinese, who might be boat dwellers and not always in port, or border dwellers who were so often away in China proper. Another great problem in so large and cramped a community has always been sewage disposal. Fortunately for the peace of mind of the business-like and frugal Chinese, tidal and other factors always made impossible the needless squandering of such valuable natural resources as goes on in places like England, where large pipes are perpetually discharging virtual gold-mines as far as possible out to sea every day. No: this valuable commodity is sold to highest tender for transportation, in Chinese junks, to parts of the coast where the population are not so richly fed. These vessels were commonly called 'Fu Fu boats'.

Many years ago a current population census was being discussed by the Council's Assembly, and officially estimated figures were under fire from a Chinese member who was a merchant of wide interests. 'Quite ridiculous,' he said. 'My figures can prove it.'—'Your figures? What figures?' asked His Excellency the Governor in puzzled tones. The Chinese councillor then explained that he owned the firm which had had the sewage disposal contracts for many years. The number of junk loads per head of population was an essential and constant factor in his business calculations. He could not afford to be wrong. And so, from that day, the census figures were an approximation based on the sewage returns. Perhaps they still are.

In many other ways too the benevolent domination of large business interests is apparent. It is banks and merchant firms which control the property and public utility companies and helped to found, finance and run the clubs. Most of them inevitably have some tie with shipping, and their reserve launches are often available for large bathing picnic parties to outlying islands on fine week-ends. Their executives own most of the race ponies, and it is in their stables that the lesser man may often keep his hacks or polo ponies, probably rejects from the racing stables, without undue expense. But the majority of Europeans, as distinct from Britons, seldom penetrated fully into the British way of life except at events such as race meetings.

There were many reasons why the upper levels of the mountains of the island were among the first to be developed for the white man's habitation. There was little level land on the island between mountain foot and sea front until extensive reclamation had been effected at the turn of the century and what there was was needed for wharves, godowns, business and government offices. Again, the very sheltered nature of the harbour made it airless and stuffy on shore in hot weather. Before the days of household refrigerators, let alone the newer development of air conditioning, the more great buildings were crowded into the limited space, the more the sun's heat was retained throughout the long hot season. The small mainland plain was also unpleasantly shut in by the Kowloon hills at its back and, as a small and ancient Chinese walled city already lay there, it seemed the natural habitat of that in-between world of the less prosperous sections of the community. The higher orders of government officials and the executive personnel of the big business houses had homes built for them on the midriff, bosom, shoulders and head of the Peak, leaving all that was sordidly commercial or commercially sordid in the unmentionable nether regions below. With labour costs negligible, very lovely sites were dug and blasted from the precipitous hillsides to which there was access by narrow paths from the not much wider roads which followed the folds of the mountain's torso at various levels. The narrow garden paths led steeply up or down from the road, and two paths which left the road side by side would probably diverge rapidly to sites on either side of rock spur or gully. Often the houses to which they led were invisible one from the other. Many of their inhabitants were family men, and sociable, and young newcomers to the colony would make themselves known by making a formal call. The embarrassment was considerable, to a young man, of wending his way up or down a long narrow path in full view of windows of the house, only to find on arrival that the occupants were holding a formal party or were sunbathing on the lawn. So over the years a social custom evolved. At each path entrance stood a two–three-foot white post with letter box attached and with name of householder as well as name or number of house inscribed thereon. A small movable panel in this box could be adjusted to read either 'In' or 'Out'. Neither was to be construed by a stranger calling for the first time as an invitation to proceed farther. But to friends, if they had not been specifically invited, 'In' meant that the household were entertaining and did not wish to be disturbed. Scornful young men newly arrived from England used to ridicule such rigmarole but, like many strange and seemingly complicated customs, it had its advantages. A green young junior assistant just out from home could be taken round several miles of Peak roads by a friendly senior in quite a short time. The old hand would point out the boxes of socially inclined households, especially those with pretty young daughters or nieces in residence, and into each would go a couple of the young man's visiting-cards—one for the head of the house and one for his wife. An invitation to dinner or to some social gathering would usually follow. The older generation were only too grateful for such means of finding company for their young folk.

Many years ago these visiting-card boxes attracted the attention of the *Sporting Life*, which used to appear once a week in England in those days in many pages of pink newsprint and was known as the 'Pink 'Un'. Not only racing, but racy stories were a speciality of the 'Pink 'Un'. One of Hongkong's most respected British residents of those days was a lively little man of the name of Percy Tester who was a leading stockbroker and steward of the Jockey Club. He was unmarried and for quite a time shared a house on the Peak with a business friend named Shiner, who owned the unfortunate initials 'W.C.'. The resulting inscription on the box at their path's entrance was too much for the 'Pink 'Un'. It read:

P. Tester

W. C. Shiner

which drew the comment: 'Strange occupations in the Far East.'

Hongkong lies near the extreme meeting point of the prevailing south-westerlies of summer and the north-easters which blow down across the Pacific from about November to February or March. Inevitably the change from winter to summer is accompanied by low cloud and sea mists, which sometimes enshroud the whole of Hong-kong down to about 250–500 feet above sea level. These conditions may last for six weeks to two months, with occasional breaks of bright but changeable weather and humidity ever on the increase as warmer weather approaches. There is no rain worth mentioning at this time, but the Peak dweller has his head literally in the clouds for days on end. The English airing cupboard is replaced by a spacious drying room which, in earlier days, was heated by a stove and, until suitable electrical appliances were devised for warming wardrobes and hanging cupboards, nothing could be left out of the drying-room overnight. Slippers or shoes left by the bedside acquired mould and mildew by morning and matches became unstrikable. But when summer comes and clouds rise high or disappear, the Peak stands sparkling clear out of the sea of murk that envelops the steaming, teeming city of Victoria below. At such times ten minutes in a car or the funicular Peak tram can bring a drop in temperature of about ten degrees and the sweat-sodden city worker finds his body moisture almost too chilling to be comfortable. So one or two changes of clothes a day are not unusual, and many people keep complete changes in lockers in their downtown clubs.

The immense development of building in Hongkong will presumably have greatly diminished wild life on the island since the last war. But in the twenties wooded hillsides abounded in a species of small deer which, although seldom seen, were the bane of enthusiastic gardeners on the Peak and, of course, snakes abounded. Of these the most common were probably the common cobra and the bamboo snake. The king cobra, or hamadryad, was also, I believe, to be found on the wilder rocky mountainsides of the New Territories, but I have never heard a first-hand account of one. Pythons also were not uncommon, but did not grow to vast jungle proportions, and were more of a menace to poultry, stray dogs and small deer and all kinds of vermin than to humans.

Of birds there were no tropical jungle varieties in the Hongkong islands and, on the mainland, it was chiefly the game birds such as duck, pheasant, snipe and the like which abounded. I have often seen the exquisite little kingfisher hunting along the streams of the mainland and, farther north, I have glimpsed the charming golden oriole. On the Yangtsze basin much fishing is done for man by captive or domesticated cormorants. They are an interesting sight sitting in a sedate row on the half-deck of a sampan with rings about their necks to prevent them swallowing their catch.

The 'walky-walky duck' is a great feature of Chinese peasant life along the rivers. There he lies as a decoy, with sufficient clipping of his wings to prevent effective flight, and probably secured by a scarcely visible line to some immovable object. The Chinese use him mainly, not to attract his fellows for shooting, but as the nucleus of a, so to speak, free range duck farm.

There is a demand for ducks' eggs and duck feathers are a valuable merchandise.

The unwary would-be foreign sportsman who manages, in apparently open country, to stalk large quantities of sitting duck must not, of course, fire at anything that is not on the wing. But sometimes, while he fumbles with his safety-catch, they are away and only one, rather slower than the rest, is barely airborne. If the man is inexperienced he may consider this bird fair game once it is in the air and let fly before the unfortunate 'walky-walky' duck has reached the end of its tether. This is of course a heinous crime in sporting circles, and I must plead guilty to having committed it once when I was very young. But my companions on that occasion were kind and generous-hearted and it was never told against me.

CHAPTER FIVE

DRAMATIS PERSONAE

No account of the life of the foreigners on the China Coast between the wars could be easily comprehensible without some picture of the communities as they existed when the period started. To this must be added some description of those sections of the native population with which they had most contact. 'Native.' How this word's ignorant ab-usage has distorted its meaning and given it a derogatory flavour! And how ridiculous it becomes as a generalization about the inhabitants of a country such as China. To the native Cantonese, the native of Amoy, Hangchow, Nanking, Changsha, Chefoo, Chungking, etc., is about as much a foreigner as a Turk or a Pole is to the Basque.

The Chinese, then, or those of them with whom the white man came into contact.

It is perhaps useful if one can first appreciate the long tradition of 'squeeze' or 'perks' or 'rake-off' which had permeated the whole of Chinese life through countless ages. Let us begin with the class that were servants of foreigners. That superb domestic servant, the Chinese house boy at his best, is traditionally employed at a very modest wage with his food and housing thrown in. In small households the boy, who might be anything from seventeen to seventy-one years old, would be cook also; or perhaps a cook, experienced in the mysterious fads, foibles and habits of the different kinds of white man, would acquire also the almost more delicate skill of being a house boy or personal servant as well. Sometimes a bachelor of modest means would content himself with a 'cook boy' only. But, once his master's status in life was raised, the boy became a personage far too important to occupy himself with the menial tasks of swabbing and sweeping, filling coal buckets and so on. Then would appear a coolie, often some elderly 'poor relation' who had failed to better himself and knew not the gimmicks necessary for the pleasing of the white man, without prompting in his own and only language. The preparation of food was, and presumably still is, something of a rite in China, and a house boy's dignity, which is known as 'face', would not be smirched by such a task, as it would be by scrubbing the front steps, nor again by pressing trousers or giving a shine to polo boots. No boy of real standing, the Jeeves of even a very minor tycoon, could spare the time for being anything but butler, valet and household manager. If the minor tycoon suddenly got married then, equally suddenly, a dainty little Chinese girl, 'the amah', might become ensconced in the servants' quarters, who might, or might not, be the wife of the major-domo, but was certainly major-domo, personal maid, sewing maid and confidante to the lady of the house. Thus was the precarious balance of power, such a problem in some households in Britain, neatly established. The better class house boy has a very real code of honour, and if sometimes it seemed to transgress Western codes, there were times when their sturdy loyalty, which can flourish only in an atmosphere of mutual trust and respect, transcended anything in the Western ethic. But 'squeeze' is inherent in the Chinese way of life and, to the house boy, was an understood part of his emolument. Every supplier of goods or services to the household paid toll, and failure to do so could only result in mysterious happenings to goods before they came before master. What appeared to be the same egg which had arrived fresh at the back door a half-hour previously became strangely addled when it came to be poached for master. If a would-be employer was so simple as to offer double or more wages upon condition of no 'squeeze', he just was not 'with it', as we say nowadays. No boy of class would accept such terms with any intention of adhering to them.

But, as I have said before, the code of honour in business dealings throughout China was a high one, despite the tradition of 'squeeze'. In so many respects did their codes differ from ours. Human life, for example, was always expendable. How ridiculous, therefore, to the average Chinese, the absurd consideration shown to animals by the foreigner. Life was always too uncertain in the old days to bother much about maintenance, whether of machines, animals or human workers. When worn out they must be replaced. In these conditions the white man, and most especially the British who had been there so long, represented a stability and security not to be found elsewhere. I think that this was probably the basis of the excellent relationship which so often existed between employer and employee. There were of course the rougher white elements whose culture did not always match their technical qualifications. But in the roughest of them there was usually a sound core of fairness and honesty.

There is a very old tale of master and servant relationship which is perhaps relevant.

A certain bachelor, who was of the rough diamond type and very quick-tempered, once utterly lost his temper with his boy when the latter was attending him as he dressed in his bedroom preparatory to going out one evening to a formal dinner.

It was one of those occasions when everything seems to go wrong and, in the end, master's temper took complete control. 'You bloody fool, Wang!' he shouted and, grasping him by the scruff of the neck, flung him violently out of the room. One swift kick in the appropriate place completed the treatment and, as poor Wang tumbled headlong down the stairs, master marched back into his room and slammed the door. But his violence had dissolved his anger and, in a moment, he began to feel deeply ashamed of his outburst. So he rang the bell and, when Wang arrived: 'Wang,' he said, 'I am very sorry to have done that, and I feel ashamed. Here is a dollar to show you that I mean what I say.' Wang bowed low and, with profuse thanks, retreated. A moment or so later different and very hesitant footsteps could be heard coming up the stairs. 'What the devil now?' wondered master, almost ready to be irascible again. There was a knock at the door, so timid as to be almost inaudible. 'Come in, blast you!' shouted master, and in came his old house coolie. 'What's the matter now?' asked master. 'S'pose wantchee something, what for Wang no come?'—'Master,' said the coolie, 'Wang no likee my come. But s'pose anytime master wantchee some man kick down stairs my anytime can do fifty cents.' Master's reply is not recorded.

The most successful relationships were understandably where master and employee were each prepared to accept the other's point of view without necessarily understanding it. The Chinese are riddled with superstition, much more so than we are, for all our not walking under ladders, not cutting our nails on Fridays or Sundays, nor sitting down thirteen to table, nor helping others to salt. Walking through the Chinese paddy fields along the narrow paths which are designed primarily for wheelbarrows, you may hear the squeaking and creaking of a wheelbarrow from some distance on a still day. But, if you offered oil for his wheel to the coolie propelling it, he would be horrified. Everyone knows that the air is full of demons and devils, and what better to frighten them away than the hideous squeaks of the wheelbarrow? From time immemorial Chinese fishing craft, which are often equipped with eyes, painted one on each side of the bow, so as to see where they are going, have unfairly used a special device for the deception of the innocent, simple-minded devils which, as everybody knows, are constantly thronging the air. One of the playful or spiteful pranks in which devils delight is, of course, to lean heavily on the top of the mast of a boat and sink it as they fly over it. But the unsporting Chinese have an answer to that one: on the top of each mast is invariably fitted a length of whippy bamboo which, when leaned upon, just bends and the junk is saved. Very unfair to devils are the Chinese.

The less educated Chinese had no conception of the meaning of medicine as we understand it and, if an injection is given, it is just a sort of white magic: 'B'long velly good joss.' Similarly their water supply was never safe to drink unboiled and, that the white man should be able to turn on a tap in his 'Concession' and drink the water, the tap must be 'very good joss'.

Here is a cook story, which I have placed in Hongkong, though it was at one time so famous that, like Shakespeare, many others would have liked to claim it and I have heard it attributed to places as far away as East Africa.

A man and his wife were entertaining a married couple to dinner and his guests were much impressed by the excellence of their after-dinner coffee. If it was not presumptuous to ask, where did they get it? Their hostess was pleased at the compliment and gladly gave the information, which helped not at all, as they appeared to use the same supplier and pay the same price. There could be only one explanation, and here again it would be gratifying to the hostess. Obviously it was all in the way the coffee was prepared by that master of his trade, *her* cook. So the cook was summoned and bore his blushing honours thick upon him. But, when asked to explain his method, he became noticeably reluctant. So he was told that, if he was parting with a cherished secret, great would be his 'face' when it became known who was the master coffee-maker of Hongkong. So, 'Makee boil', he said, which did not take matters much further. 'Makee boil?' asked his mistress. 'How fashion? In what and for how long?' The cook was tongue-tied with embarrassment and it was some time before he could be persuaded to utter another word. 'Missy,' he stammered at last, 'makee boil in old sock.'—'Old sock? What old sock?' demanded the outraged lady of the house. 'B'long master sock,' came the nervous reply. Four horrified British voices joined in one great shout: 'Master's sock!' At once the cook added, in apologetic extenuation of his crime: 'Please, please, missy, no b'long clean sock.'

The Grand Panjandrum of the Chinese side of any large foreign concern's business was a gentleman known as a compradore. It is possible that in very early days his standing had not been high, as the same name is still used to describe the ordinary concern, comparable to the family grocer at home, from which a household would draw most of their supplies. But in later years the compradore of a big banking or trading house was a personage of very high standing indeed and, although his department would function as before, he was often given the status of a director. He would be a Chinese of wealth and repute and would deposit substantial securities by way of guarantee. He would then oversee all Chinese contracts, especially those to do with labour, and would personally guarantee all Chinese staff and make good any deficiencies for which they might be responsible. He also acted as banker for foreign staff and an order signed 'on' him was locally as good as a cheque. 'Compradore please pay' ran the wording of the printed form and, if some young men were sometimes in a position where they felt like underlining the 'please', the compradore was usually understanding. I do not know the origin of the name, but I can remember some confusion arising when the late Commodore Grace, R.N. (a son of 'W. G.'), once called at my father's house in Hongkong. My father's number one boy came to him and said, obviously puzzled, 'One master have got outside, wantchee see you. He say he b'long compradore.' I fancy that my father was more amused than was the commodore.

Another word of, to me, uncertain origins is the word 'pidgin'. I believe that 'pidgin English' is a term long used in countries other than China for a sort of lingua franca which undoubtedly grew up between the traders of old and the natives of the countries concerned and, as wide travelling sailors represented the English side of the exchange, they brought with them snippets of the various tongues they had encountered elsewhere. Of course, the Portuguese were earlier traders even than the British in Far Eastern waters and probably some pidgin English stems from Portuguese origins. Be that as it may, the word 'pidgin' on the China Coast means business or job. 'This b'long fool pidgin,' one would say to a boy who was making a mess of something he had been given to do. 'This no b'long my pidgin,' he would say of some job which was not his responsibility. I think that ignorance of these origins has led to the use of the phrase 'Not my pigeon' and the like in England in comparatively recent years. Basically pidgin English has much in common with nursery English—a breaking down of language to its simplest forms without grammar as we know it.

It is important to remember that, from earliest days, Chinese were, if anything, more socially aloof from foreigners than vice versa. Business dealings might be expedient and proper, but their homes and families were separate from such things. Of course early British traders were very much adventurers, and many of them were perhaps rather rough. Also there were few if any womenfolk with them. Any social contact was thus bound to be a lopsided affair and the effects of this have lasted to the present day. But, with the Portuguese and the Dutch, most of the stand-offishness was on the Chinese side and was somewhat broken down in course of time. Over the centuries the Portuguese and Dutch had early begun to intermarry with whatever race was native to their place of exile, but the Chinese were, if anything, slower to accept unto themselves the offspring of such unions than were the foreigners. With the Portuguese, especially, such unions tended to be prolific, if only because their faith was Roman. But, where the British Empire's white races were concerned, such unions were seldom, in the early days, between any but the very lowest elements on either side and, as a result, 'Eurasian' was something of a dirty word. In India the position was for a long time similar. Many of such Eurasians as might wish to elevate their standards of living and culture could find their faith something of a stumbling-block as they multiplied too fast and, if they were good parents, they found the task beyond them.

The vast majority of the Eurasians on the China Coast are classified as 'Portuguese' from Macao, or occasionally 'Macanese' but, as to the various racial mixtures involved, let me instance one family known to me personally. There were at one time three men bearing the same name on my staff in Hongkong: an uncle and two nephews who were not brothers. Uncle Fernando, the real old chief clerk type so often seen in old-time offices in England, could, in the appropriate dress, have passed any day as an Indian. Nephew Carlos was more nearly like a Chinese of the rather flat-faced type than anybody else could be, except perhaps the carefully selected Japanese fifth column men of the early Sino-Japanese war period. The third of the group could well have passed as of a rather heavily built Mediterranean type, or indeed as a pure Portuguese. And yet they were all closely related.

In later years, with the growth of understanding and social mixing;

with emancipated Chinese girls of good family teaching in missionary universities; with their being educated in America or perhaps Britain, the picture changed. Of those from the old days who were of good stock, many had survived as outstanding members of their communities, whether living as Chinese or as Europeans, and their new generations have been proving their quality in many lands. Where there is a gap of many centuries between Western culture and a lack of it, the difficulties besetting social integration are extreme. In countries such as China, where there has been a most pronounced culture, albeit of its own special kind, for longer than the Western world can remember, the hiatus is not too hard to bridge. British nationals in the China scene included, apart from the Eurasians, people of other races, and many of these were Indian. The Sikhs, in particular, had in the first instance come largely as soldiers, police, armed guards or watchmen. In early days, and indeed even more recently, it was difficult to be certain of the loyalty of local born recruits to such jobs, if a choice between loyalty to their employers or their fellow nationals arose. But the Sikh was equally a foreigner as well as being warlike in disposition. Much, too, of early British trade with China was developed through the East India Company, and Indian merchants were soon established and many Indians of all sorts followed. China's comparative proximity to Australasia attracted also a number of Australians and New Zealanders, both men and women, as these new territories developed. Hongkong dockyards built tonnage for Australian shipping lines: a New Zealander was closely associated with the early days of breakaway into the interior of Mao Tse Tung and other founders of China's last revolution. Of other foreign nationals, the most important were probably at one time the French, Germans, Japanese, Americans and Russians. But though the last named became, perhaps, the most numerous after the Russian Revolution in 1917, their standing collapsed. To a lesser extent this happened to the Germans also after World War I, but by the thirties they were commercially as firmly established as ever. No longer could any of the odium attaching to foreign traders who still claimed the protection of their extraterritorial rights apply to the Germans and they not unnaturally took any advantage they could of this. The Germans were still recognized by their own nation, whereas the Russians, equally unprotected by extraterritorial rights, were refugees from their homeland and were without passports or national status. In the thirties, as the power of Hitler grew, Shanghai became a refuge for thousands of stateless persons from many parts of Europe. Some of them had just become *persona non grata* with Nazified authorities in a number of countries. In this respect Hongkong differed from the China ports and its white population remained largely British. From earliest days it had been Hongkong's essentially British character which was its main characteristic despite its population being largely Chinese. Chinese business men from China proper would, if they could not settle some commercial dispute amicably, sometimes agree to let the Supreme Court in Hongkong decide their case for them. They would gladly pay all costs and agree to abide by the court's decision. Sometimes, in times of upheaval in their own country, political refugees would come to Hongkong for asylum.

Part Two

CHAPTER SIX

BACKGROUND TO THE TWENTIES

For the origins of events in China during the early twenties a brief look back is necessary to the happenings at the beginning of the century. There had been considerable unrest in China from about 1896, and this culminated in the famous Boxer Rising which led, in 1900, to the siege by the Boxers of the foreign legations in Peking and their relief by an International Force in the same year. In 1901 China and the Western powers signed the Peace of Peking and, in the same year, Sun Yat Sen, then a man of thirty-four, was trying unsuccessfully to establish some form of democratic government. In 1904 Japan declared war upon Russia and, in the course of the fighting in Manchuria, a Manchurian brigand chieftain of the name of Chang Tso Lin fought on the Japanese side and rose to prominence. By September 1905 it was all over, and at the Treaty of Portsmouth Russia ceded Port Arthur and Talienwan to Japan. In the same year Sun Yat Sen first publicly stated his three principles, Nationalism, Democracy and Socialism, and formed the Chinese Revolutionary League which was designed to enlist the financial support of Chinese overseas in spreading his revolutionary ideas throughout the country. His operations were largely conducted from abroad, for obvious reasons, and at one time there was a price of £100,000 on his head. On one occasion in London he was kidnapped and held at the Chinese Legation there, but the intervention of Sir James Cantlie, the surgeon who had known him in Hongkong and, through him, the Lord Salisbury of the day, secured his release. Sun had much to do with the inner organization which finally led to the revolution against the Manchu Government in Peking in 1911. Sun Yat Sen founded the Kuomintang Republican party, and on 5th January 1912 became provisional President. On 12th February the northern leader, Yuan Shih Kai, who was much more a man of action, was appointed to reorganize the country and Sun resigned in his favour. The Chinese silver dollar, based on the old Mexican dollar and then worth about two shillings, became known as the yuan and bore Yuan Shih Kai's head upon its face.

In 1913 Chang Tso Lin became military governor of Fengtien Province which was another name for Manchuria, and in the following year Yuan Shih Kai dissolved Parliament and ruled alone. But two years later, in 1916, Yuan Shih Kai died, and in 1917 Sun Yat Sen placed himself at the head of a movement for forming an Independent Republic of South China. But he was by character a theorist and propagandist rather than an administrator and he made little headway. This year of 1917 also saw the outbreak of the Russian Revolution, which was to have far-reaching consequences for Russian residents of Manchuria as well as of Russia itself. After the end of World War I, on 11th November 1918, many consequences quickly followed. In 1921–2 the Washington Conference took place, and this is mainly remembered in Britain for its provisions for the limitation of tonnage of capital ships in the world's navies. But various provisions were also made in relation to China. Section 7 established that the powers would withdraw their armed forces as soon as China 'shall assure the protection of the lives and property of foreigners'. China had provided a fertile recruiting ground for 'labour battalions' which served in large numbers behind the allied lines in France, and the personnel of these, when they were shipped home after the war, were very amenable to the new doctrines of Socialism which required them to form themselves into labour unions on the soil of Hongkong and the foreign Concessions. Such ground was ideal for attempting the organization of labour against capital, especially as it involved the fostering of a nationalistic spirit against the foreigner. In Hongkong in particular there was a good deal of labour unrest, and it says much for the persuasive powers of the organizers that they were able to bring about large-scale strikes there, where conditions of employment for Chinese were so incomparably superior to the conditions obtaining in China itself. Of course British service personnel took over essential services where necessary, and the condition of the interior mechanism of some of the ferry boats, which maintained an unfaltering service between island and mainland, was something of a shock to the orthodoxy of British naval engineers. They found it hard to understand how some of the craft had ever run under their Chinese engine-room staffs—with string and brown paper, almost literally, taking the place of approved materials. What a pity that the lesson of this experience was forgotten when, at the time of the Suez crisis, the capacity of the Egyptians to keep things going without us was scornfully disbelieved.

At about the time of this unrest in Hongkong the now Duke of Windsor, then Prince of Wales, was engaged in 1921–2 upon his world-wide empire cruise aboard the battle cruiser *Repulse*. The Hongkong authorities heard disquieting reports of an underlying anti-imperialism in India during his visit there, and now he was to come to Hongkong, where agitators were inciting the Chinese to boycott the imperialist prince, and mysterious posters to such effect were making their appearance overnight in prominent places in the city. The authorities were faced with a difficult problem. To cancel the prince's visit to Hongkong would be a serious admission of defeat; but to submit him to the slightest possible risk of an undignified withdrawal in the actual face of the popular clamour would be disastrous in the extreme.

The discussions seemed to be getting nowhere until at last an old councillor well versed in the workings of the Chinese mind spoke up. 'Your Excellency and gentlemen,' he said, 'I don't really know what all the fuss is about. You have everything organized: processions of pageantry and colour; military bands; all the hillsides and the harbour and the larger buildings to be illuminated with coloured lights; firing of salutes; fireworks on an unprecedented scale. Do you really think that the Chinese population are going to take any notice of posters which ask them to stay indoors, of agitators who want them to do anything to upset such a glorious party? Carry on with your programme as arranged and I guarantee that there will be no trouble.'

And so it was.

Of course in the matter of organizing strikes it was different. Few if any of the Chinese 'working class' in Hongkong were without dependants or some sort of family connections in China itself, and the threat of reprisals was adequate to ensure a good turn out. Least happy perhaps of all the colony's labour force, when it came to striking, were the domestic servants.

To them their jobs meant also homes and food, and to give them their due many of them were attached to the kindly but pathetic beings whose seeming helplessness in domestic matters gave them such an easy and remunerative living. They left their foreign homes with reluctance. How could the homes continue without them? Would they be there to come back to? They had grave misgivings. But of course these were as baseless as any foreign ideas that Chinese could not keep engines going with the aid of brown paper and string. After World War II my wife, who had spent the whole of it in England, chafed at the lack of enough to do in our Hongkong flat. Protocol forbade that we should do without servants, but she was determined to give ours afternoons off and such unheard-of things. Our servants soon got used to it and worshipped the ground she walked on, but when such ideas were first proposed to them their anxious concern for this helpless little white woman—who incidentally had driven ambulances in the Welsh mountains in winter, and in the Liverpool blitz—was pitiful to see. It was rather touching for a bystander to watch their tender briefing of her in the arts of making a pot of tea or boiling an egg. She thanked them gravely, and only a faint twinkle in her eye betrayed her impulse to giggle.

As the years passed China became more and more disorganized. Any central authority which Peking might have wielded since the revolution in 1911 had steadily weakened. Various provincial governors who had always thrived on extortion from their luckless subjects now found that efficiency paid larger dividends than they had ever dreamed of. If a neighbouring province was ruled by an inefficient muddler, then of a certainty the troops there would be ill equipped, and probably seldom paid. It was just too easy to offer them all a lump sum down payment in consideration of their handing over their province to a neighbouring governor. What loyalty need there be to their own ruler, who treated them badly and was not even the representative of a national authority? Of course, until he got the new taxation system going in his latest acquisition, the new Governor might find himself short of funds. This fathered another bright idea—to print local banknotes of his own and pay the troops with them. An edict was then issued cancelling, absolutely, any of the old notes which were not handed in at once. If the financial position was very serious the time limit could be made so short that nobody in outlying districts heard about it in time to get their money to the Central Bank of the province. Notes brought in late did not have to be honoured, and this was very profitable to the Governor, who had of course started by commandeering the bank. To refuse to accept the new notes offered by the troops was treason and punishable by death. This soon led to the strong as well as the unscrupulous Governor enlarging his sphere of influence until he ran his head against the boundaries of someone comparable to himself. Not all of these men were evil: some genuinely hoped that they could rule various provinces better than the existing incumbents, but it was a sorry state of affairs for the people.

At this point something more needs to be said on the subject of currency. Long before the advent of foreign currencies and ways of trade, the Chinese economy was based upon silver—silver bullion. Weights in silver were estimated in Chinese ounces, or taels, which, for silver, were the equivalent of about $1\frac{1}{3}$ ounces avoirdupois. There were other taels, just as we have more than one kind of ounce. Haikwan taels were customs taels and another tael was the Kuping tael. Ingots of a particular shape were produced in an infinite variety of sizes and of no precisely ordained weights and were stamped with the 'chop', or seal, of the person or body issuing them, as a guarantee of their standard of fineness. When used as currency they were weighed in the presence of the interested parties and their value agreed as so many taels and fractions thereof—or 'tael cents'. All such calculations would be made on the spot with the Chinese accountant's vade-mecum, the frame of beads known as an 'abacus', and more of this anon.

When the requirements of foreign trade brought in the Spanish and Mexican silver dollars, which were followed by a Chinese dollar equivalent, the value of this was about Tael Cents 70, or ·70 taels, which meant that a tael equalled about Mex. Dollars 1·40.

With the various provincial currencies behaving, in the days of the war lord type of local governors, rather like the seed that fell upon stony ground, springing up overnight and withering away again in the noonday sun, no man of substance would hold his money reserves in anything but solid silver. Thus the prosperous provincial who failed to hand in his banknotes on demand, in time for registration, would have recourse either to selling goods or livestock at forced sale rates or, better still, to broaching his little hoard of silver.

The really competent provincial governor simply could not lose.

For the expatriate, as for the Chinese man in the street, the silver dollar had long been the standard unit of currency for the more mundane transactions of normal life. You bought your household supplies or paid your ricksha or bus fare in dollar currency. You paid your surgeon's fees and your rent, or bought houses, horses, motor-cars and the like, in taels. Perhaps the tael could in some ways be compared to the English guinea; neither appeared as part of the coinage but each played its part in its own sphere. I do not believe that the Chinese dollar has ever been worth more than about two shillings to two shillings and threepence in the last forty-odd years, and that it could ever, in such a period, have been worth defacing for gain is a stark commentary upon the standards of life among the Chinese poor. Imagine splitting, into two thin slices, a coin rather larger than our own half-crown, extracting the silver, replacing its bulk with a base metal and then putting the two sides together again so neatly that the operation left no discernible scar. But coins so mistreated did not ring true, and one test which I was taught to apply involved holding the coin between finger and thumb with only one's nails touching the surface on either side. One then blew smartly upon the rim of the coin and held it very quickly to one's ear. Good silver gave forth a faint but unmistakable ringing sound; base metal gave forth no sound at all.

As regards the abacus, I remember something I was told in about 1925–6 by a rather senior gentleman of the Shanghai Municipal Council's Finance Department. He wanted to know what use, if any, my office made of calculating machines, as he was expecting a call by a sales expert from some very well-known manufacturer of such things. Next day he told me that he had had his caller and had suggested a competition between him with one of his machines and two or three of my friend's own clerks, picked men, with their abacuses. The result had astonished even my friend. There had, he said, been 'not much in it'. The dexterity and nimbleness of both fingers and brains of his experts had to be seen to be believed. You can buy an apple from a grubby-fingered fruit vendor on the ferries that ply round Hongkong and watch him peel it for you with the same one hand that is holding it, all without touching the flesh of the apple at all. He cannot afford to take too long about it—it delays his sales to other customers.

Meanwhile Chiang Kai Shek, born in Ningpo in 1887 and thus twenty years younger than Sun Yat Sen, had long graduated from the Military Academy at Whampoa. There were German instructors at this academy and Chiang had emerged with far more than a smattering of the military arts and had soon shown himself a capable leader of men. This earnest young soldier, later connected by marriage with Sun Yat Sen, had all of the latter's idealism and a good deal of practical ability as well. The people of China were heartily sick of all their provincial war lords, and when Sun Yat Sen, the dreamer, died of cancer in March 1925 the people of the south were quick to support Chiang Kai Shek, the man of action, who rose in his place. Chiang was determined to overthrow all the corrupt local rulers and establish good government throughout the country. But he had no intention of paying his troops and buying his armaments by fleecing the people, and unfortunately the

Western powers could not recognize nor help him so long as Peking was still the accepted official centre of government. So in desperation Chiang turned to Moscow, where there were no such scruples, and a mission, headed by one Michael Borodin, was quickly sent with ample funds to support its work. It was Sun who had originally called in Borodin's mission, but it was the emergence of Chiang, after his death, that enabled it to become effective. It was Borodin and the mission's chief military expert, General Galen, who enabled Chiang to master practically the whole country, and before long to compel the foreigners to surrender their long-cherished extraterritorial rights.

In the far north, Manchuria or, as the Chinese named it, the province of Fengtien, had long, as I have said earlier, been under the virtually undisputed sway of Chang Tso Lin, who had been appointed its military governor. The situation in Manchuria itself had its own complications. It will be remembered that Chang Tso Lin had first risen to power through his association with the Japanese in the Russo-Japanese War, and I do not know whether his choice of sides was in whole or in part dictated by any of several influences: choice of the seeming lesser evil; preference for men of his own colour; better payment.

Manchuria had long been the scene of much inter-racial conflict: the Manchus themselves, whose earlier conquests had placed the ruling Manchu Dynasty upon the imperial throne in Peking; the Russians whose territories enclosed Manchuria on two sides; and then the Japanese, whose powers there had been almost complete after the Russo-Japanese War. As long as the old Russian Empire existed, Russian people in Manchuria had some status. But they were almost all of a class inimical to the new Communist regime in Russia, and were therefore technically without any national status whatever. As the old ruling classes and bourgeoisie in eastern Russia became more and more oppressed by the new masters of their homeland many of them fled in desperation, and their easiest route was across the Amur River into Manchuria. Many of their younger women managed to escape by sea from the Russian port of Vladivostok, their passages being paid at lowest rates by the keepers of dance halls, cabarets and brothels in the China ports, especially Shanghai, where it was sometimes said, in the twenties and thirties, that erudite and entertaining conversation was as like to be found in the brothels as anywhere. Any white man, whatever he might be like, was always sought after in the hope of persuading, inveigling or trapping him into marriage. Such a marriage brought with it a passport, if nothing else. There was a heartrending story of a young British assistant in a large bank in Harbin who was called upon one evening in his quarters by an aristocratic looking old Russian gentleman whom he had met a few times across the counter. The old man brought with him three daughters between the ages of seventeen and twenty-two. They were well enough, if rather shabbily, dressed, but their father explained that, in order to keep up appearances, one must cut costs somewhere, and they had not had a proper meal for three days. In anguished pity the young Briton summoned his domestics and commanded his larder to be stripped for a really good meal, and it was eaten within half an hour. Within another half-hour it had reappeared and a doctor, who was hurriedly sent for, explained that their systems were too unused to good food to be able to cope with such a repast.

The old man had known that the young one's employers would not sanction his marrying when he was so junior. It would involve them in housing problems and in raising his salary beyond that of his fellows. But he had hoped that he would accept his pick of the three as a gift, as cook, housekeeper, mistress or combination of all three. It was better than letting her starve. The young man's manager was understanding and sympathetic next day, but if he helped where would it end? How could the young man take a girl on, on any basis, without wanting to help her sisters, her parents and who could tell how many other relations? So cables were hurriedly exchanged and the young man was transferred that day to another branch a thousand or two miles away. As a result of this and other like incidents, no British concerns ever afterwards stationed unmarried men in Manchuria.

Such then was the Manchuria over which Chang Tso Lin ruled. It is a rich and fertile land, and Chang Tso Lin was rich, powerful and an experienced military leader. In Peking the death of Yuan Shih Kai in 1916 had left a void, and there were plenty of men who would have liked to fill it. Soon one soldier had emerged, capable by Chinese standards of those days, and probably of a more rigid integrity than was usual. His name was Wu Pei Fu and he seems to have been more of a strong man than a political schemer, so it became apparent before long that a head-on clash between Chang in Manchuria and Wu in Peking was inevitable. Wu Pei Fu knew that his supremacy in Peking would never be secure until he had conquered or eliminated Chang Tso Lin. But, after the death of Sun Yat Sen, the power of the Kuomintang Party, which he had founded, grew apace. Then its new young military leader arose, and Wu realized that if he did not deal with the Kuomintang they would never be satisfied until they had, sooner or later, dealt with him. So he was faced with a possible war on two fronts and decided to stabilize his northern boundaries as far as possible while he met the threat from the south. But the Chinese, south of the Yangtsze, did not take kindly to the, to them, virtual foreigners from the north, and Wu's troops, who followed the age-long behaviour pattern of Chinese soldiery, made certain of the inhabitants' hostility by their treatment of the despised southerners. By the summer of 1926 Chiang's troops had advanced, in places, as far as the Yangtsze River and the northerners were holding on desperately to the walled city of Wuchang, which lies on the south bank opposite to the cities of Hankow and Hanyang which are only separated by the swift-flowing tributary, the Han River, at its junction with the Yangtsze's north bank. Each of this trinity of cities, known collectively as Wuhan, had its own special significance in the struggle.

Wuchang was the terminal point of the railway which ran through Changsha, an important provincial capital to the south, and down to its southernmost terminus at Canton some six hundred to seven hundred miles away. From Wuchang a ferry ran to Hankow which, apart from being a transhipment port for all cargoes and passengers bound to or from the middle and upper river, was also the southern terminus of the Peking–Hankow Railway.

Hanyang was a large centre of iron and steel industry, so the immense importance of Wuhan, as a whole, to anyone who wanted to control the lower Yangtsze basin, is understandable.

CHAPTER SEVEN

PARTURIUNT MONTES

'The mountains are in labour,' the Roman poet Horace wrote, and this perhaps describes the state of affairs in China in the mid twenties. But Horace's deliberate anticlimax of a 'ridiculous mouse' being born did not follow. Chiang Kai Shek's rapid and successful strides in the south had roused the people far before him on his progress to the Yangtsze River, that rambling but massive boundary across the heart of China from the Pacific to the High Plateau of Tibet. As so often happens, it was among the students at the universities, which were foreign sponsored, that the temperature rose most rapidly. The foreign powers had promised, by treaty, to withdraw their troops and gunboats as soon as China herself could protect the lives and property of the aliens in her midst. All right then: here was a great new leader, sweeping all before him with a disciplined army that did not destroy as they conquered. Let the white man keep his word. But the students' impetuous manifestations of nationalism created disturbances unlikely to generate confidence. Foreign armed forces had not withdrawn, and were not likely to with such goings on. Too much of a paraded show of force might in itself be something of an irritant, and the tendency of the international authorities in Shanghai was to play down demonstrations as much as possible and avoid what is nowadays termed a confrontation. The International Settlement's police force was largely British officered, although various other nationalities were represented, including, for example, White Russian survivors of the old days of Imperial Russia. The police were supported by a substantial body of citizens known as the Shanghai Volunteer Corps, which included various national units such as the Scottish Company, the American Company and the Portuguese Company, as well as the Armoured Car Company, the Shanghai Light Horse and several British companies known as A, B, C, etc.

In mid May of 1925 I was in Hongkong and was ordered north to Shanghai in the last week of that month to join my employers' great office there. I left Hongkong in one of the ships of my firm's Calcutta–Japan service and we were off the Yangtsze estuary, less than twelve hours' steaming from Shanghai, on the fateful 30th May. There had been no indications of anything out of the ordinary in the situation to the north when we had left Hongkong, and we passengers were astonished when the captain told us that he had just had wireless instructions from Shanghai not to call there but to proceed direct to Kobe, which was his next port. I must admit that I was delighted at the thought of a free trip to Japan, but I was to be thwarted. Less than a day later new orders came, and I cursed to myself as I saw the curving wake of the ship as she turned about. It was almost exactly fifteen years later that I finally saw Kobe, and May 1940 was not an ideal time for an Englishman to arrive in Japan.

The man I was to work directly under in Shanghai met me on our arrival at the wharf and, after depositing my luggage at some lodgings he had arranged, took me to our firm's large office building on the water-front. The spacious office room we entered had in it many busy Chinese, but there were a number of larger desks distributed at suitable vantage points which were either vacant or tenanted by tired-looking men in khaki uniforms, or maybe just heaped with tin hats, rifles and equipment. The Shanghai Volunteers were fully mobilized and on round-the-clock patrols throughout the Settlement in support of the police. Even the older men belonged to a 'reserve company' which, in emergencies such as this one, had a considerable share of duties. Commerce had to be attended to as and when circumstances permitted. Of course in 1925 only the youngest and greenest, such as myself and the older men, had not seen service in World War I. Among the much older men were a few veterans who had fought in the Boer War at the turn of the century.

I soon found out what had happened.

Student demonstrations had been going on for some time, and anxiety to avoid rough handling of the participants had been taken as a sign of weakness. May 30th was a day of a race meeting at a partly Chinese-run international Race Club on the outskirts, and many British, including the most senior police officials, were there. Meanwhile student disturbances began to develop in the city's main shopping thoroughfare, the Nanking Road, and in the end the police felt forced to arrest some of the offenders and take them in custody to

Louza, the district police station of the area. Soon a mob had formed and was rapidly inflamed by the excited students into attempting a frontal attack upon Louza to rescue their friends. The officer in charge had a limited force at his disposal, but once the mobs had begun to gather it is difficult to see what force, short of a battalion or two of trained troops supported by armoured vehicles, could have achieved without violence.

Finally, he gave orders to fire above the heads of the mob, but with little effect. So the next volley was aimed and there were many casualties and the mobs dispersed and fled. Some time later a court of inquiry was held which was jointly presided over by a British and an American judge. They found that the police officer had had no alternative, but that he had been put in such a situation only because his seniors had not had the foresight to provide him with more men. This was a not unnatural conclusion, but student disturbances had long gone on and it had been felt that to take them too seriously was to give the organizers too great a sense of their own importance. It is easy to be wise after the event.

Be that as it may, the authorities did not wait for the court of inquiry before mobilizing every possible means of law and order enforcement. All able-bodied white men in the Settlement were called upon to play their part, and had just to carry on their normal occupations at such moments as were left to them from patrol duties, sleep and food. Most foreign business houses included white women among their staffs, and arrangements had also to be made for their safe escort between home and place of business. Sometimes a man might come off duty in the business district at two or three in the morning and about three or four miles from home. He never knew where he might be when relieved, so could make no advance arrangements for transport; taxis were sometimes hard to come by. In these circumstances the warm, welcoming atmosphere of one or two of the best-kept brothels was particularly inviting on a cold winter's morning. To those who could afford their charges, a hot bath, a room to change in and a first-class breakfast were readily available. One youngish employee of a big foreign organization, whose 1914–18 war service had gained him N.C.O.'s rank in the Volunteer Corps, once came off duty in the small hours and decided, as a bachelor, that he was in need of home comforts and feminine sympathy, even on a financial basis, and entered one such establishment. A charming young Russian lady welcomed him upstairs, and he was somewhat taken aback, on entering the room, to observe leaning against the wall in a corner a perfectly good British service rifle which was obviously the property of the Shanghai Volunteer Corps. When he left he took it with him, determined to unmask the irresponsible rascal who must have left it there. But another shock was in store for him when he got to Volunteer headquarters. The number on the butt plate was easily checked with the armoury records, and he discovered that the rifle had been issued to one of his own directors—and a married man at that! It took him more tact than he had ever known himself to possess to get out of that situation.

A more serious incident occurred involving the Shanghai Light Horse, although fortunately it passed off without any consequences, as by a miracle no lives were lost. The stands of the Race Club, with stables handy, were the obvious place for a mobilization headquarters and billet for the Light Horse with their sturdy little Manchurian ponies. The club was just outside the congested downtown district of the settlement, and the Light Horse comprised an armoured car and a Lewis gun squadron as well as their cavalry. Only men accustomed to handle Lewis guns were allowed to use them, but days went by without opportunity to practise, and these men were business men who led their own lives when not on duty. In such difficult times it would be too much to expect such men to abstain from beer and other liquors when off duty. The only trouble was that emergency duty could always descend upon them at the most unexpected moments, and one day it happened. To a party of troopers in the club bar came an SOS from the Nanking road, half a mile away. Student snipers were in occupation of the flat roof of a vast department store and were firing upon passers-by in the street. A man had been dispatched to lead them to the spot and point out their target. By the time he arrived drinks had been hurriedly swallowed and a Lewis gun section was aboard the armoured car and raring to go. As they approached the spot their guide told them to open fire upon the roof of the store. But unfortunately there were two such stores, one on each side of the road, and they chose the wrong one. Worse was to follow. 'No, no, you fool!' yelled the exasperated guide. 'The other building!' The gunner was far too excited to play his part of a trained soldier properly. He traversed the gun in a wide arc to bring it to bear upon its proper target. He got it there, but unfortunately he forgot to release the trigger *en route* and a hail of bullets swept their straight course down Shanghai's busiest thoroughfare. Not an incident to be proud of, but what else could be expected in all the circumstances of the time?

However, the general state of preparedness of the Settlement authorities gradually had its effect and a sort of uneasy calm returned. Of course Shanghai was easily accessible to the sea, and the cruisers and destroyers of Britain's China Squadron were always represented in the harbour and could always be doubled in numbers at short notice.

But farther up the great valley of the Yangtsze life was not so simple. The various provincial war lords who had long looked upon it as their own preserve were much more disturbed by the threat from Chiang Kai Shek in the south than by the, to them, usual pattern of threatened punitive expeditions from Peking. Each was trying by one means or another to establish himself more firmly, to eliminate weak neighbours in order to strengthen his own position. Chinese armies of the older pattern were moving hurriedly hither and yon. Rolling stock on railways was being seized, sometimes for possible use in an attack on neighbours, sometimes to deny those neighbours the facilities for doing likewise. British ships which berthed at way ports *en route* between Shanghai, Hankow and ports beyond were liable suddenly to be boarded at gun point by thousands of ill-clad, ill-armed and ill-paid Chinese soldiery who demanded free passage. Often considerable bodies of such troops would be encamped on the river bank and would while away their boredom with target practice at conveniently passing shipping. In many such places the river might be several miles wide, but the shifting currents of its silt-laden flow often ran, deeply, only close under one bank or the other. The only navigable channel might in such case run for many miles close under the lee of a river bank swarming with trigger-happy troops. By the time punitive gunboats arrived the troops had sometimes moved and the site was vacant or occupied by their relatively innocent successors. One fairly successful stratagem was employed by the Royal Navy on a number of occasions, and the idea probably originated from the famous 'Q' ships, the disguised warships that did so much to combat the submarine menace to our shipping in World War I. When a Chinese military encampment was known to be in a particular place, and had been giving trouble there, a little gunboat would be lashed alongside an innocent merchant ship at the last port before the trouble spot. She could be lashed to port or to starboard according to which side of the river held the encampment. When the peaceful-looking ship moved into the danger zone and small arms fire began to rattle against her sides and endanger the lives of the captain and helmsman on the bridge, she would suddenly put on a little extra speed and cast off her satellite. As she drew away the little gunboat would emerge from behind her, its full armament blazing at point-blank range. The first psychological effect was tremendous, as these vessels each carried two mighty six-inch naval guns in addition to lesser armament. But unfortunately their guns were of typical flat-trajectory high muzzle-velocity naval type, with armour-piercing high-explosive shells. When aimed at the informal encampments of Chinese troops on river banks of plain mud they buried themselves feet deep before exploding: much noise, much flinging of enormous showers of earth into the air, but little loss of life.

Prince George (later, Duke of Kent) was a young naval officer who had newly joined the staff of the Rear Admiral Yangtsze (R.A.Y.). He spent quite a time in Hankow, on and off, and was, simply by virtue of who he was, something of a problem to the British authorities there. As 1926 wore on and the victorious troops of Chiang Kai Shek drew nearer in their northward advance towards the Yangtsze, more and more white strangers began to appear. No doubt there were also many oriental newcomers, but these were not so noticeable to the eye of the foreigner. The numerous alleged White Russians, who came to earn their living in Hankow by means which varied according to sex and individuals, all claimed to be White Russians fleeing from the persecution in their homeland. But even to them any Red sympathizers in their midst were indistinguishable from the rest. And even among the White Russians there were crooks and thugs. Some of these men were hangers-on, attached to cabaret performers, night club hostesses and prostitutes, and these eked out the incomes they extorted from their women by preying upon the frequenters of such establishments. It was reasonable to suppose that any white man issuing forth from such a place in the small hours would be an easy prey—and they usually were. Into such a troubled neighbourhood P. G., as we called him, could not be permitted to go unescorted at night even on supremely innocent excursions, such as to a cinema, let alone to a café for a glass of beer. For the most part, a husky young lieutenant of H.M.S. *Bee*, the gunboat flagship, was detailed to accompany him, and I believe that they got on well together. Other hazards, such as the occasional bullets that whistled through the streets from across the river, once Chiang's troops began to besiege Wu Pei Fu's garrison of northern troops in Wuchang, were taken as a matter of course. But on the occasions when his official escort was on duty P. G. had to stay on board. However, fortunately there was in Hankow at that time an enormous young Irishman who was then on the staff of Shell's Far Eastern company, the

Asiatic Petroleum Company. This young man, Ronnie Parr, had been runner-up in the public schools' heavyweight boxing championship not many years before and fitness was a fetish with him. At every sport he touched he excelled, and represented Hankow in interport matches at cricket, rugger, polo, water polo and so on. But boxing was still his great love, and the joint naval squadrons of all the Western powers on the Yangtsze had never been able to find a boxer who could beat him. Stories used to circulate of unfortunate Russian thugs who were ill advised enough to molest him in dark alleys at night. He never touched anything stronger than beer and, though he might spend many hours under an overhead fan in a night haunt on a hot and sticky tropical summer's night, he was never the worse for wear when he emerged. Rumour had it that any attackers who didn't escape used to end up in hospital, but however that might be nobody had been heard to accost him for some time and he was an ideal escort for P. G.

Meanwhile the social life of the British in Hankow and other such settlements continued in the way normal to it. These little pockets of Britons varied, of course, their way of life according to their size. All formed part of larger international communities, but in ports such as Hankow, Tientsin and, to a lesser degree, Tsingtao, the British were numerous enough to be able, if they wished, to be in some degree independent of the other foreign nationalities. But in the tiny little way-port communities this last word only had a meaning if all nationalities co-existed in amity. If a man or a woman were known as a stinker, he or she had no more friends amongst their own nationals than among any other. The community usually cured them, but if it didn't it broke them.

Wherever the big firms operated their European staff had to be housed, and this meant owning considerable blocks of suitable property in the great ports of Hongkong and Shanghai and, to a lesser extent, in Hankow and Tientsin. Elsewhere a large building with offices on the ground floor, and probably a wharf and godowns close at hand, would house the agent, as he was called, on the upper one or two floors. Inevitably, in the bigger ports, this led some firms into property development, and in Hankow, when I was in charge of the department that ran Lloyds' Agency, I was also, at a very young age, in charge of a property department with an annual rent roll of the equivalent of some £30,000–£40,000. A large proportion of the foreign community lived in such houses and flats, which were to be found in building estates where Chinese street names, such as San Kiao Street, jostled with good old names from Scotland, like Lockerbie Road. In those days, there was no flying home to England for leaves and most men worked a four- or five-year stint, at the end of which they would get upwards of six months at home with passage paid and a time allowance of three months for travelling—which was not excessive. Many a household, if they expected to return to the same place, usually tried to keep their homes intact by letting them furnished for the period of their absence, often to the people who were temporarily replacing them. Sometimes of course the relief man was a bachelor who preferred to live in an hotel or club, and in such event personal contacts usually secured a good arrangement with some foreigner of like standing. But on one occasion in Hankow, in my predecessor's day, something went wrong, and for some reason a man left the letting of his house, for nine months or so, to a plausible Chinese contact. The house faced on to a square with grass lawns in the centre and some fifty or sixty other houses sharing its amenities, and the Chinese quickly secured a foreign tenant whose actual nationality was somewhat obscure, but who gladly paid an exorbitant rent for many months in advance. The new household was a bit of a puzzle to the lady residents of the square that spring. Nobody ever met any of the inhabitants nor even discovered who they were and, gay though they appeared to be, with sounds of music and much illumination every night, the usual channels of gossip via Chinese domestic staff seemed blocked up entirely. And then, summer. Few houses were proofed in those days against mosquitoes, which were plentiful and occasionally of the malaria-bearing *Anopheles* type. But most people submerged themselves under mosquito-nets and had fans turning and windows wide in the humid heat of summer nights. In such conditions of trying to sleep, one was apt to be sensitive to noise, and it was far too hot, very often, to cover even one's body, let alone one's head and ears, with a sheet. So it wasn't long before the leading ladies of the square were getting up to peer in the middle of the night from their darkened windows at the mystery house, all of the windows of which were blazing with light and emitting, so it seemed, different forms of potted music from each. There were no radios in domestic households in China in those days, so this musical feast must mean a separate gramophone and a separate person to put on and to change records in every room in the house. It was very puzzling. But at last one morning the ladies, who were catching up on their sleep after their husbands had gone to business, were rudely awakened by nothing less than a fracas in their own select square. It was bright daylight, and they could see quite plainly some half-dozen or so young men on the front steps opposite, expostulating wildly with a female apparition in the doorway. The apparition was responding in a harsh voice suggestive of bad language and was shaking her fist. What made it still more strange was that the young men were all in the garb of the lower deck of the U.S. Navy! And then police appeared, and before the end of the day the house was locked up and a surprising number of hard-working young ladies had to find a new place of business—or give up. I wonder which they did.

It would be wrong if I have given the impression that life on the China Coast was all laughter and luxurious living. There were often long periods of relative stability in the lives of older married people, but younger men, especially bachelors, were a sort of mobile reserve which could be, and frequently was, used to plug gaps due to illness or misfortune over a front that extended for thousands of miles. And in the very small communities the whole of their area was a potential prey to squabbling, racketeering war lords, and if a few white people got mopped up in the course of some operation it was just too bad. In such places there was ever present the possibility of a sudden alarm which would involve the evacuation of women and children within a few hours. The wise man also kept a large store of tinned food, and perhaps a little English or American paper money, in case the local currency became suddenly debased overnight. So although there was plenty of gaiety, there was often a feverish phreneticism about it. We were so often on the brink of something—we knew not what. But the compensations were many: in one place sailing might be superb, and golf also, and bathing almost all the year round and glorious mountainous country for hiking; in another the sailing mediocre, the country flat and the bathing limited to the club's swimming-pool, but with a varied night life that went on till morning and theatricals and Russian ballet and Cossack riding schools and cross-country riding and golf that was adequate. Elsewhere it might be the pheasant, snipe, partridge, woodcock and duck shooting. Whatever was the special attraction of any place was always well organized and relatively inexpensive there.

Hankow lay at a much lower level than its sister cities of Wuchang and Hanyang, and was boxed in at the back by an enormous dike which came to the Yangtsze's edge below Hankow and that of the tributary Han on the other side. Within this area lay, behind the town, the Race Club and the country houses of the top executives with, beyond them again, Chinese market gardens and small holdings as far as the Changkung Dike. Beyond it lay a vast area of gently undulating grass land stretching as far as the eye could see and dotted here and there with little knolls. Every summer all this grass land was flooded to a depth of many feet, and as the water rose the little knolls became submerged also. But they served a purpose, as they provided temporary refuges for anyone caught by the floods when they were too far from the safety of the dike with its motor road top. As autumn was followed by winter the floods receded and the land dried out, leaving miles and miles of fertile land which, by about March or April, was thick with succulent fresh grazing. Those of us who rode limited our riding for the rest of the year to the congested market gardens and farm lands within the dike. Racecourse, polo ground, flat farm land: it was a dull life for the little ponies. But once the far country had dried out some of us would ride up to and over the dike, and in a matter of seconds our ponies were transformed into mad things. Plunging and leaping playfully, almost like frisking young lambs, they could test anybody's capacity to stay in the saddle. It was one of the most exhilarating experiences I can remember in a fairly long life. I had come to Hankow in March 1926 at twenty-four hours' notice, with a suitcase, to fill a gap for a fortnight; but another emergency prevented the more senior man intended for the post from arriving, and I stayed there just over two years. My heavy luggage was packed up and sent after me. In my twenty-four years in the Far East I had many such emergency moves.

To return to events around the Yangtsze in the second half of 1926. The country was in a state of great unrest, not only from Hankow to the coast, but above Hankow, to Ichang, to the Gorges and beyond.

There was little pretence at legality on the part of any of the contestants for power in the upper Yangtsze province of Szechwan (sometimes spelt Szechuen). As the Japanese were to discover later, it was not an easy region to invade, and the squabbling bandit chiefs of the area may well have thought that if Chang Tso Lin had risen from banditry to respectable domination of Manchuria, it should be equally possible in their remote province. One result of this was a large and nefarious arms traffic in which a number of foreign adventurers made fortunes and some of them lost their lives. This traffic was largely financed by the smuggling downriver of opium, and consuls of some foreign nationalities were not too scrupulous about allowing ships of dubious ownership to register under their national flags. Any merchant officer who consented to command such ships was running grave risks, as he was expected to, and the rewards were great if he survived.

Enough has been said of the hazards of navigation in the Gorges in daylight. After dark the dangers were beyond description. But it used to be done, with the object of evading seizure either by the vigilant customs or by the equally vigilant gangs of hijackers employed by rival bandit war lords.

Chief of all these miscreants was a man named Yang Sen, and so powerful did he become that he even ventured downriver as far as Ichang and tried to establish himself there. But, despite his preoccupation with the advance of Chiang Kai Shek, the northern general Wu Pei Fu was able to send a well-armed and comparatively disciplined force which quickly ousted Yang Sen and drove him back into the more mountainous regions up the river.

So it was that Yang Sen established himself at Wanhsien, a riverside port which lies about half way between Ichang, at the foot of the Yangtsze Gorges, and Chungking. Wanhsien lies in still mountainous country some sixty or seventy miles beyond the last great Gorge. It had long been a local centre of authority if not always of government, as we understand it and, as Yang Sen's main base, was relatively well fortified.

In the conditions of the time it was obviously impossible to allow British ships to carry Chinese so-called troops, and their masters were forbidden to do so in any circumstances. This infuriated Yang Sen, who openly boasted that he would force ships of any nationality to carry his men whenever he wanted to.

It so happened that in August 1926 the S.S. *Wanliu* of the China Navigation Company, a local venture of the great Alfred Holt's Blue Funnel Line's Far Eastern agents, was approaching Yun Yang, a town about forty miles below Wanhsien. Several large sampans full of Yang Sen's troops pushed off from the foreshore with the intention of boarding the steamer. In obedience to his orders, the captain refused to stop, but the leading sampans persisted in an attempt to get on board, with the result that one capsized and several soldiers were drowned. Yang Sen seized upon this incident to demand a huge sum in compensation from the ship's owners, claiming that the military pay chest had been on board the capsized craft. When this absurd claim was rejected, Yang Sen's troops seized another of the company's ships, the *Wanhsien*, upon her anchoring at the port of her name, to detain her until his demands were met.

At this point it may help to clarify the story if I give a brief summary of the disposition of British gunboats on the Yangtsze as a whole.

The entire force was under the command of Rear Admiral Yangtsze, based at Hankow, and consisted primarily of some half-dozen general purpose gunboats which had originally been designed for service against the Turks on the Tigris and Euphrates rivers in World War I. With a main armament of two six-inch guns they were powerful little ships for operation in flat country, but quite unable to manœuvre in the rapid-ridden waters of the upper Yangtsze. These were the Insect Class: *Bee* (flagship), *Scarab, Mantis, Cockchafer, Ladybird* and *Gnat*. Their complement was fifty-four officers and ratings. For use in more narrow and tortuous channels, including the upper Yangtsze, R.A.Y. had at his disposal a number of ships named after birds and mounting six-pounder guns: *Woodcock* and *Woodlark* (total complement twenty-six each vessel), old and very small but suitable for use in the shallower Siang River, which runs south from the Yangtsze to Changsha and the Tung Ting Lakes; *Teal* and *Widgeon* (complement thirty-one each vessel), newer and more highly powered for use on the upper river as far as Chungking.

In order that the two upper river gunboats could get away to Shanghai for annual refit, the Insect Class *Cockchafer* was specially fitted with more powerful steering gear, which made it possible for her to operate in the Gorges area during the high-water months from about April to November. At extreme low water her length made it impossible for her to manœuvre there in safety. She therefore spent the summers on the upper river, while *Widgeon* and *Teal*, in turn, went away for refit, and when they were both back on station she herself went to Shanghai for the same purpose.

Thus at the time of the beginning of these events the Senior Naval Officer Upper River, Commander Paul Berryman, was in *Widgeon* at Chungking; *Cockchafer*, under Lieutenant-Commander Acheson, was at Wanhsien and *Teal* was away on refit.

The Merchant Fleet, which was the object of Yang Sen's spleen, was that of the China Navigation Company, and all its upper Yangtsze ships had names beginning with Wan: *Wantung, Wanliu, Wanhsien.*

H.M.S. *Cockchafer*'s captain, Lieutenant-Commander Acheson, promptly sent an armed party on board the *Wanhsien* to demand the withdrawal of the Chinese troops.

Unfortunately, while the argument was going on, another China Navigation Company ship, the *Wantung*, arrived in harbour and had barely anchored when she too was seized. Despite the consequent serious depletion of his small crew, Acheson sent another armed party on board *Wantung*, but he was now in no position to work and fight his ship effectively and his position became impossible.

Yang Sen sent an ultimatum to the *Cockchafer* that he would fire upon her unless her two boarding parties were withdrawn at once. Unfortunately the only other commissioned officer of the *Cockchafer*, her first lieutenant, was away on sick leave, and all that Acheson could do was to withdraw his boarding parties, report the situation by wireless and await reinforcements.

Berryman in *Widgeon* immediately sailed for Wanhsien with the British Consul on board, but struck a rock and, though the damage was small, repairs delayed her for a few days, and this delay enabled Yang Sen to concentrate all his troops in Wanhsien on the river bank opposite to where the ships were anchored.

When *Widgeon* finally arrived Yang Sen had had some light field guns posted to command the anchorage and refused to see the British Consul or discuss the matter. He insisted that his outrageous demands be met in full and threatened to open fire upon the gunboats if they moved. An impasse had been reached.

By this time the light cruiser *Despatch* had arrived at Hankow. R.A.Y. immediately ordered the requisition of the Indo-China Steam Navigation Company's S.S. *Kiawo*, then at Ichang, and instructed H.M.S. *Mantis*, also there, to prepare her for service and mount one of her own pom-poms on board her and make ready a position for a second one. Meanwhile he sent H.M.S. *Scarab* to Ichang with the commander of H.M.S. *Despatch*, Commander Darley, one other officer and about thirty men from *Despatch* on board. This party was augmented by an officer and ten men each from *Mantis* and *Scarab*, and the whole party set sail at about 9 a.m. on 5th September in the *Kiawo*, which now flew the White Ensign, though she retained her own master and crew as none of the naval party had any experience of upper river navigation.

During the passage upriver both pom-poms were securely mounted and tested; machine-gun posts were set up and boarding parties organized in case it became necessary to board the two vessels to rescue their masters and officers. This was the first objective; the second was to seize and remove the ships if possible. When night fell *Kiawo* anchored at a quiet deserted spot several miles inside the great Wushan Gorge and, as her stone-coloured hull and red funnel with black top were distinctive, her crew spent the hours of darkness painting her funnel black and her hull likewise from the waterline upwards. But the black paint ran short, so the upper strake of the hull plating was painted red.

At dawn on 6th September, H.M.S. *Kiawo* weighed anchor and, while she was on her way, all preparations were completed and orders rehearsed. Upper river merchant vessels were not equipped with wireless in those days and an emergency naval W/T set, with operator, had been installed while she was at Ichang. But unfortunately the set failed to function, and it proved impossible to establish wireless communication with *Widgeon* or *Cockchafer* at Wanhsien. This was a grave handicap for Darley, who thus could not contact *Widgeon* and make a concerted plan with Berryman. Darley had to keep on sending in the hope that it was only his reception that was at fault and that messages might be getting through to Berryman. So he sent repeated instructions to Berryman to try to slip away and rendezvous with *Kiawo* about twelve miles below Wanhsien. But when *Kiawo* arrived there at about 4.30 p.m. the anchorage was empty and Darley had no choice but to push on and deal with the situation as he found it.

At about 5.30 p.m. H.M.S. *Kiawo*, at action stations and with three White Ensigns flying, steamed round the great bend below Wanhsien and the harbour opened to view with *Widgeon* lying ahead of the two merchant vessels and *Cockchafer* anchored below and to the inside of them.

S.S. *Wanhsien* was anchored astern of S.S. *Wantung* and, as H.M.S. *Kiawo* approached them at full speed, Williamson, on the bridge with Darley, asked him for his orders.

'Lay me alongside, Mr Master, as they used to say in the old Navy!'

So Williamson steered for the *Wanhsien* as the nearer of the two and, reducing speed at the last moment, ran alongside her. There could be no question of anchoring, so grapnels were hooked on to *Wanhsien* and made fast while Williamson kept position by necessary engine movements. The *Wanhsien* was full of Chinese troops, but they seemed dumbfounded by the sudden appearance and rapid approach of the *Kiawo*. They made no hostile move until the order was given 'Boarders Away!' when hell broke loose and all ships were at once under very heavy fire from both banks.

In all the confusion the master and officers of the *Wanhsien* succeeded in gaining the bridge deck and clambering over the rails to the comparative safety of the *Kiawo*. So far so good.

But *Kiawo* was meanwhile under heavy fire from the Chinese troops in the *Wantung* until her machine-guns forced them under cover. *Wantung*'s master, chief officer and chief engineer then succeeded in escaping to the after end of their ship but, fearing that the Chinese would sooner or later search for them, the two officers leapt overboard and swam towards a French gunboat which was lying between *Wantung* and the beach but taking no part in the proceedings. The chief officer succeeded in reaching the Frenchman, but a shot hit the unfortunate chief engineer and he was drowned. Meanwhile the master had lowered himself over the stern and remained hanging there undetected. During this time the boarding parties aboard the *Wanhsien* had been battling at point-blank range and had driven all the Chinese troops under cover. So Darley dashed on board her to rally and withdraw his men. But he was shot dead as he did so and command of the *Kiawo*'s force thus devolved on the first lieutenant of H.M.S. *Mantis*, who had been directing the fire of the pom-poms against the Chinese troops lining the shore. Actually the position of the forward pom-pom had proved so exposed that, after a short spell of firing during which several of its crew were wounded, it was left out of action until later in the proceedings. Everything possible having now been done in the *Wanhsien*, the boarding parties withdrew, the grapnels were cast off and *Kiawo* steamed up to *Wantung*. The latter's fire had been completely silenced by *Widgeon*, so Williamson was able to nose *Kiawo* gently up to her stern, and her master, Captain Bates, was able to scramble over *Kiawo*'s bows to safety. Thus rescue of personnel had been completed and, as there could be no question of any attempt to cut out the two merchant ships, H.M.S. *Kiawo* steamed clear to take stock of the situation.

Meanwhile *Widgeon* and *Cockchafer* had been hotly engaged. When the firing began, the *Cockchafer*'s captain, Lieutenant-Commander Acheson, had dashed for the bridge, but was seriously wounded as he did so. As mentioned earlier, he had no commissioned officer to support him, so he gallantly fought his ship lying down on the bridge. J. R. Masson, the shipping line's agent, who was on board, stood over Acheson reporting on the battle and transmitting his orders throughout. With no rear protection to shield its crew, it would have been suicidal to have attempted to man *Cockchafer*'s forward six-inch gun, but the after gun's crew rapidly closed up, loaded, and very soon its roar was punctuating the clamour of the battle. Acheson directed its fire upon the field guns stationed on the foreshore and, at such range, his gunlayer could not miss. After scoring one hit upon the *Kiawo* the enemy guns were quickly destroyed by the bursting six-inch shells and, while *Kiawo*'s pom-pom fire wreaked havoc among the Chinese troops massed upon the foreshore, *Cockchafer*'s six-inch gun was elevated to fire over the town at the previously plotted position of Yang Sen's headquarters. As the target was out of direct vision there is no knowledge of whether the target was hit, but subsequent rumours had it that shells had fallen close enough to cause Yang Sen to retreat hastily into the countryside. I have also heard it said that almost entire streets of Chinese houses in the town collapsed from the slipstream as the great shells tore close overhead. Perhaps, having regard to the flat-trajectory type of gun involved and the sloping nature of the ground, some of the shells actually tore like express trains up the streets and between the houses rather than over them.

Widgeon for her part was quickly busy against her own individual enemy, a battery of field guns so posted on a bluff upriver from the town as to command the entire harbour. *Widgeon*, with her two six-pounders, silenced the battery after a short duel, and several bright flashes were observed which indicated that the battery's ammunition had blown up. *Widgeon* then concentrated upon the S.S. *Wantung* with rifle and machine-gun fire until all surviving troops were driven under cover.

So the little *Kiawo* withdrew with her dead and, with a flash signal to *Widgeon* of her intentions, sailed into the gathering darkness. The whole action had taken less than ninety minutes. By the time Williamson reached his safe anchorage, about ten miles downstream, he was only just able to see the big tree which was his mark for anchoring. Both engine-room telegraphs had been shot away and a chain of messengers had to be organized to pass verbal orders from bridge to engine-room. This must have made manœuvre extremely hazardous in such tricky waters, but by 8 p.m. *Kiawo* was safely at anchor. Her only serious damage from gunfire was the blowing of a water tank clean out of the ship from its place above the bridge. Night was spent by the able-bodied in effecting necessary repairs, whilst a like service was performed for the wounded by a naval surgeon with the help of volunteer assistants. Alas, a dangerously wounded lieutenant and rating both succumbed to their injuries before arrival at Ichang early the following afternoon, but the remainder of the wounded were taken ashore to hospital there. Soon afterwards *Widgeon* and *Cockchafer* arrived at Ichang, having managed to slip away under cover of darkness.

Thus closed the Wanhsien incident, with the loss of the lives of seven British servicemen, in addition to the unfortunate chief engineer who was drowned—Commander Darley, two lieutenants and four ratings. All the wounded who reached Ichang alive survived and, considering that four officers and thirty men boarded a vessel crowded with troops and fought it out at close quarters, the casualty list was remarkably light.

The next step was for all the naval personnel components of the expedition to return to their respective ships, and *Kiawo* was instead manned with officers and crew from H.M.S. *Hawkins*, the flagship of the China Station. Every available gunboat was now concentrated at Ichang, and all preparations rapidly made for the most powerful squadron possible to proceed to Wanhsien as soon as it was able and knock out Yang Sen and his bandits once and for all. But Yang Sen had already had enough and had no illusions as to what sort of force the second expedition would comprise. He indicated his willingness to talk and the new expedition meanwhile waited at Ichang. The negotiations soon ended with the return of the captured ships to Ichang and the whole affair was thus closed.

Meanwhile, in Hankow, the tempo of events was beginning to accelerate. The dictates of naval policy did not at that time permit of any ship being immobilized for six months in a place like Hankow and, as the river waters began to sink towards their winter low levels, it was apparent to British and Chinese alike that the *Despatch* would soon have to leave before the channels became impassable to her. Even destroyers drew too much water for the depleted channels, and the gunboats were spread thin over the many river ports which lacked a British Concession police force, such as we had in Hankow, and a Hankow Volunteer Defence Corps with an armoured car of its own. On the Chinese side everything was beginning to take on more of a planned pattern than ever before. Behind the scenes Chiang's Russian advisers were watching the steady diminution of British Navy forces at Hankow with keen interest and satisfaction. There were no university students there for them to work upon. But in such a large centre of industry and commerce there was plenty of malleable material of other kinds. The Western powers had promised to withdraw naval and military forces as soon as the Chinese themselves could guarantee law and order and protection for the lives and property of foreigners. Why didn't they get on with it? It was all very well for them to complain that there was too much manifest anti-foreign feeling for them to be able to withdraw without risk to their nationals. Why, it was the very uniforms that inflamed the populace. Let them withdraw and give the Chinese the chance to prove their case. Of course they would guarantee the safety of the foreigners, if the foreigners would meet them half way. The British, naturally, as the predominant foreign power on the spot, were the target for most of the propaganda. Besides us, only the French and Japanese still held their own land concessions in Hankow, their own spheres of influence and their own administrations and police forces. Russian and German Concessions of the old days had long been converted into special administrative districts, Numbers I and II. These were well enough run on international lines with the Chinese having a part to play in them. Useless to suggest that their successful development and survival had, in great part, been due to their being neatly sandwiched between British, French and Japanese Concessions whose sturdy strength had bolstered them. Of course the reservoir of workers was not limited to Hankow alone; there were the other cities of the trinity, Hanyang and Wuchang, where there were no foreign influences at work, save a few missionaries. These latter, from the Chinese and Russian point of view, were nuisances to be found anywhere in China and would, they thought, soon peter out without their supporting bases in cities where the foreigners' influence was paramount. Processions were organized, ostensibly just to celebrate some Chinese feast day, or to recruit members for the newly formed unions. But it was not long before reasons were found for these processions, many thousands strong, to wish to parade through the British Concession, which was so tiny an area that such a large body would be impossible to control by the limited forces of law and order at its disposal. Even on the supposition that the great horde would be in a reasonable state of mind, disposed to be orderly and amenable to being disciplined by Concession police and Volunteers, it was obvious that no good could come of it. It was also reasonably apparent that no good was intended to come of it. Barricades were set up at all points where Concession roads crossed into other territory. The big harbour office of the Chinese Maritime Customs with its massive clock tower stood on the water-front of the Chinese city just fifty yards or so beyond the British Concession boundary. Next beyond it, and on technically Chinese soil, stood the office building of Butterfield & Swire, agents for the Far East of the great Blue Funnel Line and managers of its local associate, the China Navigation Company, whose ships had been involved in the Wanhsien incident. A bare hundred yards inside the

Concession, whose boundary road ran back next to the Customs House and at right angles to the river, stood the three-storeyed old-style office block of Jardine, Matheson Company's Hong Building, as it was called, with spacious quarters above for the agent, who was also a junior director and was expected to house important visitors or the more senior transient staff who might be changing ships there on their way to or from the middle river.

In the middle of the wide road which separated the Hong from the river foreshore and was known as the Bund, stood a tall electric light standard and, as more and more processions began to seek entry to the Bund, a small breastwork of sandbags was erected around it. In front of it steel trestles, festooned with barbed wire, could be quickly erected, and this defence was destined to play an important part before long.

Normal berthing for ships at Hankow was at large pontoons or hulks anchored off shore and approached by gangways of planks. With the seasonal rise and fall of the river the moorings could be adjusted accordingly and, by the end of the year, with the river at its lowest winter level, the planks traversed about a hundred yards of shelving mud foreshore.

It is difficult to remember exactly when the disturbances began to build up, but there was already considerable tension by October. The new regime in China appeared to scorn the old Chinese moon calendar, or it may have been that the Western calendar was sometimes easier for the provision of pegs to hang demonstrations upon. The 10th October, for example, became the Double Tenth (tenth day of tenth month). Exactly what anniversary it was, apart from my birthday, I was never sure, but I spent the whole of it as part of a thin and inexpert khaki line in the boundary road next to the Customs House with a not very friendly mob surging around me. But those were early days and the agitators and organizers had, fortunately, not yet perfected their techniques. Besides, a cruiser was still in harbour. I remember other tense moments as one of two men on guard at a barricade on night. Our full number was three but, as a mob advanced towards us in the darkness, the third man had run back for reinforcements.

It was a nervous moment for the two of us when the mob's leaders reached the barbed wire and began to try to remove it. Even a fixed bayonet, a round in the breech and a full magazine failed to inspire much confidence. And then, suddenly, headlights at a street corner behind us and the Defence Corps' one and only antiquated armoured car lumbered on to the scene. In a matter almost of seconds the expanse of road before us was empty, deserted. Such was the pattern of the disturbances of the late autumn, probing our weaknesses and rehearsing their techniques. Later, amongst the British, Christmas and New Year festivities of a sort continued as circumstances permitted, though the gaiety was rather thin and feverish. Over 620 miles from the sea was a long way to be inside a country surrounded by people who were growing daily more hostile.

And then, on a Saturday morning, 4th January 1927, information came through of large mobs gathering in the Chinese city, beyond the Customs House.

At the Jardine hulk lay the aged H.M.S. *Woodlark*, smaller even than the Insect Class gunboats and with a total complement of twenty-six men. These had been reinforced by a half-dozen or so Royal Marines, and a composite landing party was formed to make a line across the Bund with the lamp standard and its sandbag redoubt to support them from the rear. By noon sufficient crowds had gathered to make the situation threatening, and it was known that there was a large build-up of mob still to emerge from the adjacent Chinese city. Jardine's agent, W. S. Dupree, who was also chairman of the Concession Council, decided that something must be done, and quickly, to gather in all women and children from outlying areas on the other side of the Concession and concentrate them for safe and speedy evacuation in case of need. So, as telephones had become suspect means of communication, he set off in an open truck, leaving two other members of staff and myself to keep an eye on his wife and two small children whom he had left in their quarters above the office. Meanwhile, through official channels, the British Consul General was demanding that the Chinese themselves should disperse the mob, to avoid bloodshed. But there was no response until it was apparent that the British service men were not going to be goaded into indiscretion. In charge of the tiny landing party was the young first lieutenant of the *Woodlark*, Pugh Cook by name, with a cane in his hand and a revolver in a well-buttoned-up holster to which he drew his men's attention as he enjoined them not to draw and fix their bayonets until they saw him draw his revolver. The uproar of the mob was becoming such that there was a risk of his subsequent commands being unheard. For a time Pugh Cook strode up and down before his men as the front line of the mob drew near. I deliberately say front line and not leaders, as the leaders were well in rear and the front line consisted almost entirely of small children being designedly pushed forward by adults behind them. If the brutal imperialist troops could be provoked into firing or other violent action, it was reasonable to suppose that the brunt would fall upon the children and this would obviously make splendid propaganda. To anyone who knows the attitude of Chinese to children (except perhaps girls in time of famine), this is proof of how un-Chinese the whole of the agitation was. The little line of sailors and marines was widely spaced to enable their small number to cover the whole front, whilst keeping a machine-gun team inside the breastwork: the men in the line stood in the formal 'at ease' position with rifle butts on ground. As the surging mob drew nearer brickbats, chunks of stone and broken pieces of metal drain gratings were flung at the line of troops over the heads of the children in front and many of the sailors and marines were injured but stood their ground. Soon the line was infiltrated and one man got a wound in the thigh from his own bayonet, drawn from its scabbard from behind his back.

Meanwhile, inside the adjacent Hong building, we were watching the scene with some anxiety. It was important not to let our faces be seen at the windows upstairs; the Chinese domestic staff were certain that any glimpse of us would serve only to inflame the mob; but we were able to peep from behind curtains, and it was apparent that, if there was not a quick change for the better in the situation, Mrs Dupree and her two young children would be in grave danger. However unreliable the telephones, an effort had to be made to get a message to Dupree. And then, just as the telephone began to ring, the mob began suddenly to recede and the landing party formed up and returned to H.M.S. *Woodlark*. We learnt later that the Chinese authorities had at last decided to act, but had made it a condition of withdrawing the mob that the provocative imperialist troops should be withdrawn, and the maintenance of law and order entrusted to the Chinese themselves.

When we answered the telephone it was Dupree himself. Tugs and launches had been laid on from a neighbouring Concession's Bund and almost all women and children had been evacuated; he would drive a truck himself and collect his family in about twenty minutes. As we talked on the telephone we were peering surreptitiously through a window, and it was apparent that the mob was already re-forming, though more as a loose crowd of loiterers than a solid mob for the moment. So we warned Dupree to be ready for trouble and to stay at the controls with his engine running, leaving it to us to get his family on to the truck. The crowd scattered at the unexpected sight of the great truck, and as it drew up the Chinese servants flung open the front doors and we bundled Mrs Dupree and her children and some basic hand luggage aboard. In seconds they were away with much intimidating roaring of low gear and we were back inside with the great doors slammed again before the crowd came to its senses. Although the landing party had withdrawn, little *Woodlark* still lay at the pontoon with binoculars trained on the Hong, and machine-guns and naval guns to back them up. It was apparent that the Chinese in the street were not prepared to risk any more overt acts of violence so close to so many threatening muzzles; not, at any rate, in daylight.

Behind the Hong lay the great cargo yard with its concrete godowns and, behind these, another street which ran parallel to the Bund. We debated the possibility of escape the back way but had no means of knowing what mobs might be awaiting us in the street beyond. We considered the chances of a dash across Bund and foreshore to the safe protection of the *Woodlark*, and decided that it could only be attempted as the last desperate venture. The afternoon was wearing on and, with January daylight hours in Hankow about equal to those in England, the beginnings of darkness were not far away. The sky was grey and overcast. If we were still there when the mob broke in after dark what should be our pattern of behaviour? Surrender watches, rings, money and other valuables and hope not to be battered to death? It was an unpleasant thought. And then, suddenly, rain began to fall. In ten minutes it was coming down heavily; in fifteen minutes the Bund was clear. In twenty the rain had passed and a small hatless figure was to be seen strolling along the Bund, hands in pockets and whistling. It was Dupree, and as he caught sight of us he waved and gave us a hail. As he did so a gleam of sunshine appeared and he shouted: 'Come on, you blokes; nice day for a stroll.' Our ordeal was over. So too were the mobs, and the phoney character of all the disturbances was soon apparent. Hankow Chinese friends disgustedly disclaimed any responsibility for the disturbances and told us that the mobs comprised hardly any local people at all. Their manner of speech had given them away and they were waterside riff-raff imported from various parts of the Yangtsze Valley specially for the purpose of creating a disturbance. When the rain scattered them they dispersed entirely and were never seen again. But the British were taking no more chances. All women, children, sick and aged had been got safely away by ship and, on the Navy's orders, all remaining Britons were to concentrate by that same night in a large concrete modern block of offices and flats which stood farther along the Bund, next to the British Consulate and just opposite the hulk where the gunboat of the senior naval officer lay. It was the Yangtsze headquarters of the Asiatic Petroleum Company,[1] a subsidiary of Shell and, although all the main armoury of the Volunteer Corps had by this time been evacuated, a number of shot-guns, revolvers and two Lewis guns with ammunition found their way into the building, with anything else which seemed likely to be of use, from the odd bottle of gin or coil of rope to signalling lamps and flags and suchlike. One imported article was a medicine ball, a large round object covered in leather and weighing some 14 lb., which is used by athletes for physical training, being tossed from one man to another for catching at close or medium range. This used to be used on the flat concrete roof four storeys up, and one day of course someone, showing off his strength, tossed too hard and high and the medicine ball sailed over the parapet. Some of us were near enough to get to the edge in time to see it land on the pavement with an earth-shaking thud and were able to see the reactions of Chinese passers-by, none of whom, by great good luck, was hit. This unidentified object was evidently some fearsome secret weapon of the unpredictable British and they fled in terror, so that we were able to recover our treasure without incident. Miraculously it seemed virtually undamaged and survived the whole period of our incarceration. Everything was quickly organized within the building, and we were all split into sections with various duties to perform. One section at a time was always on guard duty and all sections except the specialists participated in the rota. The specialists were the organizing headquarters and the signals section which had to maintain a twenty-four hour watch for signals from the Navy. We had a number of trained ex-service signallers amongst us and also one advertising man who had once been a professional telegraphist. This gentleman's morse flashes were so rapid as to be almost unbeatable in any company, and the Navy, who were being very tolerant of our slowish reception rate and very substandard dispatch rate, got a sudden shock when this wizard first came on duty.

Within two days of our entry into our stronghold, two British destroyers made their appearance and were a very welcome sight. It is perhaps worth mentioning that the arrival of these vessels represented a very considerable feat. Their normal draught, which was at its deepest aft, was more than some of the winter channels between Hankow and

[1] That experienced and admirable writer, Maurice Collis, refers in his history of the Hongkong Shanghai Banking Corporation to another building as our headquarters, but I can assure him it was the Asiatic Petroleum Building.

the sea permitted. All possible stores were therefore shifted forward to lighten their sterns, and the two ships set out with one experienced river pilot, in the leading vessel, between them. They steamed day and night and, from what I heard in their wardrooms later, had a most adventurous journey. To run aground in the dark, as they several times did, at their speed, meant to embed their sharp bows in the mud. In such narrow channels the full use of their great stern power, to back off, was liable to run them stern first into mud banks or rocks on the other side—a precarious voyage, gallantly and skilfully accomplished, if a mere landsman may be permitted so to remark. These vessels so strengthened our local force that it would now be possible, in case of need, to detach small gunboats, such as the *Woodlark*, in case any British farther up the river got into difficulty. Soon afterwards all who wished to be brought out from the middle and upper river ports were evacuated by one means or another, to join the Hankow community or to go on to safer Shanghai if they were not sufficiently able-bodied to be allowed to remain there. But all British shipping had ceased to ply the river, all banks in Hankow were closed for safety and all factories, including cigarette factories and cold storage plants, had shut down. The whole commercial life of the river was dormant and the Chinese were soon negotiating anxiously for the self-imprisoned British to emerge. In the end our naval authorities permitted this, but we all had to find living accommodation afloat or on the Bund so as to be well under their watchful eye. I myself spent two or three weeks in the agent's quarters in the Hong, about a week in the cabin of a tug alongside the Jardine hulk and a few days as a guest of H.M.S. *Gnat*.

There seems little doubt that it was the left-wing radicals of the Kuomintang, not Chiang Kai Shek himself, who forced the issue in Hankow, and in January 1927 they formed a Provisional Government at Wuchang. But later in the same month their forces captured Nanking and their troops were allowed to run amok there among both Chinese and foreign residents. So close to the sea, Nanking was readily accessible to fairly large ships, and a County Class heavy cruiser, which was stationed there, opened fire with eight-inch guns to stop the looting and rapine. Chiang had nothing to do with this ugly incident, and from that moment a rift began between him and the wilder elements of his party, which widened rapidly into an open split.

The next item on the Chinese agenda was, of course, Shanghai; but Shanghai was too vast an international community to be jeopardized in such a way as Nanking or Hankow, and arrangements were immediately set in train for an International Defence Force, several divisions strong, to be sent there. Its senior commander was a Briton, Major-General Duncan, and his chief of staff Colonel Viscount Gort, V.C., who was to command the British Expeditionary Force in France in 1939–40. Their arrival put new heart into the people there and speedily relieved the tired Volunteers of anything but their routine training duties, thus enabling them to get on with their commercial and professional occupations.

Meanwhile something like normality had returned to Hankow except that the British civilian population was diminished by the absence of all the women and children and any men who were non-essential. However, the large quantity of navy personnel helped to provide the numbers for all games, and special outdoor activities were organized for the many lower deck men who wanted exercise at times when the civilians were at work. And at this time a very heart-warming thing occurred. In some buildings on the Bund, close to the Jardine Hong, many Germans had offices and flats, and had from windows watched the whole performance on 4th January between British sailors and marines and the mob. It was less than nine years since the 1918 armistice, but many Germans came forward and said that they had never seen anything like the superb behaviour of our men. They would never forget it, and they wanted to do everything in their power for any British service men who ever came to Hankow. Among these Germans were many ex-soldiers, including one ex-cavalry officer of their crack Uhlans.

Of course the great exodus from Hankow had left large blocks of British property untenanted. But one substantial country house in the land beyond the racecourse was taken over by Michael Borodin, head of the Russian Mission, and a great number of the houses and flats under my personal control were soon let to members of his staff. They had plenty of money to spend, and any uncertainty about the reliability of their tenancy was offset by the large rents which they gladly paid, sometimes two or three months in advance. I have a vivid memory of a little woman who once called at my office. Her appearance and manner were distinctly woebegone and she told me a plaintive tale. She was quite young and good looking, and her pathos stirred my young heart. It seemed that she was the wife of a British subject by birth who had Communist leanings and who had gone over to Moscow since their marriage. What was a wife to do? She was sure that the British community would ostracize her and she threw herself upon my sympathy.

She wanted to rent a house. As far as I was concerned her sob stuff was beside the point. Houses were empty. She was prepared to pay cash down in advance before she had even seen the house. She did not look like the madam of a brothel. O.K.

But I must admit to having been touched by her seeming forlornness. A few weeks later another month's rent was due and the Chinese rent collector could get no satisfaction. Her house was near to my flat, in which I was by this time installed, so I called in at lunch time. When I rang the bell the door was opened by a hard-faced woman whom I hardly recognized. It was a great shock to my young susceptibilities, but looking back now I wonder whether the second appearance was as much of an act as the first. She was obviously shaken when she saw me at the door: at the exposure of her previous act or because she was expecting some of her husband's associates? Who knows? But despite the prosperous Communists who had money to spend, much of my firm's large residential property close by to my flat was vacant. I myself lived in a comfortable first-floor flat over a corner shop with a row of empty houses next to me along the side street. One of my messmates was our firm's Ichang agent, who had had to fly for his life by boarding a ship under cover of darkness with a minimum of luggage and was waiting in Hankow until Ichang had sufficiently calmed down for him to return. He was a bachelor in those days, and had taken a great pride in the many possessions with which he had adorned his house at great expense. It nearly broke his heart to leave them behind, but he had given about three months' wages to his house boy and hoped that he might manage to preserve them. But the impermanence of the situation was fully apparent to his house boy. To such, the only stable thing in China for years had been the white man and he was determinedly loyal to his master. Not long after his master had arrived in Hankow, the boy appeared. He had paid the owner of a Chinese fishing boat handsomely, packed all the delicate valuables with loving care into crates and got them aboard under cover of darkness. Some 350 miles they had sailed downriver to Hankow and here he was. We had an adequate staff of servants in the flat, but something had to be done for such a paragon and room was found for him in the servants' quarters, behind the flat and adjoining the empty houses in the side street. He fitted in well with the other servants, and everything went smoothly until our next quarter's electricity bill was presented. It had increased substantially, but nothing either my house boy or I could think of could explain the increase. Time went on and another account came in. This time—and it was summer weather—the account had doubled, so I telephoned the power company and reported it, suggesting that they check meters and circuit. This they of course agreed to do, but with the natural stipulation that if no fault was found we would pay the cost of the checking and testing. I was fully confident and I laughed at this proviso—but too soon. The electricians discovered that the paragon who had been allotted the end room had succeeded in linking the supply in his room to the next door empty house, and the next, and the next. He had been running a very remunerative lodging house business for Chinese refugees from trouble spots. They had been too glad of accommodation in a well-built foreign house to jib at having to keep out of sight and entering precariously through a window after dark.

But how could one sack a chap like that? To me the interesting thing was the moral code of such an individual: faithful to the death in great issues but unable to resist a bit of illegal 'perks' if offered—even at his master's expense. Very typical.

There was little trade at first in revived Hankow, but the currency quickly depreciated at about this time, and only silver-backed deposits in foreign banks maintained their value. An immediate result of this was an upsurge in the export trade. To secure foreign bank credits, native produce was willingly offered at a discount and, as a result, was in great demand in world markets. Japanese shipping, at about this time, experienced quite a protracted boycott and, with thousands of Chinese continually demanding passage from one point to another as conditions became disturbed in different areas, much of the leeway of the previous months was made up by the British merchants and shipping lines.

By the summer Chiang Kai Shek was supreme in his party, and had established a moderate government in Nanking. But he was getting restive under the dominating influence of the Russian clique and that part of the Kuomintang who supported them, and he began the ousting and replacing of all the Russian top brass. This did not find favour with the left wing of the Kuomintang, and their power was such that Chiang resigned in August 1927. But he still had a numerous and powerful following, and in December of the same year his marriage to Soong Mei Ling, sister-in-law of Sun Yat Sen, further identified him with the constitutional elements in his party and strengthened his claims to recognition. Meanwhile Hankow had become reasonably settled again, though with still a large naval force always in the harbour. Many British women and children came back to their homes at the end of the summer. I cannot remember whether it was in this year, 1927, or the previous one that Charles Lindbergh brought his seaplane down on the Yangtsze in Hankow in the course of his famous round the world flight. At any rate, there was a smallish British aircraft carrier in port at the time, which gave its hospitality and help to the famous flier.

Meanwhile, in the north, Wu Pei Fu's position had been much weakened by Chiang Kai Shek's victories over his armies farther south, and from Manchuria Chang Tso Lin's armies began to threaten him and soon assumed power in Peking. But it was not long before Chiang Kai Shek, whose military leadership was sadly missed, was recalled, and early in 1928 he was reinstated as head of the Nanking army which shared the general march on Peking from the south. He was in Peking by May 1928, and Chang Tso Lin left by rail for Manchuria; but his train was bombed *en route* and he died of his injuries.

When Chiang Kai Shek had resigned earlier, there had been a partial return to power of the Russian clique, but Chiang's position was now immeasurably strengthened. It was apparent to him that the Russians had not forced the British to surrender their Concession in Hankow out of love for the Chinese but in the hope of supplanting the British. He had no intention of allowing this to happen and decided to get rid of them once and for all. Late one night in the early spring of 1928 representatives of authority called on every house in the area that housed Russians in Hankow and they were all taken away, the majority for deportation. I heard about it the following morning, which I think must have been a Sunday, when I dropped in to the wardroom of the British duty cruiser for a beer. Also present when I got there were several consular gentry, including, I remember, both a British and a Belgian consul. The British Navy and all the European consuls had apparently known all about what was going to happen. The Chinese had approached them and requested their co-operation. This fortunate Chinese decision avoided any violence or bloodshed. Elsewhere, I heard later, many Russians were not so lucky, and the story in Hankow was that in Canton, where there had not been the same liaison with the foreigners, the Russians had been butchered wholesale. Chiang Kai Shek was now, comparatively, master in his own house and was duly elected President, which office he held until 1931, but I question whether he was privy to the brutalities which occurred in Canton. Anyway, I doubt whether Moscow has altogether forgotten what happened in 1928, nor have the Chinese forgotten the would-be dominance of their Russian advisers that led them to it.

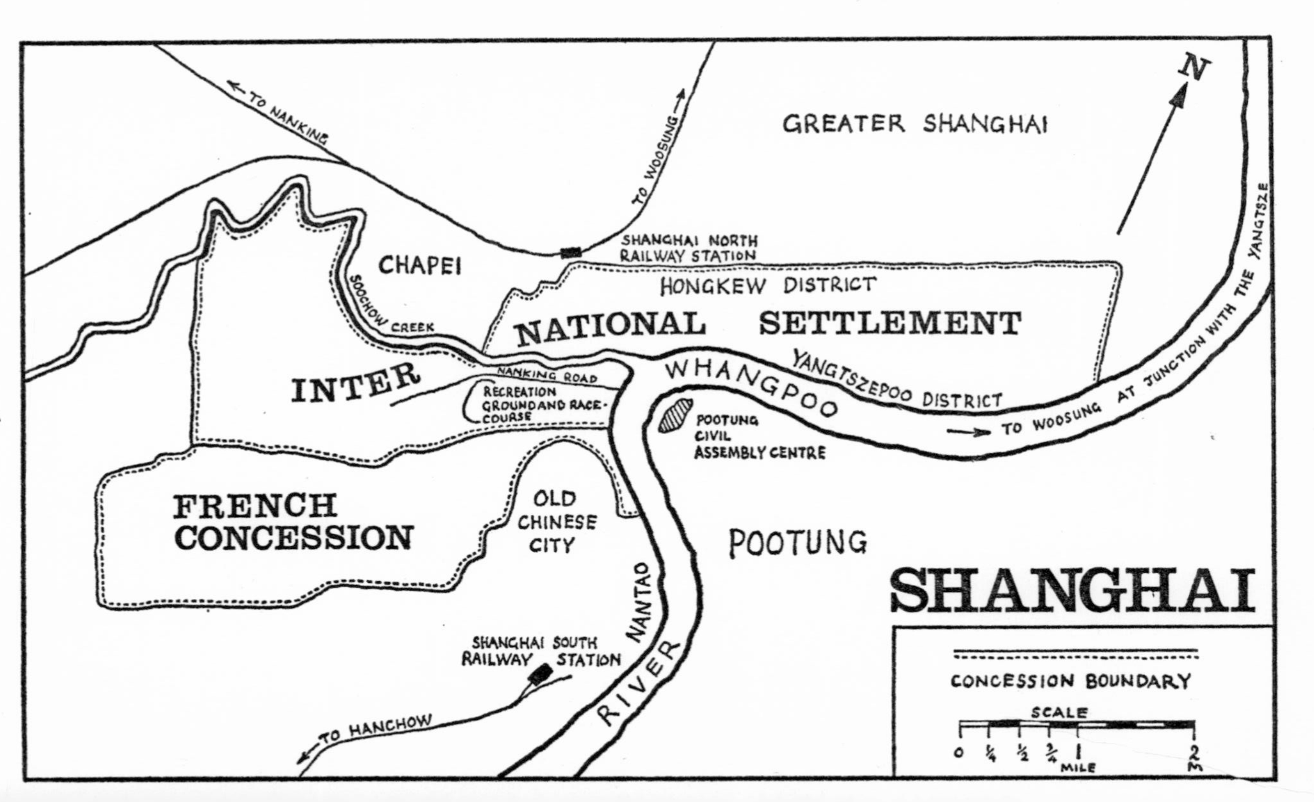
N
TO NANKING
TO WOOSUNG
GREATER SHANGHAI
SHANGHAI NORTH RAILWAY STATION
CHAPEI
HONGKEW DISTRICT
SOOCHOW CREEK
INTER NATIONAL SETTLEMENT
NANKING ROAD
RECREATION GROUND AND RACE-COURSE
WHANGPOO
YANGTSZEPOO DISTRICT
TO WOOSUNG AT JUNCTION WITH THE YANGTSZE
POOTUNG CIVIL ASSEMBLY CENTRE
FRENCH CONCESSION
OLD CHINESE CITY
NANTAO
POOTUNG
SHANGHAI
SHANGHAI SOUTH RAILWAY STATION
TO HANCHOW
RIVER
CONCESSION BOUNDARY
SCALE
0 ¼ ½ ¾ 1 MILE 2 M

Part Three

CHAPTER EIGHT
LIFE IN SHANGHAI

THE year 1928, then, soon began to show promise of better things all round.

Mao Tse Tung had, in October 1927, established a mountain base for the Communists at Chingkangshan in Kiangsi Province near the border with Hunan, about 250 miles south of the Wuhan cities. But I do not think that Chiang Kai Shek or anybody else, except the Communists themselves, thought that he could fail to master and unite the country in the end. The Chinese political situation remained confused from the spring of 1928 until well into 1931, and this chapter will therefore concentrate chiefly on descriptions of various typical facets of social and commercial life in the foreign communities at that period.

I had left Hankow for home leave in mid April 1928 in a mood of deep depression. I had, I suppose, been too long in the middle of the worst of things and had seen only the gloomy side. In those days, although my employers' head office was in Hongkong, as befitted a British concern, the great office in Shanghai was actually bigger and almost as important, as it controlled not only many industries in that vast city, but also all the many branches and agencies in China along and north of the Yangtsze, several of which had substantial industries of their own.

I remember my astonishment at the almost jubilant mood which prevailed in the Shanghai office when I arrived there on my way home. Exports, thanks to the depreciated currency, were booming; freight and passenger income had been an all-time record, thanks to a boycott of Japanese shipping and to the fear which skippers of Chinese flag vessels had of venturing anywhere where they might be appropriated rather than temporarily commandeered. But by then I had already written to my father, who at that time held a senior government post in

Malaya. I had told him of the seeming end of all prospects in China and had inquired about chances of a job in Malaya. So, although my mood was now already changing, I had arranged to leave a P. & O. boat at Singapore and catch the following one at Penang, after staying with my father at Kuala Lumpur. In an interview there a very kindly tycoon offered me a job, but advised me not to take it, as I would lose much seniority by joining a new organization at that stage in my career. But by that time he was preaching to the converted, as I had almost made up my mind before he spoke. Still, I had a very pleasant stay in Kuala Lumpur with bathing and tennis, and even some polo, which, if not very good, was of far too high a standard for me. When I left Hankow there had been no Chinese tailors capable of making clothes for Englishmen. Such craftsmen had not returned as yet. So I had decided to travel in any old rags and repair my wardrobe in Kuala Lumpur. As I stepped ashore at Singapore I was greeted by a completely strange but very smart and attractive young lady. She was a friend of my parents and was expecting me to lunch at the Europe—Singapore's most lush hotel of those days. Any presentable garments I had were in my luggage and I was garbed in a stained old pair of rather ragged khaki shorts and correspondingly shabby clothing on my top half. But she assured me that I was quite all right, and that in any case guests and lunch were waiting. I shall never forget sailing into that majestic hostelry in tow of such a graceful and delectable tug, only to find that I was the guest of honour of a party of about eight to twelve people, right in the middle of the great dining-room. What a tribute to the charm of my hostess and the delightful good manners of them all that my embarrassment was soon forgotten.

My father retired that year, and the next time I visited Kuala Lumpur was twenty years afterwards, when I went to the church and saw a memorial tablet in his name.

Whilst I was on leave I was glad to forget China for a while, but when I came back some months later I paid more attention to what had been happening. In July 1928 China had unilaterally abrogated all 'unequal treaties', but Shanghai, to which I found myself posted on my return early the following year, was for the time being little affected. Tientsin, which I did not visit until the summer of 1931, still had its British Concession when I arrived there and a number of foreign troops, which included detachments of British, American and Italian infantry.

In Shanghai business and social life for the foreigner had returned almost to normal. Only remnants of the powerful international 'Shaforce' of the previous year remained. Cross-country riding had been resumed in areas far beyond the boundaries of the Settlement and French Concession. Sailing of a sort was popular on distant stretches of the river beyond the limits of the port; many of the well-to-do operated large well-found houseboats and would cruise in peace and safety for miles along the inland waterways connected to the Whangpoo River. The Whangpoo, it will be remembered, is a largish tributary of the Yangtsze, which flows into its estuary at Woosung on the south bank, and Shanghai has sprawled along both sides of it, about nine miles from Woosung. Most of the more numerous of the foreign nationalities had their own clubs. The Cercle Gaulois, unassailably French; the Country Club, equally British; the Columbia Country Club, very American, but penetrable to British guests of American members, and so on. But, apart from numerous sporting clubs for golf, racing, cross-country riding, etc., the Shanghai Club and the Cercle Sportif Français were the two most international. The Shanghai Club, on the Bund, was a strictly business and residential club, although it had such amenities as excellent card and billiard rooms and a bowling alley. Last, but not least, it was the proud possessor for many years of the longest bar in the world, until one day an American visitor told us that one still longer had lately been built in that country—just to beat ours. Ocean-going liners which berthed farther upstream would often swing there and proceed backwards to their wharves which were at a narrower part of the river.

America was still much under the influence of prohibition at that time, and when an American President Line ship got her nose in the mud just outside the door, so to speak, of the Shanghai Club, a delightful cartoon appeared in next day's *North China Daily News*. The ship had been endowed with arms and legs and tears were streaming down its face. 'Driest ship in the world fails in its attempt to enter longest bar in the world,' ran the caption.

The Cercle Sportif Français was, as we say, a very different cup of tea. Any self-respecting country club had swimming-pool, tennis, bowls and a hall suitable for badminton, balls and entertainments. But the French Club, as we called it, had a superb ballroom and orchestra, with regular tea and evening dances, gymnasium, badminton, grill-room and a notable cuisine. Its only pretensions to being French lay in its being sited on French Concession land and being run by an almost entirely French committee. Membership was not difficult to anyone prepared to pay its reasonable entrance fee and nationality was irrelevant. Some British ladies of the *grande dame* calibre might be heard to remark that they wouldn't be seen dead there, the company was so mixed and dubious. Of course the fact of the matter was that, if they had been seen there, they would have seemed dead by comparison; I must not stigmatize only British ladies—there were others, not excluding French women, who agreed with them.

I must admit that though I played a good deal of bridge in those days, and had played with adults since the beginning of my teens, one experience of the card-room there sufficed me. Of course every nation in Shanghai celebrated its national day in its own characteristic way—St Andrew's, St David's, St Patrick's, St George's, Bastille Day on 14th July, American Independence Day on 4th July, and many others.

Cross-country riding was a popular sport in Shanghai and at many other China ports in those days, but fox hunting as we know it in England was not practicable. Even in such places as there might be foxes, the riding was limited to certain very definite tracts of country and, should pursuit of a quarry take the hunt unawares out of the prescribed area, there was trouble with the populace. Over the permitted areas stewards of the Hunt Club would range along paths in the off season, making the necessary financial arrangements with the country folk to permit their land to be ridden over.

In the season scrap paper trails were laid over distances of about six to ten miles with one or two checks to let the ponies get their wind. These checks sometimes involved a mere petering out of the trail and sometimes, in country rather congested with walled villages and farms, about a quarter to half a mile of bright-coloured paper instead of white might be laid, along which the hunt was bound not to exceed a trot. Paper hunts, these rides were called, and the club was the Paper Hunt Club; but the rides were competitive, with a silver cup for the winner, and they were very similar in character to point-to-points. In the Tientsin and Hankow areas the obstacles often included small mud walls, but in Shanghai they were chiefly ditches, creeks and irrigation canals. Only people who had lived and ridden in the area for years ever really knew what was coming next and, on a mount of less than fourteen hands, one had little chance of studying the ground ahead. Ditches would yawn unexpectedly at the pony's feet and, left to himself, a good pony would do a sort of cat jump which could easily unseat the unwary. Many miniature ditches, known as grips, might be about a foot wide and two feet deep and these were only a danger if they were not seen. This happened once with me and my pony put a foreleg in and snapped it when at a fast canter—unpleasant for me as well as for the poor pony. Occasionally a pony, especially in inexperienced hands, might bolt aimlessly off the trail and suddenly stop short with four-wheel brakes in front of some obstacle he didn't like the look of. Chinese ideas of sanitation differ from ours, and all household sewage in the outlying farm and small village communities is stored in one or more large open receptacles. These are usually huge vats or 'kongs' sunk in the ground, and from them the manure is ladled as required on to the adjacent vegetable gardens. Small wonder that the foreigner mistrusts native-grown lettuce, radish and other raw vegetables. But for the rider the trouble is that, when his pony stops so abruptly, he is liable to be catapulted over the animal's head into one of these kongs. When this happens none of his friends will go near him for days, and he longs to be able to get away from himself. Young people who had done some fox hunting at home were disposed, at first glance, to be somewhat contemptuous of our China riding country. But closer and more practical experience of it usually changed their attitude. Almost all the Manchurian ponies, which were called China ponies, had been imported from the wild state at four years old or more and, if they had passed through the hands of Chinese jockeys before coming on to the hacks and hunters market as rejects from the race track, some of them had been very badly handled. They often had mouths like iron.

On the whole relations between the paper hunters and the country folk were smooth enough, but now and again some village head man or his appointee would hold on to the largesse distributed, or an unfair share of it, and then there was trouble. Perhaps fifty or sixty ponies and their riders, thundering in a mass at an open ditch ahead, would be dismayed by the uprising of countrymen from their hiding in the ditch. They would suddenly appear, straight ahead, uttering harsh cries and brandishing a variety of weapons in the shape of Chinese agricultural implements. Six-foot bamboos, topped by ugly looking forks or scythes, can be very formidable and pandemonium ensued. If subsequent inquiry did not establish a firm basis for future peace, the club would withdraw from that part of the country altogether. Next season, or even earlier, polite hints from the farmers would be followed by deputations upon the stewards. Would the hunt please come back? The subsidy was the only stable thing in a world of uncertain markets and shifting prices; the farmers would guarantee elimination of the trouble-makers—and so on. The costs of subsidy were largely borne by the parent Shanghai Race Club, whose stewards encouraged horsemanship in every way they could as a means of developing jockeys for racing. There were no strictly professional riders at any of the China race clubs, but a tycoon (the local parlance is Taipan) who owned race ponies would often employ young men at salaries not strictly compatible with their commercial merits—if they were competent jockeys.

In social life in Shanghai the numerical balance between the young people of the two sexes was better adjusted than in Hongkong, where the young daughters of senior members of the community were scarce and in great demand. Hongkong, being both a naval and a military base, had a perpetual ebb and flow of young service officers with time on their hands. Navy lads could organize exotic board ship parties and launch bathing picnics to the outlying bays; the army often had real horses and none of your China pony stuff. The ordinary civilian, whose free time during the day was limited to week-ends, often found the competition too strenuous. But Shanghai was a different matter: there were many young women office workers of all nationalities. I remember two secretaries in my own office, one of whom was Swiss, and the other, the best secretary I ever had anywhere, a White Russian. The latter's father had been a relict of the old days of Imperial Russia and, as an inspector of the Shanghai Municipal Police, had been so seriously wounded in an affray with armed robbers that he had had to retire young. I was glad, when I left after the last war, to be able to organize a transfer for the girl to our Hongkong office. Once there she was able to get proper papers and emigrate to a new life in Australia, a worthwhile acquisition to any country. Of course the intensification of Chinese passenger traffic on coast and rivers, often little more than a cover for surreptitious troop movements, added to the difficulties of running regular services. Piracy had long been a menace, and the most common mode of operation had been for a number of pirates to join the ship in the guise of harmless passengers. To search every one of the hundreds of Chinese who might board the ship at any way-ports, and their baggage as well, was an impossible task. The only way to control them was to turn engine-room and bridge into small fortresses with well-armed and ruthless guards safely ensconced within them. No local bigwig would be averse to getting free passage for his troops on the same principle and the harmless-looking but enormous bundles of clothing, bedding and other personal possessions could easily hide fire-arms or lethal knives. Of course opium was another problem. The profits of this illicit traffic were so immense that resort was had to all sorts of ways and means. A story used to be told that a captain of a British gunboat, on deciding suddenly to inspect the inside of a barrel of part of his six-inch main armament, discovered strange packages hidden there. His Chinese steward got the sack. Another story, a sad one, was of a young Merchant Navy officer, not long appointed to command a river steamer on the middle Yangtsze. He was a competent officer but was not versed in local procedures, and one night he mysteriously 'fell overboard' and his body was never recovered. Nothing definite was ever found out, but rumour had it that investigations led to the belief that he had been approached ashore by certain mysterious parties who hoped that he would accept gifts. All he was required to do was to be not too insistent on the searching of various nooks and crannies of his vessel. But he was an honest man, and however much the offers were increased he still said 'No'. To the mysterious persons there could be only one answer. He was exorbitantly greedy and probably wanted a share of their profits. So arrangements were made and he was disposed of. I have no certainty that either of these stories was true, but they could well have been. The occupation of armed guard on a coaster or river steamer became quite popular, chiefly with Indians and Russians, who also filled many jobs which corresponded roughly with that of commissionaire in high-class London hostelries. The less choice establishments also had custodians who were just as formidable and didn't bother to use finesse on trouble-makers. All this helped to relieve the imbalance in the ratio of unattached young Russian women in Shanghai, but I was never clear how the young Russian males had got there in the first place. No cabaret owners would want to import them by paying their fares. Possibly they had come from Manchuria—or from Russia via Manchuria, and for tough young men this was probably not too difficult.

Professions such as medicine and the law involved their own problems. In, or adjacent to, the lesser communities there were usually missionary organizations with highly competent doctors and nurses attached to them. In places such as Hankow and Tientsin there were small partnerships or firms of doctors to enable at least one of their number to get away for the nine months or so at a time which they required for home leaves and to get themselves up to date. In Shanghai and Hongkong there were several of such partnerships which were large enough to allow of some degree of specialization by one or other of their numbers in all the different branches: surgeons; physicians; ear, eye, nose and throat men; chest specialists; orthopaedists; gynaecologists and so on.

My many friends among them used to complain sometimes of the spotlight of unsought publicity which was always upon them in such a tight-knit community.

A young surgeon, with no professional engagements booked, might take his wife or his girl out dancing on a Saturday night. At midnight or later a message might find him: an emergency appendix for the following morning. On the Monday, at their usual coffee get-togethers, the ladies of the port would discover that one of their nearest and dearest had been operated on, at 6 a.m. on Sunday, by a surgeon who had been seen by other ladies 'dancing and drinking, my dear, drinking whisky till the small hours' of the night before.

For all this, they gave, on the whole, magnificent service. One man in particular stands out in my memory: Alex Skinner of Hankow.

A big raw-boned Scot, he must have been at least fifty at the time I have in mind and, with his partner away, was in sole charge of the health of the British and some others of the community, during one of those sticky summers with shade temperature rising by day to 100° F.–104° F. and falling in one's bedroom at night to 98° F.–100° F. and the humidity at saturation point.

A young man arrived down from a hill station with peritonitis. His appendix had burst on the way down. Skinner operated; there was another crisis and he operated again, and so it continued for several weeks. During all this time Skinner, whose wife and family were away, dossed down on a camp-bed in the hospital corridor outside his patient's room so as to be immediately at hand.

I remember running into Skinner one evening in the street near his home. I seldom saw him drink, but on this occasion he almost forced me to come in and 'have one'. He was near to breaking down with the strain. 'Just operated on the poor b——r again', he said. 'What right have I to go on submitting him to this when his chances of survival are so small? I feel like a bloody butcher.' But he saved him.

On the other hand, he could be bluntly rude to the *malade imaginaire*. On one occasion a very social lady came to him. 'Doctor,' she said, 'oh, doctor, I can't sleep.'—'Why not try going to bed?' he asked, giving her a shrewd glance of appraisal.

On another occasion a woman came to him and complained of feeling unwell. 'You smoke, don't you?' he asked. 'About how many a day?'—'About sixty,' she replied. At which he remarked: 'I'm afraid you'll have to cut that down a little.'—'Oh, doctor, I couldn't possibly do that.'—'I see; well then, there's only one thing for it. Double your smoking and then we'll neither of us have to bother for long, will we?'

Another remark of his which I treasure was made to me. A polo injury had necessitated massage of my left thigh and the Russian masseuse, to whom he had entrusted me, seemed to be making little impression on the muscles which were troubling me. I told him this and he asked me at what time of day I was having my treatment. When I told him that my business did not allow me time until six o'clock of an evening he said: 'Good God! Six o'clock in the evening at the height of the summer! What the hell's the good of that? Poor girl's exhausted all her strength by then, lifting the faces of fat women all day.' What a picture it conjured.

I could recount many tales of professional men, an Irish doctor in Shanghai and an Irish barrister in Hongkong, both of whom I knew personally better than I did Skinner, who was much my senior in years. But I think that a story well worth recounting is of a little chartered accountant in Hongkong, a brilliant man who, in his youth, had been an outstanding athlete. Unfortunately when age and increased pressure of work began to deny him his athletic outlets for his energy, the need did not dawn upon him for curbing his natural and voracious appetites until too late. He got fat. He got fatter. He got very fat indeed. It was said that he used to travel home always by Blue Funnel Line and that they used to rig a cabin for him with a special harness to help him in and out of bed. His trouble was that his arms and legs were too short and he could not always manage to get his own shoes and socks on and off; they were out of reach.

At the Hongkong Club his needs were recognized, and when he was in the club a boy was always in attendance in the lavatory to render him any necessary assistance. On one occasion, having partaken very freely of fluids before, during and after his tiffin, as lunch was called, he rushed into the 'Gents' in great haste and the boy hurried to minister to his front buttons. There was a good deal of fumbling below that bulging waistline and he exclaimed at the boy in angry impatience.

'Master, master, no can findee,' protested the boy in self-justification.

'No can findee, God damn it! You had it last.'

There were naturally the clergy in each community of any size, quite apart from missionaries. Among them were many splendid men, such as Dean A. C. S. Trivett of Shanghai. Men who were interned with Trivett during the Pacific war have spoken very warmly of his fine example, and I do not think that I have heard anything but praise for their clergy from any men who endured even less tolerable conditions in the camps elsewhere.

I have mentioned massage a little earlier, and a great luxury of life in China, for those who knew how to make use of it, was the availability of first-class massage by Japanese women for a very few shillings.

I remember what seemed to me a disaster which befell me about a week before my first Christmas in Shanghai. I had been persuaded to venture upon a roller-skating rink, and as I launched myself gingerly, for I had not roller-skated for years, I was clutched with great clumsiness by a member of our party who was one of those buffoons who always thought that outrageous behaviour was expected of them. If he had been a competent skater it would not have mattered, but he was not.

I came down with my right ankle bent almost double on the floor beneath me with the buffoon on top, and on top of him a succession of other bodies that stumbled over us as we lay. How I escaped a fracture I shall never know, but the sprain was very severe and the chagrin at being almost completely immobilized for Christmas almost as bad.

I managed to hobble to a ricksha and get home to my digs in a state of deep despondency. But the stout old American dame who was my landlady laughed at my worries. 'That's all right,' she said; 'we'll get hold of Buffalo San. She'll hurt, but she'll fix it.'

How the broad, square Japanese woman, who appeared with almost magical speed, ever came to acquire such a name I do not know. I lay on my bed with my arms above my head so that my hands could grip the bedposts, and Buffalo San set to work. The pain was almost unbelievable, but Buffalo San was relentless and I am proud that I managed to confine myself to some groans and one or two yelps or squawks. Screaming would not have stopped her. But by the end the swelling had been a little reduced and the ankle felt better. I took my courage in both hands and booked her again for the next evening.

After four or five treatments, getting progressively more endurable every time, I was able to stand normally, to walk and even to dance. My Christmas was saved.

A year or so later I was to discover an establishment, less than half a mile from those digs, which was presided over by an amiable female water buffalo—a Japanese woman whom we called Auntie. But perhaps the description will mean little without some brief information about the water buffalo. I am uncertain whether this is its correct name, as I believe that the term 'water' buffalo applies strictly to a variety found in the Philippine Islands, which is smaller than the more common Asiatic type, the Indian Buffalo. Anyway it is far larger and stronger than the ox and its natural habitat is swamps, so that it is an invaluable worker in the waterlogged paddy fields. More of this buffalo anon. Auntie was constructed on similar lines with a face not unlike a large, round, golden melon out of which someone had cut a large, horizontal slice—her smile.

Auntie's standard treatment was to enclose you naked in an electrically heated box in which you sat with only your head protruding and with two other small openings in the lid through which fingers, but not arms, could be exserted. Ten minutes of this were followed by being laid out on a marble slab, scrubbed with a loofah and soap and dried and wiped down with eau-de-Cologne. And then a sort of operating table where one was pounced on by Auntie and at least one of her minions, who were young girls in their late teens with all the charm and pretty smiles and cooing noises of the best geisha girl and fingers like talons of steel.

The stiff muscles from the first football or rugger games in the winter, or the first long cross-country ride, would be softened and soothed and made flexible again.

Sometimes too on a hot summer evening, when sleep seemed impossible, I would go for a bath and massage and return so utterly relaxed that I could go to bed and sleep immediately.

The whole treatment cost only about five shillings.

On one occasion a friend and I were saddled with a very drunken, very aggressive young man who wouldn't go home, and managed to decoy him to Auntie's by dark hints which suggested to him quite another sort of establishment—lovely young girls, etc. etc. While one of us helped him from the taxi, the other slipped in and warned Auntie of what was coming. Auntie was delighted. 'I fix him,' she said with her broad sliced melon grin. She certainly did, and the way she and her slim little girls worked him over was compensation to us for all we had suffered at his hands earlier in the evening. He came out very, very sober.

But more about the water buffalo. This animal is thoroughly domesticated by the Chinese for use in their rice fields. If it were less muscular, its enormous bulk would make the going difficult in the deep alluvial mud. It thrives and revels in such conditions and ploughs its happy way in the sole charge of a tiny Chinese child who sits astride its neck, piping shrill orders and kicking and hitting to obtain instant obedience. But let something rouse its ire, such as the alien smell of a white man, or maybe of his pony as well, and its head will go down in a ferocious terrifying charge at a speed no horse could emulate on such terrain. If it makes contact it will pound and knead its prey relentlessly in the mud, and it is said that even a tiger is no match for it.

When a white man first comes to China he may have strange preconceived notions about his own healthy lack of smell and the revolting smells which seem so dear to the populace. But the water buffalo thinks otherwise, and so does the Chinese farm dog. Certainly a perfume is a sort of smell and a smell is a sort of perfume, and when it comes to fine distinctions it is obvious that we and the Chinese do not, so to speak, smell nose to nose. I can recollect sharing the back seat of his limousine with a Chinese banker for a rather protracted drive in Shanghai one winter. He was wearing a superb gown richly lined with fur, and just to sit next to it almost made me feel warm. But the skin had quite obviously not been cured, as we would understand the expression, and I was nearly overwhelmed.

On the other hand, some smells which we would dislike are evidently equally distasteful to the Chinese. I remember one tour of the Chinese city in Shanghai with a Chinese business man, when we stopped at an entrance of what he said was a factory. 'Human Hair Factory. I think better I go in first. You wait.' A few moments later he was almost tumbling out again, his face distorted with disgust. I did not go in.

That was when I first learnt about the human hair industry. The teeming millions of the unwashed lowest orders never cut their hair after the end of summer: it was too valuable in assisting body warmth. When the warm weather returned they would have their hair shaved right off and no doubt they were glad to be rid of the lice that went with it.

This plenteous crop then went to a factory where it was first boiled long hours and, presumably, with many changes of water. This was the process which carried the smell that had intimidated my Chinese friend.

And now something of commercial life and of the rivalries between the business interests of the different nationalities which made up the trading communities. Even amongst the various nationals of the great powers there was something of an atmosphere of the 'haves' and the 'have nots'. The British had not been all that much longer established than the others, but they seemed to be more readily accepted by the

Chinese as a permanent feature of life than, say, the Americans. Perhaps the mere fact of the International Settlement in Shanghai, for example, having been jointly established by Britain and the U.S.A., meant little. Perhaps, through the old East India Company, associations stretching a long way further back had acclimatized the British and Chinese to each other. But there was something else. In my day Chinese seemed to accept the British as there to stay with their age-old father to son family organizations and their massive and impressive office properties and other outward marks of permanence. Sometimes a personal private plane might bring some American tycoon to a vast and luxurious rented suite in a large hotel or apartment house where he would hold court for a week or two, or more. Chinese would flock to large and luxurious receptions and the tycoon would be impressively telephoning Manila, San Francisco, Detroit, Chicago, Washington on and off all day.

But then he would disappear. Obviously his world-wide interests made it impossible for him to stay in any one place too long, but this aspect of the matter would not be readily discernible to the Chinese. I have endeavoured to show earlier how the seeming permanence of the British through thick and thin, midst rebellions, robber bands, unscrupulous officials and looting military helped to develop that atmosphere of mutual dependence and trust between the Briton and his Chinese employee or associate.

Some other white peoples acquired like status, but not all. And not only had the British been early in the field, their interests had been widely multifarious. The same man or group of men would preside over the fortunes of a shipping line; a large import trade whose goods were carried in those ships; a large export ditto; banking interests to finance the commerce; wharves and godowns to accommodate ships and cargo; docks to repair ships or build new ones; engineering concerns to supply equipment; insurance companies to cover the risks; factories and mills; mines; what else can you think of?

In insurance, in particular, which was my main concern during my time there, the newcomer would cut his premiums beyond the limits of prudence in order to get a finger or toe hold. He might then find that some forty or fifty years of experience of the coverage of bulk rice shipments between, say, Thailand and China had shown an overall average of x per cent damage. He had now signed a year's contract to pay for all losses and had received $(x-5)$ per cent for the privilege. Where such contracts ran into millions per annum, it was no laughing matter.

I remember once when I was in Tientsin there was a little matter of coastal bullion shipments. These were always a good indication of the direction in which the main tide of goods was flowing and, when an area was importing more than it was exporting, bullion would flow out instead of goods. Naturally such trends were well known to all, including the pirates, and even the big insurance groups operating in that field could not absorb the whole risk without 'reinsuring' or laying off a large part of the amount with the world's leading insurance market, London. My British competitors and I had been doing this sort of thing for years and were in close touch with the prevailing sentiment in the London market. We knew just how far the London market were prepared to go in rate cutting. We knew that the amounts involved were so huge that neither could easily cope without the other. We made no secret of our rock bottom minimum rate of premium, but did not bother to explain publicly why we could go no lower.

The Germans in China had, in World War I, lost much of the standing of nationals of a major power but, unlike the Russian expatriates, they still had a nationality and a busy, thrusting, industrially developed homeland. They were not of a race to shrink into obscurity when they lost their Concessions at the end of World War I. On the contrary, they made capital of their position. They were not there with the compulsive backing of arms: they were there as equals, to trade on equal terms with the great race who were their hosts. It was not long before their great trading houses were prospering as much as they had ever done.

And then came Hitler.

Most of the older German residents had had little personal contact with their homeland in the period immediately after the First World War. When Hitler arose, the majority of them disapproved of him as openly as they dared. Many of them, too, had memories of the Japanese as their on-the-spot enemies in that war and had had plenty of dealings with them since. They wanted no part of Hitler nor of any *entente* between Japan and the Third Reich.

Moreover they were well aware that if they went home they would rapidly be milked dry of any fortunes they might have amassed overseas.

When Jardine, Matheson & Company decided to start a brewery in Shanghai in the thirties they had no difficulty in securing the services of one of the best German brewmasters. He had spent years abroad and had no intention of going back to Germany to lose there all that he had earned by setting up breweries all over the world.

The Chinese themselves had plenty of tricks of their own too.

Sudden illness of an agent (or local manager) for my employers in a port that did a large tea trade resulted in a man experienced mainly in shipping to be asked to go there to fill the gap in a hurry.

One of his first duties on arrival was to inspect a large consignment of tea which was lying in bulk in a godown prior to shipment. Wisely he took his head Chinese of the local set-up, his compradore, with him.

When they got there he was astonished to see the old Chinese whisk an enormous horseshoe-shaped hoop of metal from under his gown and, gripping it firmly, plunge his arm deep into the mound of tea before them.

'B'long magnet,' he said with a knowing grin. 'Sometimes have got plenty iron filings inside heap. Make very good weight. No make very good tea.'

No iron filings were found on that occasion.

Sometimes even the experienced could put a disastrous foot wrong. The head export buyer of one large merchant house suddenly decided, on one occasion, to corner the world market in goatskins, of which China was the main source of supply. But world markets elected not to play, and the firm concerned found itself saddled with this huge quantity of merchandise—and no buyers. A bad time was definitely had by all, but the firm were large enough to carry the loss, and no doubt the gentleman enterprising enough to take such a gamble speculated more successfully the next time. I think that directors preferred executives who thought big enough to make mistakes to men who were not sufficiently enterprising; but they had to be more often right than wrong.

The shipping man whose experience, when added to a good intelligence service, enabled him to judge from reports of upper river water levels, and to send in the first ship of the season across the Tungting lakes south of the Yangtsze to Changsha; the skipper whose judgment enabled him to hold his ship for one more day at such a place when the water levels were falling—these were the men that counted.

I remember once joining the S.S. *Kungwo* at Kiukiang on a summer evening for return to Hankow, about a hundred miles farther upriver. The *Kungwo* was far the largest river steamer on the Yangtsze, 4,636 tons gross, and was the pride of the fleet which my employers operated, though two of their other vessels were between 3,500 and 4,000 tons.

Something had cropped up at Hankow which necessitated my hurried return and I explained this to the skipper, an alert little old Scot named David Christie, and asked him our estimated time of arrival. 'Just a minute,' he said, and summoned the chief steward. 'That master just now come aboard b'long tall man have got red hair; he b'long Customs River Officer, Mr Sexton?' When the steward confirmed this, Christie turned to me with a bright gleam in his eye. 'Dupree [the Director] wants you back in a hurry so I think I am justified in being a bit unconventional. With a bit of luck we may make history.' He then explained that, with the summer flood waters in full spate, the ship would make slow time 'over the ground', but that we were at a bend of the river with much of the surrounding country flooded. When Sexton appeared Christie asked him whether he had been in those parts for a survey of levels. Upon Sexton admitting this, Christie asked him how much he knew about the water levels in the adjacent countryside. Deep enough and in sufficient width for a navigable channel? Good.

'I expect you wouldn't mind making Hankow a bit early,' said Christie, 'so I'm going to ask you to stay on the bridge with me as long as we are off the recognized route.'

So off we went, and soon after leaving port were steaming gaily across the countryside, with here and there a farm or small village on a knoll or hillock standing out from the waste of waters.

'Full Speed Ahead Christie' was our skipper's nickname on the river, and he deserved it.

One navigational hazard at Wuhan was sometimes met at the point where the tributary Han River joined the Yangtsze's north bank between the cities of Hankow and Hanyang. It drained mountainous areas of Honan Province to the north and its flow was dependent on different circumstances of geography and weather from those which affected the main Yangtsze itself or its tributaries from the south. Perhaps half the width of the Thames at London Bridge, it poured into the Yangtsze deep and strong and almost a torrent. But its spates often swelled faster than those of the Yangtsze and petered out sooner, and the main river, at the junction, could well be a foot below or above the level of the Han.

Even large, well-found tow boats, capable of towing a string of enormous barges against powerful currents on the bosom of the great Yangtsze, have been known to break their backs at this hazardous confluence.

Another form of transport on the Yangtsze was by means of vast rafts of timber upon which the crew and their families made their homes while the great mass floated downstream from the timber-growing areas, diminishing as it went with every sale effected *en route*. In theory they could hardly have failed to be a serious menace to night navigation, but in practice I heard of no untoward incident of any importance.

The worst sufferers were the dwellers on or near the banks when any disturbance up the river sent foreign warships scurrying up to the danger area. Twenty knots was, I think, the speed that a young naval officer told me his cruiser had averaged up to Hankow from the river's mouth in one emergency. Waves in her wake wrecked junks in large numbers and devastated areas of the river bank's villages and towns. Compensation was paid, of course, but it took a year or more to settle.

All that I have now written for many pages has an aura of timelessness about it—we must re-enter time and history.

Chiang Kai Shek fought one war with a Kwangsi provincial clique early in 1929 and was quickly victorious, but many others followed swiftly. Not one of the local war lords in any part of the country was, in the final issue, prepared to give up his provincial status with all the rewards he was accustomed to expect from it and subordinate himself to central authority that really wanted to govern.

In 1930 Chiang secured the support in the north of the 'Young Marshal', as Chang Hsueh Liang, son of the old Manchurian leader, was called, and stabilized the position there for a time. But the whole stage was too vast for Chiang to control or oversee in person and, if he himself clung to idealistic notions of governing the country, the vast majority of his supporters of all ranks were in the game for what they might get out of it. The country was a natural forcing bed for Communist ideas, and Mao's left-wing party gained more and more support throughout all classes except the officials, the soldiery and their hangers-on.

China did, in January 1930, unilaterally abolish extraterritorial rights, and this meant the end of the old mixed court in Shanghai which had previously dealt with all cases involving parties of more than one nationality, whether Chinese and foreign or two sorts of foreign. But this passed almost unnoticed by the average foreigner.

CHAPTER NINE

HANKOW AND HONGKONG

By 1931 it was clear that the country was thoroughly disunited and was likely to remain so. Nothing could reconcile views so diametrically opposed as those of Chiang Kai Shek and Mao Tse Tung.

To Chiang Communism meant the upheaval and destruction of all his most treasured beliefs—the Chinese way of family life and all the customs and behaviour patterns of thousands of years.

To Mao the corrupt practices of the old regime were the complete justification for his revolutionary ideas; the old system, or lack of it, must be rooted out once and for all.

The Chinese have long regarded themselves as being intrinsically superior to every other race on earth. Any temporary superiority of Western races was, in their eyes, due entirely to a certain technical adroitness gained by their rapid advances during the period of China's isolation. This isolation had been maintained by adherence under reactionary regimes to outdated customs. Throw off these shackles of the past and who would be able to stop the most numerous race on earth? When one considers the many fine qualities of the Chinese at their best, one can readily understand their feeling as they do. Industry, endurance, ability to exist and, one might even say, flourish under conditions of near famine and squalor, immense patience, a huge sense of fun and gaiety.

If Chiang could oust the Communists and unify the country, it would be a sad day for Japan. If the Communists ousted Chiang and associated themselves with Moscow, it would be worse.

So Japan did the one thing which at that time could unite Chiang and Mao, in however uneasy a partnership.

Japan decided to act in Manchuria.

Mao Tse Tung had declared a Kiangsi provincial Soviet government in October 1930. In January 1931 the Central Bureau of

Soviet Areas was set up and in September, following an incident on the railways, manufactured expressly by her agents, Japan began military action in Manchuria. This was known as the Mukden incident and was the virtual beginning of the Sino-Japanese War.

Meanwhile, over the immense areas of the Yangtsze and Yellow River basins, a sinister stage was being set. Elsewhere too unusually heavy and prolonged spring and early summer rains caused widespread flooding. Foochow, on 6th June, reported 'the biggest inundation for eleven years'. From Canton in the far south came news on 5th July, 'due to swollen state of the river and heavy rainfall, low-lying districts flooded'.

But in the lowest two hundred miles or so of the Yangtsze basin there had been an unusual amount of snow towards the end of the preceding winter, and this had been well conserved over thousands of square miles of country by an exceptionally frosty early spring. As the strength of the sun grew and that of winter's prevailing north-east monsoon winds began to abate, the bottom reaches of the rivers were filled by the draining of the melting snows from the vast tracts of land through which they flowed. By this time too the usual spring freshets were quickening in the Yangtsze Gorges and beyond; but their gay career was checked by the massive waters building up nearer to the river's mouth.

The River Department of the Chinese Maritime Customs were always busy charting the ever-shifting channels, and their water gauge at Hankow was designed to register zero when there was a basic minimum of water there to allow of the passage of shallow-draught river craft drawing some five to eight feet. But even then there were still patches of deep water, and when the gauge registered only two or three feet vessels such as light cruisers could lie in safety at selected places in the port.

The recorded month's rainfall in Hankow for July of that year, writing from memory, was approximately 22 inches, which was a record, and by the 22nd the gauge's 'watermark' was 47 feet 3 inches, quite a substantial rise in a river at least a mile wide, and though the Bund was still above water, low-lying areas behind it were already flooding. But Hankow was not unaccustomed to such things, and in the summer of 1926 a watermark of 49 feet had been reached without disaster. Of course ground-floor lavatories and bath plugs in the lower-lying areas had tended to answer back, so to speak, as the usual pumping systems were powerless to push the effluent into such a pressure of flood waters. Strong barricades along the Bund's frontage had kept the river from coming over and the big Changkung Dike and the railway embankment, with its occasional arches well blocked by massive sandbag redoubts, had safeguarded the city's rear. But that had been five years earlier—five long years of virtual civil war between the different factions, and little had been done to maintain the dike. The Changkung Dike had been built in 1903 and its junction with the railway embankment served to cover the whole of the city's rear. The dike had a height of 55 feet and the embankment 51 feet.

By 24th July the watermark was 48 feet 5 inches and on 1st August some of the railway arch barricades began to yield, and this appears to have been due to a temporary strike of the coolies detailed to maintain them by filling sandbags. By this time the streets were being patrolled by police in sampans.

A party of British experts, led by the ubiquitous Dupree, had inspected the whole perimeter of the dike on 30th July and reported: 'Section measuring 60 feet caved in on city side: dike known to be weak in many places.' But the dike lay in territory outside their jurisdiction and they were powerless to do more than report it to the Chinese. On 11th August a section of the great dike collapsed and by the 13th the watermark had risen to 51 feet 2 inches. Shade temperatures at the time were about 95° F. and still, with occasional fluctuations, the water continued to rise, till it reached 53 feet 6 inches watermark on the 19th. Corpses were abundant, floating in the streets which were 15 to 18 feet deep in water. Quite substantial buildings, such as hotels, collapsed and there was an acute food shortage. Estimates at the time put the numbers of flood sufferers at 180 million, and in Honan Province alone over a million were estimated to have been drowned.

By 15th September the waters were steadily subsiding and the watermark was 50 feet 3 inches, leaving a few streets free of water.

The British aircraft carrier *Hermes* was then in port and when Charles Lindbergh, the famous American flier, accompanied by his wife, got into difficulties after bringing his seaplane *Sirius* down upon the still turbulent waters, they were finally salvaged after what must have been an alarming experience. Anne Morrow Lindbergh tells the story in her book, *North to the Orient*.

I have told earlier of Dupree's excursion along the dike and of his lead in the evacuation of the white women and children in the 1927 emergency. Emergencies were like pep pills to Dupree and, comparatively early in the flood, before the whole countryside had been submerged, he was the only man to remember the ponies isolated in the stables of the Hankow Race Club. Apart from his many other interests, he was chairman of the Race Club and, as such, had the feeling of personal responsibility as well as his love of ponies to spur him. Even if the floods rose little higher it would be almost impossible to feed and care for them. If the floods did rise substantially they would perish.

'Come, Walter!' he cried to Walter Johns, a young shipping assistant who was also a skilful horseman. (It was from Walter that I heard the story when I came to Hankow some three or four months later.)

As the accompanying plan will show (p. 117), the Hankow Race Club lay about half a mile beyond the Peking–Hankow railway line, which ran across the back of the Special Administrative District No. 1 (ex-German Concession). Beyond the railway the land fell away, to rise again where the Race Club property had been built up to ensure better drainage.

'It was a dicey do,' Walter told me, 'but I preferred facing the floods to arguing with Dupe. Besides, something had got to be done for the ponies, and if we didn't do it who would?'

So off they set in a Chinese sampan, and this in itself was a hazardous undertaking. The channels of the main streets had largely been converted into lagoons by barricade dams. There were the ex-British, ex-Russian, French and ex-German administrative areas to be negotiated, and each authority, with understandable mistrust of its neighbours' efficiency, had largely made its own anti-flood barriers. But any possible by-passes were undesirable, as they carried the full force of the flood and would sweep their craft away down the Yangtsze.

Walter was not clear how they got there, but when they did they found all the ponies in the stable yard and all the mafoos, as the Chinese grooms and stable boys were called, standing round and talking excitedly.

When they saw Dupree and Walter the big head mafoo rushed, babbling: 'I all time talking them you sure come save us, master. What time other sampans come?'

'You cowardly fools!' blazed Dupe. 'How fashion you think my come save you, b'long man, no save pony? My send sampan back. My ride pony home. Johns' master also makee ride. S'pose any man wantchee come, must ride pony also.' The mafoo was a full head taller than Dupree and a younger man. In panic-inspired anger, he made as if to attack his little chairman. A superb right to the point of the jaw laid him flat.

'Come, Walter!' said Dupree. 'No time for saddles. Lucky to have a bridle! Grab the nearest pony and off we go! Any man wantchee save himself, catch pony, follow quick!' In no time at all every man was astride a bare-backed pony, and Dupree noted, with grim amusement, that his recumbent victim had been quick enough on to his feet again to be almost the first to grab a mount.

It was a nightmare journey back. By this time the water was in many places up to the ponies' withers in a swirling muddy torrent laden with debris and refuse of all kinds, including corpses. If they avoided the more effective barricades, they had to battle against the full force of the flood waters. But to get the frightened animals to scramble over the barricades in such conditions was no easy task, and only the courage and leadership of Dupree and the superb horsemanship of both white men—leading, coming back over obstacles to help stragglers and going doggedly on again—got them through those two and a half miles. But the mafoos were restored to the bosoms of their families after the ponies had all been walked safely aboard a waiting ship. And not any too soon.

Dupree himself once told me of an incident which must have taken place some years earlier, as a British police chief of the British Concession (which ceased to exist in 1927) was involved, but I think it worth a brief digression, as it throws another beam of light upon that remarkable man. He was not easy to work for, as he evidently believed that any underdog who had not the guts to endure was not worth having. The occasional underdog who fought back and won would be found a job elsewhere in the large organization.

I once consulted him in the matter of finding a Chinese of wealth, reliability and standing to help me in some commercial project I had in mind for my employers.

'Couldn't do better than Yang,' he said promptly; 'one of the best friends we've got nowadays, but I had to tame him first.'

Yang, it appeared, had been concerned in some large transaction with the Jardine interests, and for some reason it had been found necessary for a sum of about $100,000 in cash, which belonged to Jardine's, to be deposited in Yang's keeping for a period.

One morning Yang was waiting to see Dupree when he arrived at his office and was apparently in a state of great upset. Out came his story. Seemingly, the night before a disastrous fire had occurred which had gutted Yang's office.

'Dear me, I am so sorry,' said Dupree; 'did you lose much of value?'

The Shanghai head office of Jardine, Matheson & Co. in the early 1920's. In the right-hand corner is the Glen Line Building. *Photo: courtesy Matheson & Co. Ltd.*

The French Bund, Shanghai. Cargoes are waiting to be loaded and shipped along the coast in the vessels moored

The consequences of running aground in the Yangtsze Gorges: a Japanese gunboat, H.J.I.M.S. *Futami Maru*, is left high and dry by the fall in the river level.
Photo: courtesy John Swire & Sons Ltd.

S.S. *Wantung* (ex-*Alice Dollar*) in the upper Yangtsze Gorges. She battles her way against a powerful current channelled by sheer cliffs typical of the Gorges.
Photo: courtesy John Swire & Sons Ltd.

H.M.S. *Mantis* drops alongside H.M.S. *Kiawo* at Ichang.
Photo: courtesy Captain A. R. Williamson.

S.S. *Wanhsien* at Ichang after being recaptured from Chinese bandits.
Photo: courtesy John Swire & Sons Ltd.

H.M.S. *Kiawo* after being bombed by the Japanese, Ichang, August 1939.
Photo: courtesy Matheson & Co. Ltd.

After the battle: British gunboats concentrate at Ichang to make a show of force, after the Yangtsze River action of September 1926. In the right centre background, *Kiawo* lies alongside *Scarab*. Astern of *Scarab* is *Mantis*. In the middle distance are *Widgeon* and *Teal*.
Photo: courtesy Captain A. R. Williamson.

A drawing made by Bryan de Grineau of the Yangtsze River action, September 1926.
Photo: copyright 'Illustrated London News'.

The British Bund at Hankow from the south, showing Jardine, Matheson & Co.'s upper and lower river steamers, lighters and hulks. The last named were usually converted barges or pontoons.
Photo: courtesy Matheson & Co. Ltd.

'Everything, everything,' replied Yang in piteous tones, 'including all the Jardine money.'

'My God, that's terrible,' was Dupree's comment. 'A nasty knock for Jardine's, but we shall survive it. It's going to be a job for you to claim on the insurance company if your policy was burnt.'

'Oh, but my policy is safe,' replied Yang. 'I kept it in my fireproof safe.'

At this Dupree sprang out of his chair, went round his desk and, taking Yang by the scruff of his neck with his left hand, gave him an almighty punch on the nose with his right. Then, letting him subside to the floor, he put his foot on his chest and picked up the telephone. 'Give me police headquarters!' he barked to the operator.

'Now, Yang,' he went on in reasonable tones, 'are you going to come clean before I get through to the chief of police? You never left $100,000 in cash lying about while you kept your insurance policy in a fireproof safe.'

Yang whimperingly admitted as much and Dupree put the receiver down again.

'Now', he reminded me when he told the story, 'he's the best friend we've got.'

I was to come to Hankow about two months after the waters had begun their definite and final fall, but at the actual time of the floods I was in Tientsin, well north of the stricken areas. I had gone there with instructions to open up and develop the activities of my department in the area and had arrived in late June. I spent about four months investigating possibilities and reorganizing the office with a view to exploiting them. I had also promised myself, when all was going to my satisfaction, some week-ends in exploring the delights of that wonderful old neighbouring city, Peking. But it was not to be. In Hankow the work of my department was being temporarily hand-led in caretaker fashion by a man who was no specialist in insurance, which was my particular line. The specialist was on leave in England, and when the emergency befell he was not quickly enough available. This emergency was typical enough in some ways of the occurrences which caused staff to be moved around at short notice. Woman trouble. But some features of this case were so unusual as to be worth recording.

Bill, the man concerned, was a splendid figure of a man in his early thirties. To another man there was nothing so unusual about him. He was a fine athlete, but there were many such in our communities. He was a pleasant enough companion, but no more than that.

I am no scientist, and whether atoms which are irresistibly attracted to each other are in any way opposites, or whether they are identical, I am uncertain. But to women of all ages poor Bill was both an irresistible body and an equally irresistible force. Unfortunately their effect on Bill was exactly the same.

A certain young married officer of a certain navy, who was serving in a river gunboat on the Yangtsze, had his home in a small upper floor apartment of, ironically enough, the Lutheran Mission Building in Hankow. He often had to leave his wife for days or even weeks at a time when his ship was on a cruise, and there is no reason to suppose that, in ordinary circumstances, anything untoward would have occurred. But unfortunately, when his wife had come to join him, she had travelled upriver to Hankow on the same river steamer as Bill. They were together for only two days, but atom had met atom and fusion was inevitable. Each was in the grip of a force more powerful than self.

Eight or nine months earlier Bill and I and my best friend of those days, a Scot named Arthur Robson, usually known as Robbie, had been living together in Shanghai in the house of a senior P. & O. Company official who was away with his wife on home leave.

Bill was a sincerely religious man, but the temptations of the garish Shanghai of those days for such a man as he were for ever leading him into sin. He seemed sometimes to think that alcohol might muffle, if not assuage, his desires, but it never did. It only muffled, or muzzled, his conscience.

He had left Shanghai, full of impeccable intentions, determined to take up again with and marry a girl at home. And then, the attractive little naval wife whose name might have been Nemesis.

How the relationship was continued during the flood conditions in Hankow I do not know.

But, from what Bill and his Hankow messmates told me later, the husband used often to chastise the little wife, and the little wife would later display to Bill all the necessary parts of her anatomy to substantiate the story. Perhaps the young husband had some idea of what was going on.

One inevitable effect upon Bill was that liquor taken to douse desire inflamed his anger against a man who could be such a dastard as to mar the lily-white skin of his lady love.

A bare 150 yards away from the young couple's quarters in the Lutheran Mission Building, Bill shared a firm's bachelor mess flat with two other men.

A nice, roomy first-floor flat with three bedrooms, each with its own bathroom.

Bill's messmates had found him increasingly moody of late. Sometimes he sat quietly for long periods, drinking whisky and oiling and cleaning a revolver.

Finally, one evening, they became alarmed and took and hid the revolver before Bill got home. Surprisingly Bill seemed to accept its disappearance quite calmly. It seemed to be just one more proof of the conspiracy into which all things, animate and inanimate, had entered against him. Just one more obstacle to surmount. He took to the whisky again; but it was a Saturday night, and his friends thought that if only he drank enough he wouldn't be able to go out; so they left him drinking moodily, almost savagely, when they went to bed.

At about two o'clock on the Sunday morning a stealthy figure crept silently into the darkened entrance of the Lutheran Mission Building. In all the alcoholic circumstances, this in itself was no mean feat, but it was nothing to what followed. The lift had closed down for the night, so Bill went up the stairs and probably could have found his way blindfold as well as inebriated. Getting to the flat, he flung the door open and switched on the light without a word.

As might have been expected, the light revealed a double bed with two heads, one male and one female, upon the pillows.

Bill was firmer upon his feet by now, but the more insidious effects of whisky were still upon him. He strode over to the bed, flung back the bedclothes and, seizing the little husband by the collar of his pyjama jacket, yanked him out of bed.

'You wife-beating brute!' he shouted. 'You're not fit to sleep with this pure girl!'

His victim may have been small, but he was awake and alert in less than a second. From somewhere handy he suddenly produced a pistol and pulled the trigger. The shot went wide and Bill quickly leapt upon him and, disarming him, knocked him down with a massive blow of his fist. Then lifting the recumbent girl from the bed, and tossing a wrap around her, he flung her across his shoulder and marched off down the stairs. Everything had happened so quickly that he was away down the dark street before the sound of the shot had fully roused the other people in the building.

The winter sun had still not risen when the young men of the bachelor flat were awoken by a thunderous knocking at the door. The police.

Bill's room, when entered, had two occupants. And that is why I was called so suddenly to Hankow.

Bill was hurriedly moved, to finish his contract in the Shanghai office, and a young naval officer and wife were as hurriedly posted to their nation's Atlantic Fleet.

Meanwhile, in Tientsin, although the Japanese 'Mukden incident' had taken place in Manchuria, there was little sign in the daily community's life of what was soon to come. As in Hankow, the Race Club, which was also in Tientsin the Country Club, lay well beyond the confines of the foreign settlements.

When I got to Hankow in November 1931 all the debris and silt had been cleared from the streets, and ground floors of all the European buildings had dried out, though many walls and pillars still showed a muddy stain up to the levels which the floods had reached. But there was still a coffin or so suspended in a tree in the countryside, and an unwary walker along a country road who put a foot into the ditch beside it might find himself sinking knee deep in the soft alluvial mud that filled it.

Belated gangs of coolies were working at repairing the breach in the great Changkung Dike, and the market gardens and small holdings within its perimeter were probably even more fertile than before.

It was three and a half years since I had last been in Hankow, in the spring of 1928 and, whilst only the Japanese and French Concessions had kept their identity, foreign influence was still paramount in the whole of the Settlement area and around it.

Peaceful penetration by the foreigner into the surrounding countryside was relatively free of hazard.

I remember one little incident when I was one of a small houseboat party that went upriver a few miles in search of pheasant and the like, one week-end.

We landed at a likely spot and, as a cock pheasant got up almost immediately, one of the party fired and brought him down. At once there was a clatter of small arms fire from a nearby village, and one of the party went forward cautiously with a Chinese servant to investigate. The sound of a shot in that peaceful district had caused the immediate assumption that the village was being attacked by bandits, so everyone loosed off at once just to show the bandits that they were on the alert. But, the village spokesman hastened to add, they had been careful to aim their weapons into the air so as not to endanger anyone. Amicable relations were quickly restored.

And now back to the main sequence of events. By the end of 1931 Japan was able to do much as she liked in Manchuria, and in January 1932 declared it to be now a republic under the title Manchukuo. At about this time she landed about two thousand marines in Shanghai in the Chinese areas adjacent to the Japanese industrial and business district. It was quite apparent that this was preparatory to the further aggressive moves which Japan was planning, and was intended to ensure their being able to control and protect their own areas of activity and influence in Shanghai when local Chinese feeling became incensed at Japanese actions elsewhere.

Already farther north in Tientsin they were tightening their grip and did not care whom they offended. I have indicated earlier the peaceful atmosphere which had obtained for many years in Tientsin where old foreign Concessions remained and foreign residents passed freely through all of them on their way to and from the Country Club and the European dwellings that lay outside the urban areas.

Now Japanese troops were very much in evidence, with check points and patrols, and delighted in stopping and delaying Britons who wished to pass. Often they would insist upon searching people, which could involve virtually stripping them in the streets—men and women alike. They acted as if they fully intended and expected to take over the whole countryside and run it as they pleased and, as for the other foreign powers, they could jolly well like it or lump it.

At the very same time they were behaving in Hankow as if butter wouldn't melt in their mouths, and British and others continued to frequent the delightful little Japanese restaurants, where sukiyaki was the favourite meal ordered.

It is important to realize how many different faces China wore for the Briton at this time, and in fact most of the time.

As another example of this, it was only the other day that a chance brought me in touch with Lionel Sackville-West,[1] whom I had known slightly between twenty-five and thirty years ago when he spent some years with Jardine's in China. He was good enough to buy me a lunch at his club, in the course of which he mentioned floods in Tientsin when he was there in about 1938–9. At one time the main streets were several feet deep in water, but I had never heard about it until now. Always a keen rowing man, Lionel had apparently aroused enough enthusiasm among the Britons to raise an eight and had found some White Russians who organized a boat to race them. This was at the

[1] Now Lord Sackville.

time that the countryside was flooded, but all went normally for a while until the Russian boat suddenly came to a dead stop—literally dead. The sharp prow of their racing boat had become embedded in a corpse.

Something of this ignorance of all but very local conditions will have appeared in the description of my feelings of despair when I left Hankow for home leave early in 1928, only to be lifted by the very different atmosphere in Shanghai on my way through. Just three days, and I felt reborn. Even the Chinese themselves, in such a vast country, were little concerned with what went on outside their own little local world. Insurance was my main concern during my time in China, and I remember being on one occasion invited to go and look over the property of a large Protestant Mission in Wuchang which, it may be remembered, lies on the south bank of the Yangtsze, opposite Hankow. I was accompanied by my chief clerk, Lee Kai Hing, who, though a Cantonese by birth, had lived sufficiently long in the area to speak the local variation of the Mandarin (northern) tongue well enough to be acceptable to the locals. The place we were looking for was not easy to find in the sprawling suburbs of Wuchang, and Lee stopped some passers-by to inquire. A torrent of conversation resulted which I was unable to follow, although I was by this time able to speak some Mandarin. We got our directions, and as we moved off Lee permitted himself a chuckle: 'They know you foreign; they ask if maybe you Japanese man.' To them, it seemed, all foreigners were alike, and I dare say that a good deal of preliminary Japanese infiltration was already going on at that time. A few years later, when the defence of Hongkong was at stake, one of the great security difficulties confronting the British was that not even Chinese gang foremen could distinguish Japanese undercover men from Chinese workers on a job on the defences.

One of the other missions in the area was of the Roman Catholic order of St Columban in Hanyang. The priests were mostly Irish or Canadians, or a bit of both, though their procurator was a little Australian who had, it seemed, been a chartered accountant 'down under' before he felt the call. I gathered that he had been an enthusiastic rider and a keen man to hounds in his day, and was always trying to arrange for him to ride with our Hankow Paper Hunt Club, of which I was honorary secretary and treasurer at the time. But our organized rides were inevitably on Sundays, presumably a priest's busiest day, and I never managed to arrange anything. Poor little Father Gabriel, he was wistful about it. The mission headquarters in Hanyang was a sort of rest centre for a large area and was also the residence of their bishop. The latter, a huge Irish Canadian of the name of Galvin, with great bushy eyebrows, explained the rather lavish amenities to me.

'Sheer economic necessity,' he said. Young priests had been coming out from their homelands and going to live amongst poor class Chinese in country districts. They had been dedicated young men and had not spared themselves. Within a very few years their health had given way and they had had to leave, which meant all the expense of replacing them. Now the situation was being dealt with more sensibly. Relief priests were sent to the front line and their young warriors came back to replenish themselves physically and spiritually at base. Billiards? Whisky? Wine? Of course.

The mission also ran a rest establishment at a well-known summer resort at Kuling in the mountains adjacent to Kiukiang, about a hundred miles downriver from Hankow. 'As pants the heart for Kuling streams' became a popular Hankow version of the first line of the hymn.

One day the bishop became confidential. Did I know of any architect in Hankow who might be prepared to advise them for little or no fee? I did, and whilst I could not guarantee his advising them for nothing, there could be no harm in my bringing him over one Sunday to meet the bishop.

Rodney Scammell was a not long arrived but fully qualified young junior in a Hankow firm of architects and accepted the invitation with alacrity.

It seemed that the priests were a veritable team of do-it-yourself experts but, in starting to build for themselves a new two-storey brick building, had forgotten until rather late that it would need a staircase. On the way our 'Scam', as we used to call him, expressed some diffidence as to his manner of addressing a full-blown bishop and I then remembered him telling me that part of his education had been at Winchester Cathedral Choir School. Obviously meeting a live bishop face to face was to him going to be rather like a drummer boy socially encountering a field marshal.

His first glimpse of the bishop visibly shook Scam. The right reverend gentleman was wearing old gumboots, stained khaki shorts and a cotton singlet, topping it all off with an aged khaki-coloured sun helmet, beneath which sprouted those formidable eyebrows above a pair of keen grey eyes. He must have stood well over six feet in his gumboots. 'Gumboots', by the way, was Scam's personal nickname for me. But the bishop's charm and ease of manner soon overcame

Scam's shyness, and they disappeared together to inspect the maladjusted—or shall I say deformed?—building, while I had a talk with little Father Gabriel about various matters, not excluding horses.

They soon came back, in great good humour, and Bishop Galvin explained that Scam had consented to walk round some of the outlying properties under their control. Would I care to come too? There were, I think, three, one of which was an orphanage and one a convent, and they were all within a mile or two. It was midsummer weather, with the thermometer in the nineties, and neither Scam nor I was as suitably attired as the bishop for trudging across Chinese farm land, but I accepted and off we went.

Each establishment obviously regarded any visit by the bishop as a special occasion, and had made due preparations for sustaining us on our toilsome journey. They had no such things as refrigerators; but bottles, hung deep in a deep well, can get remarkably cool and I cannot remember all the libations which were poured before us. Beer certainly, whisky and ginger ale I am fairly sure, but the rest is oblivion. By the time we got back to our starting point, Scam and I were certainly weaving slightly, but the bishop was striding heartily along, seemingly in no way affected.

Bishop Galvin turned to Scam and said: 'Well, Mr Scammell, please be assured of my sincerity when I tell you how deeply grateful we are to you for giving your time to come and see us and for the excellence of your advice.'

Poor Scam was overwhelmed with confusion, and as he blurted out his reply, it was apparent that he wasn't at all sure whether to say 'My Lord' or 'Sir. If I may say so, sir, it's the best pub crawl I've ever been on in all my life.'

One huge bushy eyebrow twitched, and a twinkle appeared beneath it. The bishop burst out into as hearty a guffaw as you could expect from a man of his size. What a laugh! Perhaps it was as well that no ramshackle buildings were too close at hand!

There was often a certain naïveté about Scam's public utterances, but this was his most impressive effort in my company. Alas, I soon lost all touch with him as I went home on long leave in April 1934, and when I did get back some nine months later it was to Shanghai.

During my previous spell in Shanghai I had, as mentioned earlier, messed with Bill and Robbie. Some of the circumstances of this *ménage* were much like those of a household involved in a famous tale of old

Shanghai, the only difference being that in the legend the household pet concerned was a dog, whereas with us it was a Siamese cat whose name was Benjy. 'Ha, a Jewish cat. Does that mean that he underwent the usual operation in early infancy?' inquired Robbie facetiously. But for the purposes of this tale Benjy becomes a dog. It was a small but beautifully appointed house within a stone's throw of the Cercle Sportif Français and two stones' throw from a theatre which usually housed Shanghai's Russian Ballet. There was an excellent house boy, but the true major-domo was the cook, whose culinary accomplishments, without undue extravagance, were famed throughout the foreign community. The only fly in the ointment was Benjy, a small rather unprepossessing dog. When his mistress went home on leave she was the first woman on record to do so with a hole in her heart, the wound left by her parting from Benjy. I think that if we had had rowdy parties and spilt beer over the piano, matters could have been settled amicably when the lady returned. But if anything happened to Benjy—well, it would not bear thinking of. The lady's mother was living in Shanghai, and if Benjy should seem off colour or lacking in appetite Mum was to be telephoned at once. We were immensely grateful for this escape hatch, though we had then no means of knowing in what circumstances we should eventually be telephoning Mum.

One last parting thought from our landlady. She and her husband had always believed in being prepared for emergencies and had a large store cupboard full of tins of every sort of food from necessities to luxuries and delicacies. It had now been there for a year or two, and when they returned they would throw it all away and replace it. So we were welcome to do what we liked with it; they would be delighted to come back to an empty cupboard.

'Wow!' said Robbie, his Scots instincts fully aroused. 'A party on the house. If all the grub's free we shall have more to spend on drinks; we can ask more people.' We had soon found that, to get themselves a chance of the fruits of that noted cuisine, our friends were willing to buy themselves the opportunity by inviting us to theatre or ballet afterwards. This occasion was to be no dinner party, it is true, but all the cocktail party titbits would bear the imprint of our cook's master hand.

The day came and the store cupboard had been almost stripped when the prudent streak in Robbie's national characteristics suddenly emerged only half an hour before the guests were due.

'How long have those tins been there? Two years of extremes of climate. How do we know they are still good?'

'Bit late now, old man,' ventured Bill. 'What can you do at this stage but trust to luck?'

'What can we do?' asked Robbie. 'We can open a tin and try it on Benjy. Dogs have got more sense than humans and he won't look at it if it's the least bit off.'

Bill and I demurred, but Robbie was adamant; and before the first guest had arrived Benjy had guzzled a whole tinful of some savoury delicacy and trotted off happily on his own affairs. We did not miss him.

Soon our guests were pouring in and the whole ground floor was chock-a-block with people except for a small study with a telephone in it, at the back, and the kitchen and usual offices.

Suddenly, amid the hubbub, some sixth sense told me that something was up. I looked and saw Lin, the house boy, standing in the doorway from the back quarters. He was carrying no tray of food or drinks; he was white as a sheet and obviously in the grip of deep emotion. I sidled swiftly but unobtrusively towards him and he whispered frantically in my ear: 'Master, master. Benjy makee die!' I had expected something pretty drastic in view of the way Lin's usually phlegmatic demeanour had been disturbed, but this was more than I had bargained for. 'You no talky any man that thing. S'pose any man ask you say my have got telephone call just now.' I slipped away into the study and, shutting the door, rang up my doctor and told him what I knew. He said: 'Don't tell anybody what's happened. You'll only panic them. I'll be round with my box of tricks in ten minutes. Nobody—repeat nobody—is to leave the house before I come.'

To inquiries when I got back into the throng I managed to say that it had been some rather serious personal news but that I didn't want to talk about it just then.

My Irish doctor friend Paddy was as good as his word and arrived inside ten minutes with an ominous-looking case. In response to hearty cries of 'Welcome' and 'Better late than never', he responded by holding up his hand and asking for silence.

He then explained that it was his painful duty to inform all present that there was reason to believe that some of the food they had eaten was contaminated, and that he had come armed with a stomach pump to which we must all submit in turn—the sooner the better.

I think that somehow foreign communities in China were inured to the unexpected and to emergencies, and we all submitted with, I think, remarkably good grace.

'Thank God that's over,' said Paddy. 'But before any of you go I think I had better see the dog.'

So Lin was sent for. 'Doctor Master wantchee look see Benjy,' I explained. 'You bring this side just now.'

'Master, master, Benjy no can bring,' Lin wailed piteously.

'How fashion?' I asked sternly.

'Master, Benjy makee finish. Have got run over in road, all squash,' explained Lin.

What more was there to say?

And now I was back in Shanghai again and Robbie had been moved to a job elsewhere, and Bill was no longer with us.

At this point I was lucky enough, as I thought, to acquire a tiny but comfortable flat in the far suburbs of French Town. Second floor, all mod. cons, and an excellent cook boy and his wife to care for me.

I had scarcely moved in when one day in the Shanghai Club I ran into a young naval officer in destroyers, whom I had known elsewhere on a previous commission. 'Come up and have a free holiday with us at Tsingtao. We shall be there for a month or more in the summer.' I explained that staff just back from long leave were not eligible for local leave their first summer, and he said: 'Isn't there any way you can wangle it? Be ill or something?' I laughed; little did I dream of what was to happen. A very little while later I began to feel out of sorts and developed a slight temperature, so I rang up my doctor friend who advised me to stay at home and, if I still had fever the following day, he would come and see me. When he came the following evening and examined me I had a rash and a temperature of 104·8. Measles! I was thirty-two and it was almost the only childhood disease that I had never had. Long after I was well enough to get up I was still in quarantine, and was grateful for the incomparable blessing of my excellent servants.

One day the house boy was out when an imperious ring, ring, ring came at the door. I was puzzled. All my friends knew that they could only talk to me on my little veranda from the street below. Who could it be?

The boy's wife went to the door, and when she opened it was quite unable to stop the cyclonic young red-headed female who stormed past her.

'Keep away, keep away! I've got measles.'

'Measles'—hesitantly—'what are measles?'

She was Russian.

By the time I had succeeded in explaining the position to her I felt that if she was going to catch 'em she'd got 'em. So I offered her tea while she explained what she was up to.

She was, it seemed, a protégée of a wealthy French financier and had been given the nominal job of trying to boost the sales of a local evening paper. Her way of doing this appeared to be to force her way in to unsuspecting households and, by means of a mixture of naïveté and charm, to get them to subscribe to it.

As we sat and talked the whole situation seemed so amusing that we laughed and laughed, and I warned her that if she came out instantly in a rash she might have to stay—I hoped.

We met once again, for a walk in the park whilst I was still in quarantine, but she was very much under the thumb of her financier friend and also afraid of him.

She thought he would find some way of doing me an injury if I continued to see her and insisted on breaking off the acquaintance. I was sorry. She seemed a nice girl.

As soon as my quarantine was lifted, my managing director invited me to his house in the country for the week-end. He thought the air would do me good.

Within a very short time I was ill again, and when my doctor friend arrived he at once phoned for an ambulance and I was in hospital with, I learnt later, a temperature on entry of 106.

For about forty-eight hours they struggled to keep my temperature down with ice packs, not daring to give any real treatment until they had diagnosed the cause of the trouble.

Then, late one night, I was told that I had malaria. The usual symptoms involving high temperatures alternating with low, accompanied by shivering fits, had not been present. They could only suppose that I had been bitten twice at an interval of about twelve hours whilst on that country week-end. The most painful part of the whole performance was the headaches which accompanied the collapse of the fever.

I got my holiday all right, but not with my naval friends, who were not at Tsingtao at the right moment.

When I came back, feeling much better after a fortnight at the seaside, I got passage in a little old cargo boat of the Indo-China Steam Navigation Company which my employers operated.

Strictly there was only one cabin, which was already booked, but as a member of staff I was accommodated in a spare officer's cabin and discovered that the other passenger was the lovely young auburn-haired Canadian daughter of the C.P.R. agent in Shanghai.

I suppose that the trip was normally of about thirty-six to forty-eight hours' duration, but as we went on our way the captain told us that a typhoon was working up the coast towards us and that all major shipping had turned tail and run back for shelter in Tsingtao. Our little *Lee Sang* was, alas, not fast enough to run away, so we were going to edge a little closer in to the coast than usual and hope that the main force of the gale would veer out towards the ocean, with luck.

The captain had his teenage son aboard 'just for the trip', and my nerves would not let me forget the lines about the skipper of the schooner *Hesperus* who had his daughter with him 'to bear him companee'.

It was a frightening experience, but the little ship was deep laden and wallowed rather than bounced as we managed, mercifully, to skirt through the edge of the great storm.

The trip took four days and the Shanghai papers had headlines about it when we arrived. Unfortunately they also mentioned there being only one cabin and referred to 'the passengers, Miss Doreen Parkhill and Mr Gompertz'. Poor Doreen and I took some time to live that one down.

If this succession of entirely personal anecdotes gives the impression that I am trying to imply that my experiences were exceptional, I regret it.

These were the sort of things that could and did happen to anybody out there in those days. It will be seen that there was no lack of variety in life.

The year 1935 was the twenty-fifth of the reign of George V, and his Silver Jubilee was celebrated in Shanghai by parades of British troops on the racecourse. In that same year the Saar had been restored to Germany after a plebiscite in January. In September the swastika was adopted as the flag of the German Reich and the Jews were outlawed. In October Italy invaded Abyssinia and in December Chiang Kai Shek was elected President of the Chinese Executive.

To the Japanese it must have seemed that the climate of world affairs was becoming favourable to their plans of aggression, and the accession of Chiang Kai Shek to recognized official power suggested that there might be no time to waste.

In January 1936 King George V died, and in the early months of the accession of Edward VIII the tempo of world events continued to accelerate. In January Japan withdrew from the naval conference which had limited warship tonnage; in March Germany occupied the demilitarized zone of the Rhineland; in May Italy proclaimed her annexation of Abyssinia and in October General Franco became 'Chief of the Spanish State'.

I was transferred that summer to my employers' head office in Hongkong and was to be based there for over four years.

At about that time a great reservoir was completed behind the Kowloon Hills at Shing Mun, which, the experts confidently predicted, would take good care of any likely population increases for years to come. 'Likely' is the key word, for the unlikely was soon to befall.

I brought with me the car that I had acquired on my home leave two years before and soon got into a pattern of life which I found very good. There was plenty of hard work, but Hongkong's countryside was still at that time largely unspoiled by intensive building development, and week-ends were often spent scrambling over the rugged mountainsides all day in the minimum of clothing to a final rendezvous with the car—with a chauffeur hired for the day—at some distant point of the mainland territories. Then in the cool of evening, back home well wrapped in sweaters and scarves; baths at a downtown club to save the journey up the Peak, followed by a party of ravenous hikers at dinner in a Chinese restaurant, or an excellent grill-room run by a charming Turk or, on one or two occasions, a meal at a Russian restaurant in Kowloon. Caviare was not expensive in those parts, but I found that a meal in which one consumed mountains of it, with intensive irrigation by vodka, or the less harsh variation of it, Zubrovka, undid most, if not all, the good that we had done ourselves during the day. At Chinese restaurants, rather than be for ever tossing back tiny cups of a warm Chinese wine, not unlike thin sherry, we used to consider that Chablis was well suited to accompany the Chinese dishes. This may all sound very luxurious, but it was not expensive and we had often covered fifteen to eighteen miles over mountainous country beforehand.

These activities could take place only between late October and early to mid March, as it was far too hot in the summer. Even so, plans could only be made subject to weather conditions, as the mountain ridges were not places to be caught upon when they were enveloped in thick fog.

On the seaward side of Hongkong Island and well sheltered by another island beyond it lay a little Chinese fishing village which, for some reason which I do not know, was named Aberdeen. At the Aberdeen water-front lay one or more large and well-appointed

Chinese craft which were operated as floating restaurants. Here you
might peer over the side and see a great variety of fish swimming in
ages of cane or wicker which were suspended in the water. Here, if
ou were a Chinese *bon vivant*, you might point out to an attendant
he fish you wanted and meet it, duly cooked, on your table a little
ater. I have memories of lobster cooked in a saffron sauce and other
lishes unlikely to be met in a restaurant in England. On fine evenings a
party of friends might walk together down the steep mountain paths
rom their houses on the Peak, thus ensuring themselves good appetites
on arrival. Chauffeurs hired for the evening would bring round by
oad the minimum number of cars required, and the well-stuffed party
ould thus be transported home.

I cannot but imagine that much of the simplicity of such outings
vill have disappeared by now and that the primitive old Chinese
loating restaurants are now garish floating palaces. But I should love
o be wrong.

One of the fine old customs of Hongkong was—and, I hope, still is
—the daily firing of a signal gun. At noon precisely every day the little
un booms out and, despite the nature of my employment, it was some
ime before I heard the story attaching to it.

There is a point at the top of a rocky mountainside in Hongkong
sland which is still, to this day, known as Jardine's Look Out, and
rom it signals can be observed by anyone on watch at East Point,
vhich was Jardine's old harbour headquarters in the very old days.

But a man at the Look Out could also see far out to sea and, when
he towering sails of the great tea clippers could be seen on the horizon,
quick message to the markets of the city could be very rewarding to
he firm's dealers. On one occasion the Taipan, or head of the firm, was
eturning to Hongkong aboard the clipper and certain blithe spirits felt
hat the early warning gave them time to arrange a gesture of welcome.
o, as the ship came in, she was greeted by a salute from civilian guns.

This impertinent presumption so incensed the governor or admiral
f the day that he imposed a punishment.

Henceforth, and for all time, Jardine's should be responsible for
ring the noon-day gun. They certainly did in my day and I believe
hat they still do.

The gun is a small brass cannon of a type sometimes seen in Chinese
unks in my day and probably originated in one of Jardine's sailing
hips for use against pirates.

No New Year's Eve is complete in any harbour without blowing of hooters and firing of guns and, for a Scots firm, the Hogmanay tradition demands something special.

I once attended such an occasion, an enormous reception and dance to which all staff and friends were virtually commanded at the old East Point headquarters.

At about 11.55 p.m. bagpipes and all kinds of music were hushed and the entire gathering rushed out to the quayside. There, with careful timing, the Taipan lit the end of a great length of fuse and retired hastily to a safe distance.

There were explosives experts amongst the staff, so the danger was not too great. On the other hand, the little brass cannon was loaded to the absolute limit. 'BANG!' The little gun leapt into the air and everybody unconsciously recoiled as the bagpipes resumed.

Part Four

CHAPTER TEN
STORM AND CALM

As THE year 1937 progressed, Japan's military aggression against China continued to develop and in August she captured Peking. In Hongkong life was relatively peaceful, although during the early summer the trailing skirts of one typhoon, whose centre passed some two hundred miles to the eastwards, had sufficient force to drive an American freighter ashore on Stonecutters' Island in the southern approaches to the harbour.

There is an old jingle relating to typhoons which is presumably still repeated in those parts and which runs, if I remember correctly: 'June, coming soon; July, stand by; August, come it must; September, remember; October, all over.'

By mid August, Japanese troops were fighting in the immediate environs of Shanghai and some would-be dare-devil Chinese pilots decided to attack targets in the Japanese area of Yangtszepoo, including units of the Japanese Navy. But anti-aircraft fire destroyed their nerve completely and they fled, jettisoning their bombs as they did so. Some of these bombs caused many casualties when they fell in the crowded area of the Nanking Road, which could perhaps be described as Shanghai's Oxford Street.

A young colonial—perhaps one would say nowadays 'Commonwealthian'—from a large overseas company that did business with Jardine's was attached at that time to one of the firm's trading departments. When the manager concerned came in again after having rushed out to investigate the bomb damage, the young man's desk was empty of him and his effects. He had fled and, as was learned afterwards, was already on a ship that was sailing an hour or so later. But on his desk was a lone envelope from the Shanghai Club Library. When the manager opened it he learned from the contents that a book requested by the young man was now available. Its title? *Gone with the Wind.*

But Jardine's and many large foreign concerns at once decided that Shanghai was not a place for their staff's women and children, and many hundreds of them, including one new-born baby, were quickly shipped down to safety in Hongkong.

Even by Hongkong standards that spring and early summer had been exceptionally humid, and I had developed a skin complaint which the doctors attributed to it. A rash of watery blisters developed, starting in such places as the armpits and the belt line. I was put on a diet which excluded all meat, eggs, fats, potatoes, fried or highly spiced foods, excess of salt, coffee, strong tea, beer and gin, and allowed only a minimum of whisky, say one small peg per day.

Every morning I attended at the doctor's and stripped so that he could go over the entire surface with tweezers, cotton wool and an antiseptic powder. Swimming in salt water was forbidden, and I was soon desperately wondering how I should keep strength and sanity through the long summer months. Then the doctor's junior partner developed the same complaint and spent a week-end in hospital on Mount Kellett, one of the high points of the Peak. I heard that he lay the whole week-end naked on a bed with fans playing upon him, and the rash subsided. So he returned to duty down below and, within forty-eight hours, the blisters had reappeared. The doctors were utterly flummoxed and I am proud to relate that they named it 'Gom's Disease'.

In the midst of this came the rushing influx of thousands of refugees from the north and, as far as the Jardine staff were concerned, this involved working around the clock in macs and gumboots, organizing accommodation as well as getting ourselves and all refugees under our control inoculated for cholera and other dire epidemics that threatened in such circumstances.

At the end of the first day of all this I got home to our bachelor mess, tired, soaked with sweat and, I suddenly realized, desperately hungry, as I had hardly had time to eat all day. I called loudly for food and found that only the remnants of the standard supper were available—fried sausages and mash, bacon, eggs and coffee—all foods which my diet forbade. I was too tired to care and, in a gesture of defiance of doctors and all their tribe, I gorged myself on sausages, mash, bacon, eggs, beer in successive tankards and a great cup of coffee to wind up. Next morning my skin was better, so I repeated the treatment and,

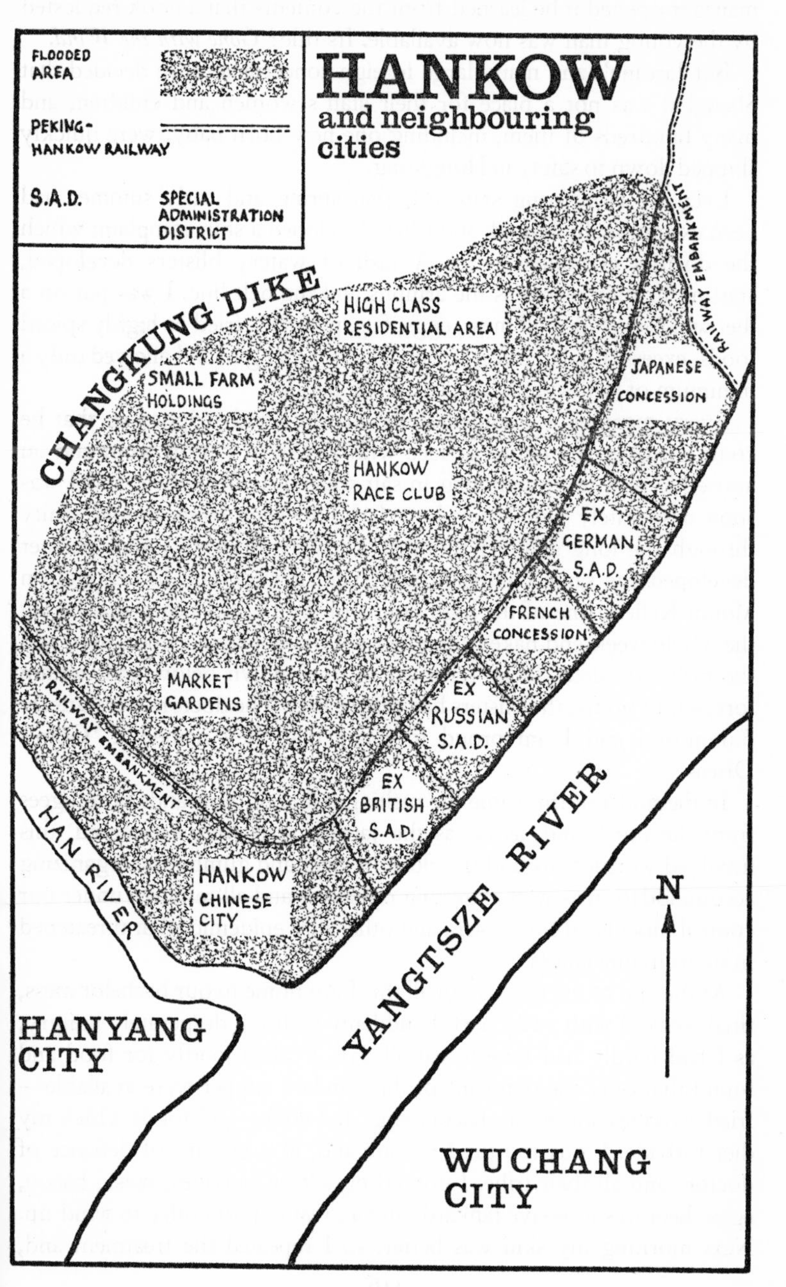
FLOODED AREA
PEKING-HANKOW RAILWAY
S.A.D.
SPECIAL ADMINISTRATION DISTRICT
HANKOW
and neighbouring cities
CHANGKUNG DIKE
HIGH CLASS RESIDENTIAL AREA
SMALL FARM HOLDINGS
HANKOW RACE CLUB
RAILWAY EMBANKMENT
JAPANESE CONCESSION
EX GERMAN S.A.D.
FRENCH CONCESSION
EX RUSSIAN S.A.D.
EX BRITISH S.A.D.
MARKET GARDENS
RAILWAY EMBANKMENT
HAN RIVER
HANKOW CHINESE CITY
YANGTSZE RIVER
N
HANYANG CITY
WUCHANG CITY

within a few days, Gom's Disease had disappeared without trace. I never heard a medical explanation of it.

Our Junior Mess stood on a knoll below the narrow road that ran round Mount Kellett near the top. It was an aged Spanish colonial style bungalow, whose spaciousness had been divided into two, known as La Hacienda. We bachelors occupied one-half, and a family had lived until recently in the other.

So we were guardians, guides and semi-hosts to a heterogeneous collection of women and children refugees in the vacant part. The oldest male of the party was a boy of about fifteen and they soon settled down into dormitories of camp-beds and anything else available.

Then came the last days of August, with warnings of a particularly virulent typhoon which looked, from its charted course, as if it might come very near to, or over, Hongkong. But this was part of the pattern of Hongkong summers: typhoons were always careering and veering around the South China Sea and nobody ever knew what they would do next. If they came too near they affected the whole social and commercial life of the community. Some Chinese merchants, with a rather dubious consignment on their hands, might always hope that, with a little guidance from them, chance might happen to cause their goods to be in lighters or lying exposed on wharves when a typhoon fell upon Hongkong. World markets are always uncertain. Perhaps local demand for goods ordered from eight thousand miles away, weeks before, had diminished. Perhaps an exporter, chancing his arm with a speculative shipment overseas, had heard disturbing reports of market conditions at destination. To such as these, typhoons, properly used, could be a godsend. Insurance companies needed to be vigilant and ruthless.

When trying to give some understanding of cyclonic storms to young schoolboys, I have sometimes likened their movements to those of a spinning top upon a fairly smooth surface such as an ordinary table. I think that the comparison is a good one. There are the two movements: the spinning and the travel. The latter occurs as the spinning object meets more or less resistance. With the top this just means inequalities in the table's surface. With cyclonic storms it is the variation in resistance in the atmosphere, plus such obstacles as mountains, large or small.

If Hongkong is like a pimple on the after end of China, the British Isles are something of an excrescence on the rim of another land mass, and the climatic result has similarities.

Our best weather experts at home would be unable to predict for certain whether any particular patch of weather, good or bad, would cross, say, the Isle of Wight or Anglesey.

Sometimes a typhoon would loiter, so to speak, with intent, around the approximate neighbourhood of Hongkong for days but, seemingly, without being able to decide whether to break in or not.

Often we felt that they did this in the later part of the week deliberately, and indeed we sometimes spent several successive week-ends unable to venture outside the harbour or on any other expedition by land or water.

Nowadays typhoons, hurricanes, tornadoes, cyclones, or what you will, are generally given feminine pet names and one is inevitably reminded that in the ancient classical world they used to call the Black Sea, which they loathed and mistrusted with reason, 'Pontus Euxinus' or The 'Kind to Strangers' Sea, just to humour and placate it. In looking back at our early September girl friend in 1937, she should perhaps have been called Medusa. In early days, before wireless messages were being received from ships at sea, quite small typhoons destroyed much life. But this was because there was no adequate warning in those times. I believe that it was the typhoon of 1906, which killed thousands of Chinese fishing folk, that was so small in area that it passed through the harbour without my father, a magistrate in those days, being aware of it in the Central Magistracy, some two to three hundred yards inland. When immersed in paperwork one morning, he suddenly noticed that it was past the time for his court to open. The weather was very stormy but he hadn't noticed that it was any more than that. He rang for his clerk of the court in some annoyance. 'Sir, there has been a typhoon,' he was told.

Medusa was not at all that sort of a girl. Sunday morning had come and gone before there was, to the uninformed, any sign of her closeness, so most people who wished to were able to have a happy day on the beach. Monday and Tuesday came and went. When Wednesday, 1st September, dawned the star of the show was still frisking about somewhere off stage. She was being capricious after her kind, and many still thought that she would yet veer off elsewhere in a fit of temperament.

But although warning signals now flew to tell us that she was near, it was such a close and sultry afternoon that many of us decided to go for an early evening swim at Repulse Bay, on the seaward side of the island. What cloud there was, was high and innocent looking; but as we lay there on the beach the first unusual thing we noticed was a sort of pinkness, a roseate glow that suffused air and sea and land-based objects alike. Then the lazy, rippling wavelets that lapped the shore were changing form and tempo. It was now a swell that we watched, slight, but gaining all the time in depth, in a relentless slow motion. 'Looks as if that typhoon might be coming nearer,' said someone. 'Let's pack our things up and get back to the Peak.' Indeed as we packed up small gusts were beginning and, by the time we were on the road for our journey of five miles or so, some of them were getting strong and, as we mounted to higher levels and were more exposed, they were becoming uncomfortably so.

At La Hacienda there was much to be done and, after stowing my car in the little stone-built garage, I joined my messmates in taking stock of the position. Old-fashioned buildings of La Hacienda's type had thick walls, and within that thickness at the window openings there were two sets of windows, as in double glazing, and great metal-bound wooden shutters reinforced with steel crossbars. In the centre of each pair of shutters was a metal screw socket. After the whole contraption had been securely shut a thick wooden bar was placed inside horizontally across the centre, with its ends in special hooped metal sockets on the inner face of the wall. The whole was then locked together by a metal screw rod which penetrated all layers at right-angles, and was finally locked home in the shutter socket by twisting a wing nut on its inner extremity.

The main purpose of the shutters was to protect the windows from flying debris, which might in a typhoon consist of anything—sheets of corrugated iron, chimney pots, sections of steel fencing, chicken coops, dog kennels—all transported bodily through the air. It was vital that all screw nuts should be tight. With any play in them the wind force would quickly tear the defences apart, and once the wind was inside the house the roof was liable to take off and join the party of the other debris, all jumbled up with the trunks of small trees, metal lamp standards—the lot.

There was also the party of involuntary campers next door. Even if they had previously lived in Hongkong and knew something of typhoons, we could not leave them to fend for themselves. Nor could we risk delay as, once the storm came close, we would have no means of getting to them. Neither we nor they would be able to open any door: it would blow off its hinges. Nor would it be safe for any living thing to be out of shelter. The air would be full of lethal missiles.

So we went in and did all we could to make the place secure, though, having been standing empty for some weeks, it had some weaknesses in shutters and other parts of the defences. We moved all the beds rather nearer together so as to pack them in close to the party wall and away from windows. The fifteen-year-old boy—I wish I could remember his name, bless his heart—had taken very seriously the responsibility of senior male in his party and was going around from one to the other, calming and encouraging them as best he could.

Then back we went and, after some food, sat waiting. There was little doubt in our minds that we were in for some sort of typhoon, really close. Already there was a continuous roar from the wind outside and its fearsome music was punctuated by sudden violent gusts, like the boom of the roll of drums in an orchestra. The intensity of these gusts continued to increase and we decided that, however tired we were, sleep, even if we could achieve it, would be risky. At any moment something somewhere might give way and life and limb might be at stake.

Like all the old bungalows of its period, La Hacienda had an old-fashioned drying-room with a coke stove and a concrete floor, where clothes were stored, and we decided that if the rest of the building collapsed this would be the room most likely to remain intact. We also realized that in any emergency there would be no time to equip ourselves, so we all retired to the drying-room, clad in gumboots, pyjama trousers, oilskins and sun helmets with their straps round our chins. The seemingly incongruous headgear was a vital part of our equipment, as it had something of the effect of a crash helmet, as those of us who had played polo well knew. All of us but one: Peter Morrison, an intransigent Scot from the Clyde, was damned if he was going to let any typhoon disturb his personal habits if he could help it. Despite all our pleas, he insisted on returning to his own bed and pretending to ignore the whole thing. So we repaired to our refuge and talked and played cards on the floor whilst the violence of the storm increased. Suddenly, above all the din, we heard a tearing, rending sound followed by a crash. We rushed to Peter's bedside, but he was still intact, so we continued our round and discovered a great heap of rubble on a piece of floor in another room, with open sky above it. An entire chimney stack had collapsed, and we suddenly realized that there was another such stack above Peter's room almost directly over his bed. We returned to Peter and this time we would brook no argument. We lifted the bedclothes and threatened to hoist him bodily.

And so the whole seven of us were assembled in our refuge when, perhaps half an hour later, there was another crash similar to the first. Peter had the grace to thank us when we got to his bed and found it piled with a mass of masonry. We went back to our retreat somewhat chastened by what we had seen, while the full force of the gusts was still pounding against the building. It was as if a huge giant had picked up La Hacienda in his two hands and was shaking it in a great paroxysm of fury against the puny humans inside it. But, slowly, the force of the paroxysms diminished and soon after midnight we were enveloped in a deathly calm. We went quickly next door and found all well. It appeared that the typhoon's full force had been against our side of the house and it suddenly dawned upon us that it was not over. The eye of the storm was now above us, giving us our little truce. When it passed, as it soon would, the typhoon would be upon us in full force, but from the opposite direction and against the less well-secured refugee quarters next door. However, the typhoon was veering as it moved and they never got the full blast that had hit us. Floors strewn with broken glass and awash but no serious damage, as we found out when the storm had sufficiently lessened for our next visit about 6.30 a.m.

The little garage had been utterly demolished, but though my car's roof was heaped with rubble no actual beams were lying across it. I scrambled in, switched on and she fired at a touch of the starter. I have had a soft spot for Vauxhalls ever since.

And so ended the story of the first La Hacienda, though I believe that a towering and palatial block of flats now stands on the site.

Our telephone lines were blown away, but it was obvious that not one of us, bachelors or refugees, could expect to stay there, whatever the weather, so quick contact had to be made with some unshattered nerve centre of civilization, the sooner the better. So I set off alone in my trusty little Vauxhall, shedding bits of garage in all directions as I got under way, whilst the others remained to salvage what they could from the wreckage. We had indeed been fortunate in the survival of our drying-room, as most of our most valuable and easily damaged clothing had been in it.

It was a strange journey down the Peak motor road. We often see the odd tree trunk across a main road in England, during or immediately after a gale. But my course was littered with them, and if they sometimes had had the tact to pile themselves in a jumbled heap, instead of sprawling all over the road, I was duly grateful.

It made things a little better that the rain had greatly eased, and when the road was not in a cutting I could snatch a quick glance between one obstacle and the next into the harbour. But the range of visibility was limited and I could gain little idea of the extent of the damage.

One of the greatest menaces to shipping in general, on such occasions, was the variety of ships. Many little ships plied the China Coast under flags which permitted them to employ scratch crews under officers of, sometimes justifiably, dubious reputation. Such ships might not be maintained in a condition which would normally permit their using the port. But in a typhoon they could scarcely be denied refuge. Faulty anchors, anchor chains and motors, tail shafts to the propeller, were among the chief dangers to other shipping. If lifeboats and davits were unsound the ship's own crew could suffer. But if, as happened on this and other occasions, small coasters, some of whose officers and crew might conveniently be in comparative safety ashore, broke adrift and careered madly around the anchorages, much damage could result. This was probably the cause of the wrecking of a three-funnelled British India liner, the *Talamba* of about 10,000 tons, and of the *Asama Maru* of 18,000 to 20,000 tons which was almost new and the pride of the Nippon Yusen Kaisha's Pacific fleet. The B.I. ship sank in the narrow deep-water Lye Moon Pass at the harbour's north-east entrance. But she was fortunate enough to lodge upon a ledge of rock on the landward side of the channel. She was easily salved. The *Asama Maru* found herself, in some incredible way, outside the pass and was blown or lifted by mountainous waves bodily on to the beach of Saiwan Bay. Saiwan was a popular rendezvous just outside the harbour for launch and sailing picnics when there was not time to go farther, and was on Hongkong Island itself. I have consulted no charts or navigation experts, but I can remember that the beach was to some extent sheltered from the main force of the sea by a shoal of rocks not far from the shore. Launches could anchor within this barrier and one could eat a meal on deck undisturbed by undue rolling, but launches could not cross it when the tide was not high. It will thus be understood that, for a liner such as the *Asama Maru* to have crossed it broadside on, the force of wind and water and the depth of the latter must have been tremendous.

All seafaring men of my acquaintance were convinced that she would have to be written off as a total loss, but the Japanese thought otherwise. How much the subsequent operations owed to their determination to salve the prestige of the N.Y.K., and how much to the fact that it was a perfectly staged setting for a demonstration of Japanese salvage skills, I do not know. But they blasted a channel through the rocks, got tugs in and towed her out.

To the best of my recollection the total toll of sea-going ships sunk or wrecked at Hongkong was about forty in that typhoon, but the B.I. and N.Y.K. ships were by far the largest.[1] I heard tell of one skipper on the bridge of his little ship who was blown clear overboard. Fortunately his life-jacket supported him adequately and he was picked up the following day at Castle Peak, about ten miles away on the route to the Portuguese port of Macao.

The last serious typhoon in Hongkong had been in the summer of 1923. In it a brand-new house built for my father on the Peak in 1922 had lost most of its modern, flat, anti-typhoon designed roof and he told me that the anemometer graph at the Hongkong Electric Company's harbourside wharf had registered its maximum of 130 m.p.h. wind velocity.

It seems that the board of the Electric Company were not entirely satisfied that it might not have registered a higher velocity if it had had the capacity to do so. The story goes that they wrote to an internationally famous firm of instrument makers in England and suggested that they design and make them a new one with a capacity of 160 m.p.h. According to the story, the experts were somewhat condescendingly careful of their client's money and were not prepared to accept the job without further confirmation that they really meant such a high figure.

But the job was done, and in 1937 the needle ran off the graph again. So how hard Medusa blew, except that she blew harder than 160 m.p.h., nobody will ever know.

I learnt later that another owner of a car like mine had left too late his return home that night from Shek-O, a country club situated on the far side of the island. As the road rises from Shek-O Bay it runs through a narrow rock cutting, and part way through this pass one of the more violent gusts caught him and, though he was travelling in bottom gear, halted him. He applied the brakes while he declutched and revved his engine for a further effort, but the car moved slowly backward and, despite his juggling with his clutch on full throttle, continued to do so. He sat and thought helplessly of the big fall from the road top at the mouth of the cutting. It seemed inevitable. But perhaps, in his struggles,

[1] Lord Kowloon now tells me that I had forgotten the *Conte Verde* of the Lloyd Triestino which was blown out of the harbour on to a neighbouring island. She was of about 19,000 tons.

he had locked the wheel hard over. Perhaps the not quite straight course of the little gorge saved him. His car came to a stop against a jutting corner of rock and stuck. He was there, not daring to attempt to get out of his car, for the rest of the night. That cut through the hill had always been known as Windy Gap. It had certainly proved its claim to the title.

All the people with whom I was personally concerned got settled into other quarters. The Taipan vacated his large mansion on the Peak and went to live in a bungalow near the Golf Club at Fanling on the mainland. The Mount, as his Peak residence was called, was put in charge of the lady head of the secretarial staff and converted into a hostel for women and children. I myself was taken pity on by a young married couple and housed in their spare room, and life soon returned to something like normal. But social life was enriched by all the young Shanghai women, married and single, whom it was our pleasant duty to look after and entertain.

Meanwhile Japan was pressing inexorably on. In August she had captured Peking, in November she was to take the Chinese part of Shanghai, despite gallant fighting by the Chinese troops there, and by December she was in possession of Nanking. All this looks important on paper, and indeed China's commercial and political life was much disrupted. But the vast hinterland remained unsubdued and aggressively hostile. As has been found recently in Vietnam, you cannot distinguish peaceful peasant from guerrilla, and Japanese patrols that ventured too far from base were inevitably pounced on and roughly handled.

But in Hongkong it was apparent that it would not be long before the fighting extended to the south, and Hongkong's New Territories' border with China proper would then be involved. Already there was increased activity in the Hongkong Volunteer Defence Corps, and we were to be semi-mobilized long before war broke out in Europe.

In the late autumn of 1937 I moved into the house of a stockbroker home on leave, sharing with two other men, H.W.M. ('Peter') Dulley, our insurance companies' accountant, and Tim Flanagan of the P. & O.

Peter, who had been an Olympic oar, had a deceptive, slightly affected manner of speaking and had been dubbed by someone, 'The Marquis of Magazine Gap'. Magazine Gap, it may be mentioned, was a well-known gap or pass through Hongkong's central mountain ridge.

Not to be outdone, Tim became Lord Kowloon and, in view of my recent experiences, I assumed the title of ci-devant Don Hacienda.

Peter was a keen yachtsman, so he inevitably joined the Hongkong Naval Volunteers. In late 1940–1 he personally commanded and navigated a little convoy of tugs and small craft to Colombo. A good effort for an amateur.

It was not until several years later that I learnt that when the Pacific war broke out Hongkong's small naval craft had been quickly sunk or immobilized, and that Peter, with all other volunteer naval personnel, had joined troops ashore in the hand-to-hand fighting. Poor Peter was killed in house-to-house fighting at Wong Nei Chong Gap, which is where the main motor road goes through the hills to Repulse and Deep Water Bays on the seaward side of the island. What chance had he against highly trained troops?

Towards the end of 1937 a new Jardine Mess was established at Strawberry Hill, a house with six or seven bedrooms close by the Taipan's mansion, the Mount. Times had changed and the mess was no longer the aggressively male stronghold which it had been when I had first lived in it about twelve years earlier. In those days the mess had occupied the entire ground floor of an immense building whose upper floors comprised flats for married staff. It was situated well above the top-level tram terminus next to military barracks on Mount Austin on the way to the Governor's summer residence near the top of Victoria Peak, the highest point of the island. No ladies were ever invited to that mess; but boys will be boys, and I have a suspicion that there were sometimes unobtrusive nocturnal visits by members of the fair sex on a strictly professional basis.

The dining-hall there was a huge rectangular room with a fireplace at one end, and almost the whole of the other end comprised two great sliding doors beyond which was the living-room complete with billiard table and a fireplace at the other end. With the two rooms cleared and the doors open, dances could have been held, but were not. Instead a number of exciting and energetic indoor games would usually take place on guest nights, which were Saturdays. One of these was indoor polo. Two teams of four assembled and sat astride strong chairs facing the backs. With the left hand, one gripped the back of the chair; with the right, one held an ash walking-stick by its ferrule end. The crook at the other end was admirably suited to striking a ball, and a real polo ball was used, with the fireplaces at each end of the two rooms as goals. The teams lined up and play commenced. Hit by our sticks, the ball would travel hard and true, and sometimes high, and mess accounts used regularly to include large items for repair of broken windows, pictures and the like. Damage to personnel was the personnel's own business, but seldom amounted to more than cut eyes, shins or knuckles. I remember one or two occasions when this and other games went on all night in the summer until, with daylight, there seemed no reason why the party should not repair downtown to the polo ground and play the game properly.

Another sport was boat races. Long window-seat cushions laid flat on the floor easily accommodated the posteriors of four men sitting astride them. Paddling along with their legs, the contestants could achieve quite a speed, and it was all very healthy and harmless.

Yet another game was 'billiard fives'. Two antagonists with one billiard ball would stand at the baulk end, and one would hit the ball with the palm of the hand to the far end and back. The receiver of service had to return it before it struck the back cushion where he stood. But billiard balls are hard and hazardous missiles, and when, in the excitement of the game, a player lifted one slightly, it could be almost lethal. It certainly broke many windows and conferred a number of black eyes.

But the occupants of the new mess on Strawberry Hill in 1937 were very different young men. I found myself president of a mess of personable and athletic young men and in this they were no different from their predecessors. But almost all had started life in Hongkong with formal social calls and had been entertained very hospitably by people far richer than themselves. How could such a young man return hospitality with an appropriate dinner-party for persons of such calibre? I was consulted, and I suggested that it was time that the reputation of the old-time mess parties was expunged, and that the top brass would delight in informal parties such as they could bring their womenfolk to for a change. They used to have more than enough of formal occasions. So the Ewo (Chinese name for Jardine's) Junior Mess started again the institution of Saturday guest nights, but on a different footing. All the silly games we could think of were played, such as passing the outer shell of a match-box from nose to nose along a line of people without use of hands. A distinguished citizen, with his face cheek down upon the floor trying, with the aid of a female face opposite, to scoop the elusive match-box from polished boards on to one nose or another, was always worth watching. The menu was usually either 'Bangers and Mash' or 'Chinese Chow'.

On one occasion the firm's managing director in Hongkong and his wife were invited to Chinese Chow, but at the last moment she rang up full of apologies. They had been landed with a temporary 'lodger' whom they could not leave alone. If they could not bring said lodger they would be compelled to stay away. Naturally I said 'Bring lodger', but I did hesitantly ask, 'M. or F.?' I was told 'F.'.

When they arrived there came in with them a charming but unostentatious woman who was introduced to us as Miss Celia Johnson; this was before the days of what was, perhaps, her most famous film, *Brief Encounter*, with Trevor Howard, but her name as a leading star of the London stage was well enough known even to us exiles. At once we were all agog. Who would sit next to this unassuming but radiant personality? The vice-president of the mess was certain that Mrs Taipan should sit at my right hand and that he, as second office holder in the mess, should have the visitor at his right. But I am glad to say that I prevailed, largely on the strength of the obvious fact that no star of the West End stage could be expected to know how to handle chopsticks, and the menu was, after all, Chinese Chow. It was my responsibility as president to care for her. So I got away with it.

I was taken aback a few minutes later when I saw Miss Johnson pick up her chopsticks with a deft dexterity far beyond my own. My mind began to function, and soon, in the course of conversation, all was made clear. As the wife of Peter Fleming, the famous explorer and writer, she had been accompanying him on a trek across South-East Asia from the Bay of Bengal but, feeling a little tired, she had left him at one of the ports of what we now call Vietnam and taken ship to Hongkong to await him there. Peter Fleming had been at school with one of our senior directors, John Keswick, so it was natural that his wife should have the hospitality of the managing director in Hongkong. They had been travelling and living 'native' most of the way, and she had learnt more about chopsticks than I had done in all my years in China. The joke was certainly on me. But it was worth it and, with such a gracious neighbour, my embarrassment was short-lived. It would of course have been delightful to sit next to the Taipan's wife, a most charming woman and good friend to our mess. But a famous actress! Wow! Not that there was any lack of spirit or vitality among our women of Hongkong. I remember in particular one, Yvonne McNab, whose father, though a Scot, was the manager of an American bank. Yvonne cannot have been more than twenty, but was as quick in repartee as she was pretty. On one occasion she was in the crowded ballroom of the Hongkong Hotel with a party, and was dancing with a distinguished and rather senior officer of one of the Services. His grip of her was becoming embarrassingly intimate and she suddenly shook herself free. 'Take your hands off me!' said a high, penetrating voice with a Scots timbre. 'I'm not one of your junior officers' wives.'

So the year 1937 ran its course in Hongkong, with social and community life among the residents as gay as usual. But events in China were already beginning to affect the little colony. It was not only people that were starting to take refuge there from China. China's currency could hardly remain unaffected by the Sino-Japanese conflict, and more and more Chinese money was coming into foreign banks and into investment in foreign concerns of all kinds. Property values began to what is nowadays called 'escalate'. Events were already taking a turn which was soon to make nonsense of the prediction of the water authorities that their recently completed reservoir would take care of population increases for many years to come.

St Andrew's Day had been marked by the usual Scots festivities. Amongst these was Jardine's annual 30th November staff race, which was regarded by the Jockey Club as 'official' and was conducted with due ceremony at the racecourse. Hongkong had not always held this race, but it was a regular feature of St Andrew's Day in Shanghai and, sometimes, Hankow and Tientsin. It was a strange contest, as it included elderly riders of 12 stone and upwards, and young men who were among the community's leading jockeys. Handicapping by weight only was impossible, so the usual sight was to be seen of riders starting anywhere from the starting-post to 200 yards ahead of it. The race was followed by Jardine's being at home to all comers in the grandstand with haggis and champagne as well as the more normal whisky.

When 1938 broke I was told that our insurance companies' accountant, Peter Dulley, was shortly going to take six to nine months' leave and that I had been nominated to take over his job in his absence. I was no accountant and, as this involved the head office accounts of two small insurance companies as well as the agency accounts of some ten or twelve world-wide and famous companies, for which they acted as feeders, in every branch of insurance, this seemed to me more of a threat than a promise. But Peter's Portuguese and Chinese staff were well organized and admirable and, as he was to be back long before the accounts would require to be finalized for the annual general meeting of Jardine local companies, the job should not have been beyond the capacity of anyone with a bit of sense and willingness to work. But the little local companies were the ones which all the Chinese knew, and investment of some of their assets in Shanghai Municipal Debentures or in well-secured mortgages in Shanghai was an inevitable adjunct to their operations in China. So all through that spring, summer and autumn, as fluctuation succeeded fluctuation in China's war with Japan, Chinese currency continued to decline and Shanghai property to depreciate. I forget whether it was weekly or fortnightly that I had to reassess and revalue in sterling the two little companies' assets, totalling in those far-off days some one and a half to one and three-quarter million pounds, but consisting of Chinese and many other currencies as well as sterling. Even the others' exchange rates varied slightly all the time, but the Chinese currency assets, on their unsteady way down, plunged, rallied and plunged again. By midsummer I was seeing spots before the eyes and believed that the cause was liver. But the doctor thought otherwise and diagnosed eye-strain and the need for glasses. The relevance of this purely personal anecdote will appear when I come to tell of life in Shanghai under the Japanese in a later chapter.

Meanwhile the intransigent Scot of the Hacienda, Peter Morrison, was becoming mellowed by the intrusion of the feminine into his life. We had had many disagreements and some rows, including one big one, but now although, or perhaps because, we were not living under the same roof, we became friends, and when he came to be married he made the very real gesture of inviting me to be his best man. I remember once going swimming at Repulse Bay with Peter and Mary, his bride-to-be. We were all three lying in our bathing-costumes in the sun on an anchored bathers' raft about fifty yards from shore when Peter suddenly took it into his head to plunge in for a swim on his own. I was somnolent, but Mary had reached a stage in her relationship with Peter when his every movement had to be watched. Suddenly I was roused by a soft but urgent cry from her and sat up. Peter was swimming peacefully seawards some fifty yards farther out, but about half way between him and us a triangular fin cut the sea's smooth surface and was moving steadily in his direction. We knew at once it must be a shark. I suppose it was not superhuman of me to be able to be calm and almost objective, but Mary—I have seldom admired a woman's courage more. If we tried to shout to Peter we would certainly alarm him, and it would be a long way back for a man in a panic and splashing as he swam to frighten the intruder. In any case to swim back towards the raft would be to swim directly towards the moving fin. To jump in ourselves could only drive the shark more surely in his direction. After frantic whispered consultation we decided that we must contain ourselves in silence. A moment later the fin veered suddenly off course and soon vanished into the distance. Later experts told me that it was almost certainly a 'mud' or 'basking' shark, a type which does not normally molest humans. After the fall of Hongkong some three or four years later, I believe that, for the first time on record, there were cases of bathers being mauled. One can only suppose that the considerable bloodshed on the beaches during the fighting attracted the attention of the man-eating varieties which were common enough farther out to sea. I myself certainly never saw such a fin again in Hongkong waters. Jellyfish, especially the lovely but notorious Portuguese man-of-war type, were the chief hazard to swimmers, though a graze by any barnacle on rock or raft almost invariably turned septic unless treated quickly.

When on a launch or raft it was as well to look deep into the water before taking a header. Its brilliant purple hue made the Portuguese man-of-war easily distinguishable, but one could be badly stung by other kinds of jellyfish. If one of them could be seen, the usual technique was to sprinkle sand over them from above—its weight as it penetrated them quickly drove them to the bottom. But the water also contained many fragments of jellyfish disintegrated by the screws of passing ships or other mishap, and it was easy to swim or dive into these without noticing them. A good wipe down in surgical spirit usually disposed of such stings with no after-effects. There was no water ski-ing, as the commercial launches that took us out had not the requisite speed. But solid, well-battened boards were often let down from the stern on tow-ropes. These were some four feet long and about two to two and a half feet wide and had short ropes attached to the forward end which, when one was erect, one could hold almost like the reins of a horse and carriage. In this way one could, in smooth water, ride behind the launch for miles; sometimes two riders together. But even in calm seas one had to be on the alert. In the open sea there was no need for passing liners to slacken speed, and if they made one's launch roll uncomfortably, what they did to the little surf board may be imagined. It plunged and reared like a bucking bronco.

A one-time local chief of the Asiatic Petroleum Company (Shell: Far East Subsidiary) was well known for his adventurous Sunday launch parties. Young people invited once, and reluctant to attempt acrobatics on the surf-board, were unlikely to be asked again. Our host, 'Bonzo' Bousfield, had his own little gimmick. While the board lay in the stern of the launch a deck-chair used to be balanced upon it facing forwards and in this would sit Bonzo in an immaculate suit of whites, with a panama hat on his head and his Sunday newspaper in his hands. When the launch was at an appropriate speed the whole contraption, complete with deck-chair, Bonzo, newspaper and all, would be lowered gingerly over the stern. Was he also smoking a pipe or cheroot? It would have been in keeping, but I forget. He used to sit back, utterly relaxed and reading his paper. The paper flapped a great deal in the breeze and this cannot have made for comfortable reading, but Bonzo was putting on his performance and was content. But long, striding, scrambling walks over the mainland hills were my favourite Sunday recreation, and, if one thinks of the basic meaning of that word, it expresses what one felt at the end of such a day—re-created.

So my arduous months as a pseudo-accountant passed. It was very hard work, but there were plenty of experts in the technicalities amongst the senior men in the firm's main accounts office, so there was no call to lose one's nerve. Anyway, my very tough chief was satisfied and I was informed that as soon as Peter Dulley returned I would be sent on a goodwill round trip to an associated concern—in those days called Jardine, Skinner & Company—in Calcutta, travelling by one of the Calcutta–Japan ships of the fleet that Jardine's controlled. A quick glance at sailing schedules revealed that I could reach Calcutta a day or so before Christmas and leave again early in the New Year. On my way back I was to break my journey for a week or more to tour Malaya and visit agents there. As I had a cousin, Denis Campbell, with the great firm of Shaw, Wallace & Company in Calcutta, I lost no time in writing to him and was promptly invited to spend my time there staying with him and his wife. A few weeks either side of Christmas are the full extent of Calcutta's tolerably enjoyable weather and, as this ties in with the British festive season, I was treated to a glimpse of the full pageantry and panoply of viceregal glory. The viceroy's superb escort of Indian Cavalry all mounted on perfectly matched greys; the viceroy's colourful ball with impeccable Western feminine fashions mingling with the brilliant saris of the Indian ladies. Calcutta was also the home of the Calcutta Light Horse and Denis Campbell was a commissioned officer therein, so, as a member of the Shanghai Light Horse, there was no question of my being allowed to escape participation in their Christmas ride. Business pressure had not given me opportunity to put a leg across a horse for over a year, and in any case the Calcutta country was full of fences, whereas Shanghai obstacles were almost entirely ditches, apart from a few low mud walls. The mounts too were Australian walers, far larger than the China ponies I was accustomed to. I somehow managed to survive the ordeal without disgrace, much encouraged on my way by friendly shouts of 'Come on, Shanghai' from the Calcutta troopers. Naturally I fulfilled my business obligations in Calcutta, but it is the other experiences that I remember. First-class, and I mean first-class, polo; rugger in a temperature equal to that of an English summer when we have one. Such games I watched and enjoyed. All too soon my ship was due to sail on her return journey and I left Calcutta with regret. My next visit was to be in course of repatriation from China about seven years later. On the way back to Hongkong I left the ship for a few days in Singapore, but it was a stay taken up entirely with business engagements, including a tour of agencies in various parts of Malaya. My only interest in it was three years later, in retrospect, when I was to hear in Shanghai the glorified Japanese version of their capture of the tragically inept fortress.

And so back to Hongkong, which was watching developments in Europe with anxiety but which was already becoming preoccupied with the presence of Japanese troops in south China, too near to the colony's New Territories border for our peace of mind. Hongkong was becoming a major supply port for China's war needs. Appreciable quantities of goods would be unloaded in Hongkong for Chinese buyers and would then vanish. With multitudes of Chinese craft of all kinds perpetually thronging the harbour, and with hundreds of miles of sharply indented coastline close at hand, there was a continuous stream of supplies entering the mainland. And then there were the coolies. They knew the country and all the devious hidden tracks through the hills. Their capacity for carrying enormous loads slung to the poles across their shoulders seemed limitless. Their speed of movement was great. Understandably the Japanese were furious.

But our sympathies were with the people of China and, pitiful though Hongkong's defences would be against determined attack by a major land and sea power, we felt that America was our sure guard in the Pacific and could not foresee anything which would change this.

And then came the outbreak of war in Europe. Most of the younger men who happened to be on leave in England stayed there and joined up, but many in the middle to late thirties were not accepted and were told to get back to where they could be of more use by keeping British trade alive and maintaining the flow homewards of many goods which war-time Britain was going to need. China had a desperate need for many things which Britain could supply, but there was a reverse side.

One strange predicament which had presented itself to Jardine's as war became imminent in Europe arose from the presence of a young German named Paul Erhardt. Paul was the son of a prominent Hamburg merchant who had had a long and friendly business association with Jardine's and who, strongly anti-Nazi in outlook, had wished his son upon us for the ostensible purpose of letting him learn the Far Eastern end of his business. But it was reasonably apparent that one important purpose of Paul's Far Eastern sojourn was to keep him away from Nazi influences and from all the trends in Germany at that time which his father felt to be harmful. How far Paul saw eye to eye with his father is another matter. Hongkong certainly didn't want to have to intern him if war broke out, and he was moved hurriedly away to the agency at Taipeh in Formosa, where he was under the eagle eye of the agent there, one Bernard, or 'Bunny', Bolton. If 'Bunny' was any sort of a real bunny it was the 'White Rabbit' sort. Anybody who knows the famous story of Britain's undercover agent in Paris whose normal outward business was that of head of a great fashion house will know that his code name was the White Rabbit. By the time I heard this tale from Bunny, the Pacific war had broken out and he had been concentrated in Shanghai along with the rest of us preparatory to internment. Bunny had had some doubts as to the soundness of his lungs, and keeping himself fit had become a fetish with him. He used to tell tales of long and arduous week-end hikes across the central mountains of Formosa. He was very much of a lone wolf in temperament and in gait and, I gather, did these pilgrimages in search of health on his own. But we all of us must relax sometimes, and when he had young Erhardt with him he may have been glad of the excuse for an occasional night out. One evening the pair of them were enjoying a peaceful beer in a bar when they were molested by a rather drunken, very disagreeable and aggressive little Japanese in uniform. Bolton did his best to ignore the man, but a Japanese in liquor is not easy to ignore, and the moment came when Bolton lost his temper momentarily and knocked the little man down with his fist. The tolerance of the ordinary Japanese man in the street towards the British was but a thin veneer at this time, as I was to discover when I visited Kobe in the spring of 1940. Now a Briton had struck down a uniformed Japanese in a public place, and the reaction of bystanders was immediate. In a matter of seconds uniformed police had appeared and seized Bolton roughly to drag him off to jail. But, whatever political feelings he might have had in Europe, Paul Erhardt had no doubt of his sentiments on this occasion. Despite the posse's unwillingness to arrest him he insisted upon accompanying them and, waving his German passport, a document thought much of by the Japanese at that time, demanded that the German Consul General be summoned at once.

During the ensuing delay it became borne in upon the young men's Japanese captors that they were going to need an open and shut case to justify them to Erhardt's powerful friends. So they looked around for the victim of the assault, their chief witness and plaintiff, but he was nowhere to be found. Feverish inquiries ensued which ended, after long delays, with the discovery that the little Japanese was himself a badly wanted man, a criminal who had been masquerading as an imperial Japanese officer and whom they had long been trying to trace. His final capture brought the little incident to an end with high Japanese officials proffering abject apologies and profuse thanks to Bunny Bolton. How he and Paul Erhardt laughed when they got home that night.

Many of our younger people, who had seen more of Paul Erhardt than I, had resented some of his Nazified attitudes and behaviour patterns. But I prefer to think of him as he appears in this little story. Naturally, he later got home to Europe to join the German Army and be killed, like so many others.

In Hongkong the Volunteers were spending all their spare time in military training and in being reorganized to take over as many as possible of the Regular Army's duties in defence.

So many like myself, who had treated Volunteer work almost as a recreation, discovered that it was no longer enough to ride about on ponies as members of the Mounted Infantry Company. Coast defences became a priority, and a number of well-used naval guns were produced and mounted at various points along the cliffs. My unit was a battery of four-inch guns at Cape D'Aguilar not far from Shek-O and its Windy Gap. They were naval guns of a type used in the older destroyers, but we were a unit auxiliary to the Army and it was the Royal Artillery who sited the guns and organized the whole affair. But whatever the type of guns to which the Army are now accustomed, their experts seemed taken aback by the ear-splitting crack of the little naval guns. Perhaps the little four-inch gun I was concerned with would have been tolerable on a gun mounting on an open deck. But it stood on a narrow, curved shelf carved out of the hillside with a wall of rock not far behind its breech. I was not present when the calibration test shoot took place, but current gossip in our battery was that the master gunner who was superintending the operation lost an ear drum as well as his 'puggaree'—that cloth wound round a topee just above its brim.

We certainly learnt to face directly either forrard or aft, with our mouths open, when our little pet was about to give tongue. But I do not know whether she ever spoke in anger. The main attack upon Hongkong was to be from the mainland and the battery was soon dismantled and its personnel withdrawn to fight hand to hand on the beaches and elsewhere. Amongst them were men of sixty and boys of sixteen. What a butchery! The year 1939 was an exceptionally busy one for me in ways not so directly connected, at first, with military or political events.

Peter Dulley was back in charge of the company's books. I myself had had a few weeks' breather after my previous strenuous year, so our director allowed his second in command to go on leave to England at the same time as he himself did an Australasian tour-cum-holiday for several months.

So that it was not only Volunteer service that filled our time, and Peter Dulley and I, both under forty, were gratified at the trust placed in us and highly flattered to be left in charge of a great organization in such uncertain times. Our chief, 'Hooky' Hall, was no ordinary man, but I have had so much to tell of 'the trees' in Hongkong that I have hitherto said nothing of the man who was, for me, very definitely 'the wood'. He is worth seeing as clearly as I can portray him.

Smallish, rather fat, but quick on his feet, red-faced, with a beak for a nose, a quick and penetrating eye and the index finger of his right hand missing. At rest, in a deep armchair after a good meal, he was not particularly impressive. But, in a flash, he could be on his feet with the sharpness of his keen mind enlivening his face and his manner, his every movement. Irascible, forthright and yet kindly and very human, he would often explode into temper, but if he had been in the wrong he quickly made amends in his own way.

On one occasion, when one of his secretaries brought him a vital document which he had been waiting for her to type, one glance at it sufficed for him to raise his hand to detain her. He read on, but there was no need for him to turn the page: the first had enough mistakes in it to initiate one of his rages. A minute or so of vitriolic abuse and the little typist fled sobbing from the room and sat at her desk with her head on her machine.

'Damn and blast it!' said Hooky to himself. 'I have been a brute. I have been unfair. I must make amends.'

He dashed out of the room, down two flights of stairs and across the road. Back he came almost at once with an enormous parcel and, with a little bow and an apology, handed it to her as she sat. It was a huge box of chocolates. But unfortunately, as he watched her unwrapping and opening the box with little coos of delight which still had an undertone of tears, his eye strayed to the document in her typewriter. Another mistake! He began to bellow anew and fled in confusion to his own office to recover himself in private.

I remember one morning, not long before 'tiffin', as we called lunch, when I was so violently and, I thought, unjustly slated that I turned and marched out of the presence before he had finished speaking.

A few minutes later his stocky shape loomed over my desk: 'Having tiffin at the club? Let's go along together and I'll buy you a gin.'

When I first came to Hongkong the mess had been full, so I had lived with my parents at their rather senior official residence. It was a good ten minutes' walk from the top level tram station, and I often missed the intended tram and caught the one which followed ten minutes later. This tram arrived at the bottom tram terminus at about 8.56 and the walk to the office took just about five minutes, so that, on more days than not, I arrived at my desk at between 9.01 and 9.02. All subordinate white staff had buzzers by their desks so that the chief could summon them at will, and it was not many days before mine greeted me before I could get my tail on my chair. Buzz, buzz. 'Look here, Gompertz,' said Hooky as I faced him in his sanctum, 'if you want to be late, be bloody late. Don't come creeping in with your eye on the clock like a —— fifth-rate clerk.' I was rather hurt at the time, but a day or so later I noticed for the first time what was a regular daily sight on the pavement outside the great office building. I was on my way back from lunch and it was about two minutes to two o'clock. Round the entrance was a large cluster of Chinese and Portuguese clerks. They had come back from lunch but they were not going to enter the building before two o'clock. No, sir!

Hooky, I may say, attended many business lunches and was usually late back—but bloody late. In the morning he was almost always in his chair by eight o'clock.

The first time I wanted sanction for an expensive cable to be sent half way round the world, he cross-examined me thoroughly before he gave his O.K. Then he remarked that nine out of ten cables sent in business were the result of failure to think of the matter early enough to write a letter. A shrewd and practical man, he had the unerring gift of analysing in a few seconds a voluminous stream of words, whether spoken or on paper. Then a terse and pungent sentence from him would resolve the whole complicated matter. When I had reached Calcutta on my visit, our business friends there had been very warmly welcoming to me and had added: 'Thank God it's you, not the Old Man.' Hooky had an immense capacity for liquor without noticeable effect, and it seems that a special duty roster was organized for his visits. Mr A would take him to the club after he had at last got him away from the office at about 6.30 p.m. He would then explain after an hour or so that he had a prior engagement which he could not break. Miraculously at that very moment Mr B would saunter casually through the room and a painless transfer of responsibility would ensue. An hour or so later Mr B's wife would ring up: one of the children was ill—she was anxious—he must come home at once. Enter Mr C.

And so it went on till the small hours, with Hooky talking hard business and downing drink for drink with a succession of seasoned Calcutta types.

In the morning he was always in their offices before they were, and ready to talk hard business immediately. Not by any stretch of imagination was Hooky a 'compulsive' drinker or an alcoholic, but if it suited him to drink he certainly could. They adored him, but found him too exhausting. His missing index finger, by the way, had been left in the trenches in World War I, but he held his pen adequately between second and third fingers and was equally adept at raising a glass. I have mentioned that he was usually at his desk by eight o'clock but, before this, he would visit the racecourse at about quarter past six and have breakfast there at seven o'clock after watching his ponies doing their training gallops. Quite a man, and a most formative influence for a green youngster such as myself.

To return, then, to September 1939. There was little doubt in Hongkong, once the Russo-German Treaty had come about in August, that Hitler was preparing for further ventures. When Britain and others finally declared war upon Germany, the news reached me and a number of others in a rather strange way. We had been under canvas at our battery position on Cape D'Aguilar and were due to be transported back by army lorries that Sunday evening. The lorries had not turned up and, after sitting about for some time surrounded by our individual equipment, we, or rather our battery commander, decided that we should start to march in the direction of home. Our isolated outpost was some distance along a narrow military road which joined the public highway close to Windy Gap. Failing our lorries, we might get picked up a few at a time by passing motorists.

So off we set, marching to the old World War I marching songs. It was not long before, round a bend in the narrow road, a motor-cyclist appeared and stopped when he met us. It was an army dispatch rider. 'They've started!' he cried, and we thought he meant our lorries. Of course that was amateur soldiers all over: thinking only of themselves. 'No, you bloody fools!' he screamed scathingly. 'To hell with your lorries! They've started the *war*!' But our transport turned up in the end.

So far as my business life was concerned, it was not more than about a couple of months before the pressure was taken off me. I had had the rather frightening responsibility of laying down marine underwriting policy under war conditions for an insurance network throughout the world, including London. But before the end of the year Hooky was back and firmly in command again. My next lark was a trip to the Philippines on about the 1st or 2nd January. Whichever day it was, I still had severe laryngitis, which some unkind friends attributed more to New Year's Eve festivities than to any other cause.

I travelled to Manila in a Dutch liner, then neutral and very comfortable, and thoroughly enjoyed my trips when I got there. These included a business visit to the mountain resort of Baguio and a turn around the islands to Cebu and Iloilo in a tiny Philippine coaster. Real South Sea Island stuff. The occasion for my visit was that, with Philippine Independence, the cash deposits which my companies were required to maintain in a bank there as a prerequisite to doing business in the Islands needed to be converted from U.S. dollars to Philippine pesos. It was a very ordinary precaution to investigate the reverse convertibility, in any circumstances, of such a currency, if one was going to lock up funds worth about U.S. $200,000 in it. And it was a good pretext for a visit which enabled me to inspect agencies while I was there.

I think that what impressed me most about Manila was the traffic in the streets. The average Englishman is usually taken aback by the breathless tempo of motor traffic in Paris. But beside Manila the scene in the Paris I remember would have seemed to be in slow motion. Miracle of miracles, I saw no accidents and an idea suddenly dawned upon me. Maybe the conscious rectitude of the ordinary British driver when he has the right of way is a cause of accidents. It certainly would have been in Manila. Perhaps the very fact that nobody ever expected the other driver to do the right thing—nobody ever went on because he knew that he had the right to—perhaps this was why the actual impacts never seemed to come. It was all very marvellous to me.

CHAPTER ELEVEN

JAPANESE INTERLUDE

WHEN I got back to Hongkong it was not for long: there was soon another trip, an emergency one, and this time I finally reached the Japan I had been momentarily pointed at for a few hours fifteen years before.

With both Hooky and his second-in-command now back in Hongkong, it was obvious that I was the mobile reserve for almost anything. It was 'almost anything' that happened. I was told one day by Hooky that the Taipan wanted to see me, and was informed by the latter that Jardine's agent or manager in Japan had just been arrested in Kobe and was in jail. 'First boat is one of ours tomorrow. Catch it,' said the Taipan. I did. Short though my notice was, it had got through to the G.S.O. III Intelligence, Major Charles Boxer, in time for him to contact me discreetly before I left. I knew Charles Boxer pretty well in those days. We were fellow members of a tiny once-a-week 'tiffin' group; we hiked over the mainland mountains together almost every week-end with two or three others. I also used to meet with him some of the cream of Chiang Kai Shek's intelligentsia who were running a Chinese periodical in English. But on this occasion Charles had some secret information to discuss. What Jardine's agent had been up to in order to get himself locked up was no concern of Charles Boxer. But there was in Kobe a prosperous concern which operated a retail and wholesale chemist's business and an aerated water factory which had the contract to supply trans-Pacific liners. Its king-pin was an unassuming little man named Griffiths. Griffiths certainly did well out of the above-mentioned business, but his commodious premises in Kobe also enshrined something far nearer his heart—a bookshop and publishing business. Griffiths, it seemed, was at heart more of a scholar and a student than a business man and had a deep knowledge and understanding of Japan and her people. News had just reached Charles that Griff had been arrested, and as any inquiries emanating from someone like Charles might prejudice Griff in whatever predicament he might be —he was one of our most valued secret agents in Japan—would I see whether I could find out anything and, if I did, send down a verbal message by one of our ships' captains? I naturally promised to do what I could but with little expectation of success. When the ship reached Kobe I was surprised to be met by our agent, Alister Macdonald himself. It seemed that there was tight control of foreign imports, but that he was allowed a personal quota of, *inter alia*, one bottle each per month of whisky, gin, brandy, sherry and port. As this had to cover his entertaining as the firm's representative, it was not much, but Macdonald had learned to adjust his social life accordingly. Alas, some misguided well-wisher in the Hongkong office had decided to increase the quantity of poor old Mac's consignment. It had come in through the neighbouring industrial port of Osaka where the stevedoring contractors had slipped it in on the quiet. But one of the Japanese staff in the Kobe office found out what had happened before Macdonald knew a thing about it and informed the authorities. It was useless for Macdonald to deny knowledge of the matter. They just did not believe him. So they confiscated the liquor and gave him a week or two in prison.

My instructions were that he was to leave Japan as soon as he was free, so he went back on the ship which had brought me. There was little time, therefore, for Macdonald to do much in the way of introducing me around the rather reduced British community in Kobe at that time. But I got an impression that he did not, for some reason, hit it off particularly well with many of them. We lunched every day in the restaurant of a not far distant Japanese hotel, and he there introduced me to a man whom he had been in the habit of meeting for lunch, with the suggestion that here was ready made company for me in my daily lunch break. The man had an Italian name and, having regard to the position in Europe in the late spring of 1940, I was surprised to find that he was actually an Italian national. However, both Macdonald and the man himself, whose name I have now forgotten, were vehement in their declarations of his detestation for Fascism as a whole and for Mussolini in particular. After all, I already knew how almost pro-British some even of the Germans in China were at that time; but I was nevertheless representative in Japan of a large British shipping agency in time of actual war and it behoved me to be cautious. After I left

Kobe it was to be about three years before I heard that Italian name again, and in rather surprising circumstances.

I found the Japanese office staff efficient and co-operative, though I bore in mind that one of them had laid information against Macdonald, and was even more guarded in what I said before him than in my conversations with the others. I felt that he had only done what he considered to be his duty, and for all I knew not only he but all of them were either paid agents or at least under the thumb of the dread Gendarmerie or Kempeitai—which, I suppose, could be roughly equated with the German Gestapo.

When I wanted to go shopping the little female secretary was very helpful with advice as to where I should shop. But once when she was leaving for the day and explained that the shop I wanted was on her route, she was polite but emphatic in her refusal to be seen in my company in public.

Before Macdonald left I was able to inquire about the fate of Griffiths. Griff, as everybody called him, had apparently been released, so I was able to call upon him at his place of business. I was not sure how good it would be for me to be seen in Griff's company, but once I had met him I found him excellent value and a superb guide and friend throughout my stay of several weeks.

I soon heard the story of how he had come to be arrested. In the late nineteenth or early twentieth century a book on Japan had been published called *Things Japanese*. Its author had been a man named Dyer Ball whose son was a puisne judge, junior to my father in Hongkong in the early twenties. Such slight knowledge as I have of this book was gleaned from my conversations with Griff. It seems that Dyer Ball's work had been an affectionate if penetrating study of the Japanese people and their customs and that he had been held in good esteem in Japan. But Griff was no less a student of 'things Japanese' than had been Dyer Ball, and he had watched the trends of the first forty years of this century with dismay. With less justification, but with equal enthusiasm to that of leaders of some other races, they had looked upon themselves as worthy to be masters of the world. It was their destiny.

Samuel Butler in *Erewhon* and *Erewhon Revisited* suggests how easily a fantastic cult can be imposed upon simple and credulous people. To the clique of power-hungry Japanese leaders their course was obvious.

The Christian Church may canonize saints: the Japanese aristocracy created a deity. They, as their Emperor's sole intimates, automatically acquired a status of almost of demi-gods. Nobody but they might approach or minister to the needs of the sacred being. To avoid becoming a puppet in their hands was almost impossible, however great the will and character of the Emperor.

To Griff all this was anathema. He deeply loved the true Japanese people as a whole. He delighted in their customs, even if some of them had developed in comparatively recent years to create an impression upon the foreign visitor. But he had the knowledge necessary to debunk all that was false and he made up his mind to do so.

As a publisher, it was natural that he should produce a new and up-to-date edition of *Things Japanese*. As a man of some literary accomplishment, it was natural that he should wish to bring the old book up to date.

Sewage disposal, he told me, was one subject upon which he touched in telling of the amenities of the Imperial Palace. Need one say more? To the ruling Japanese clique the association of such matters with their Divine God-Emperor was hideous sacrilege and Griff was as well aware of this as one might expect. But he was as determined as he was courageous.

When his new edition of *Things Japanese* was ready for publication, he waited until a time of some great religious or national festival. Japanese have not, in my experience, proved to be the hardened drinkers that some Chinese can be—especially such of the latter as are moderate but long-standing smokers of opium.

When Griff's book was submitted to the appropriate government ministry for approval prior to publication, it 'happened' to arrive at a time of universal jollification. Everyone knew *Things Japanese* and everyone knew Griff. If the latter had decided to publish a new and up-to-date edition of the former, they were delighted. A cursory glance was all that it got at the ministry. And then it was let loose upon the world and all the hounds of hell were swiftly let loose upon Griff.

But, although he was held for some time before trial and no foreigner was allowed near him, his little Japanese amah was permitted to visit him regularly, and this devoted little woman brought him clean clothes every day. He was thus able to avoid more than comparatively minor discomforts from verminous infestation. When I met him his beard, which he had been forced by lack of a razor to grow in prison, was entirely free of uninvited guests. When he had after some weeks in prison been finally called to his arraignment, he was brought into a large chamber with a wide semicircle of chairs facing him as he came in. Their uniforms left him in no doubt as to who and what his judges were. They were the dreaded Gendarmerie, the Kempeitai, and the presiding officer immediately accused him of being an enemy of the Japanese people and of spreading propaganda for the deliberate purpose of bringing their Emperor into ridicule. Griff hesitated not a moment. 'On the contrary, Honourable President,' he said, 'I am a devoted and affectionate admirer of all that is best, all that is true in Japanese culture. May I crave your indulgence in asking this honourable court how many of its members are qualified to perform the time-honoured ritual of the tea ceremony at the Festival of the Cherry Dances at Kyoto?' His judges looked somewhat nonplussed, and it was soon apparent that none of them was so qualified. 'Well, Honourable Gentlemen,' he went on, gaining power and confidence as he saw that his hunch was right; 'well, Gentlemen, as soon as you see fit to release me, I shall be happy and proud to undertake the complete instruction of any of you who may wish for such a diploma. I am not only qualified to perform this ancient and charming ritual—I am a fully certificated instructor in it.' Their embarrassment was utter and total. The only way in which they could answer him was by letting him go. So they did. Griff chuckled heartily as he told me the story, but this shy and unassuming little man certainly had guts to challenge such a court in such a daring way. He understood the Japanese.

I was privileged to see something of the night life of Kobe with Griff, and it was his simple pleasure to present himself at some of the famous Geisha houses which he had known well, and pretend, with his beard as disguise, to be a stranger. It was a delightful experience for me—the Geishas recognizing Griff in the first instant and pretending not to; Griff sure enough in his own mind that he was recognized, but playing at pretending that he thought himself undetected. It may perhaps be as well here to say something of Geishas. The Chinese too have their Sing Song girls, who are often of as good social standing as any professional entertainers in England. But the Sing Song girls never, to me, had quite the cachet, quite the poise or skill of the high-class Geisha. In no sense of the word were these women prostitues. I presume that, amongst prostitutes in England, may be found shop or factory girls, theatrical performers and all sorts. So likewise presumably there were thorough-going prostitutes amongst the lower calibres of Geishas. I remember Griff telling me of an occasion when some visitors from the States had been given an introduction to him. They were wealthy people and the party included some young girls of the débutante type. When Griff started to take them round the night life of the town there was some surreptitious whispering amongst the young girls. In the end it came out. They had heard from afar of the Japanese girl dancers who would gradually divest themselves as they danced until they were entirely naked. This seemed far more daring than any of the strip-tease acts of single performers which they had witnessed back home. Griff claimed to be *persona grata* at the best Geisha joints. All right. Let him do his stuff. Japanese think nothing of nudity, and Griff was sure that his little Geisha friends would be only too glad—just to oblige him. But it was not part of their normal entertainment duty, and he did not see why they should put themselves out for the sake of these prurient strangers. The Geishas were soon aware that there was disagreement, and when they learned what it was about were only too anxious to help Griff out of his difficulty. But he would have none of it.

'You know,' he said to the American girls, 'I find this rather funny. I was talking recently to a Japanese sailor on the water-front, and he told me that he was hoping to transfer to a ship on the Atlantic run. When I asked him why, he explained that he wanted to go to New York. "That's where they have the naked women in the night clubs," he explained.'

On the subject of Japanese ideas on nudity I may mention that my predecessor, Macdonald, had given me warning not to be too easily surprised or embarrassed. Apparently some Japanese business man of high standing with whom he had an out of business hours appointment had suggested their meeting at a well-known Japanese bath house. They duly met in the foyer and, after leaving their clothes in a dressing-room, ambled down together to the heated pool. Mac jumped in when invited, but was a little disconcerted to discover that the hot bath-cum-bathing pool was for both sexes. There was worse to come. 'Allow me to introduce you,' said his host, turning Mac's attention to two ladies who were 'altogether' ladies, one distinctly older than the other. 'My wife—my daughter,' said his host, and they all shook formal hands.

It makes me wonder sometimes whether some of our sex problems are not largely of our own making. But I believe that, like most other people, the Japanese do not care to be laughed at for their national behaviour patterns, and that they too have now acquired an almost Western self-consciousness in such matters. It might be said perhaps that they have now eaten of the apple of Western civilization and feel as Adam and Eve did.

So much then for Japan in cherry blossom time in 1940. There was very little of quality in the shops. Everything capable of being sold abroad was being exported, but her leaders were watching France crumble in the west and felt that her day was approaching.

I returned to Hongkong just as sick at heart as many in England must have been at that time. But I think that in some ways we may have felt even worse in Hongkong than anybody could have done in England. All that we held dear, all that our race stood for, was in peril. And here were we, remote and helpless to come to our country's aid. The orders of the General Officer Commanding in Hongkong were that no able-bodied Briton was to leave the colony without his permission. Britain was unlikely to send us any troops—she was more likely to take any that we had—so we must prepare to do our share by helping to defend the colony in case of need. We had long been semi-mobilized against the potential threat of Japanese troops across the border. We must intensify our training, and at the same time maintain the vital flow of Britain's Far East trade. It had early been intimated to the younger men, who clamoured to be allowed to go home to join up, that their duty lay in Hongkong. But it was not long before the military authorities let it be known that any such young men as could be spared from their civilian occupations were welcome to join the army in Hongkong itself. Any such entrants would be trained by the Army in Hongkong, and might then be posted anywhere that they were needed in the eastern theatre of war. Commercial and professional set-ups in Hongkong were not so staffed as to have any appreciable surplus, but a few young men were so released and were soon to be seen disguised as professional soldiers.

It was not long before it became evident that their faces were to be more often seen in places of relaxation and amusement than before. Discussion elicited that, whilst they were genuinely undergoing more military training than the rest of us, their hours were less arduous than those of civilian occupations, and the civilians were also giving much of their free time to soldiering or sailoring. We all felt desperately the need to be doing something useful at such a time, so the majority of those who were young enough to be acceptable to the military authorities elected to remain mobilized civilians rather than become just soldiers. All this gave us, it is true, some sense of purpose; but the benign peacefulness of our surroundings gave all our efforts a tinge of unreality. It could not, we felt, be right that our social life, our bathing, golf, tennis and race meetings, should go on. Fate must, I felt, have something fiendish in store for us—and it had.

At the end of 1940 or early in 1941, one of Jardine's young men in Hongkong, who had been desperately trying every gambit he could think of, invoked the aid of his uncle who happened to be Chief of the Imperial Staff. In the end it was agreed that a less able-bodied man in Shanghai would be brought down to take his place and he would be allowed to join up.

So Ian Bruce [1] got himself home and into the war and Ben Stafford, who though young had partial deafness and very bad eyesight, took his place in Hongkong. But the ways of fate are mysterious, and Ian, after campaigning in Europe, returned unscathed to become a junior director after the war. Poor Ben died on the beaches in the defence of Hongkong in December 1941.

In October 1940 it was decided that Jardine's insurance manager in Shanghai, who was due for leave and who was a married man with three small daughters, must be given a chance to take his family away to Australia. So the permission of the G.O.C. Hongkong was obtained for me to be sent to relieve him, and up I went in November in a blacked-out C.P.R. liner, which was my last sea trip until five years later. As an unmarried man in those days I was the obvious choice for what looked like being a danger spot. That I should turn out to be safer there than in Hongkong was not, I think, envisaged.

[1] Died, alas, in retirement in England in 1966.

Part Five

CHAPTER TWELVE
THE CLOUDS GATHER

I ARRIVED back in Shanghai in late October or early November 1940 and stayed for a short time with my old friend Robbie, who was by this time married, with a family. Ken Mason, whom I had come to relieve, soon left with his wife and three little girls for Australia and I then took over his house and servants and a little dachshund bitch called Sally.

I soon found the house too large for me alone and managed to acquire a messmate, one Jack Mothersill, who was the manager of Jardine's Cotton Mills Company in Shanghai. 'Mothers' was a charming and considerate fellow in every way but one. Earlier life in Calcutta had got him into the way of dining rather late, and when he had fed he apparently found it impossible to sleep in his bed before he had had at least two hours' sleep in an armchair downstairs.

In itself this was not serious, but he could not sleep, even in the armchair, without an accompaniment of his large radiogram playing full blast at about a foot away from his ear. It was still possible at that time to venture into the countryside on horseback, so I made a practice of rising at six o'clock for a ride before breakfast. Consequently I found Mothers's habits rather irksome when I wanted to get to sleep early.

It was not many months before I was able to contact Ken Mason in Australia by post and obtain his consent to termination of the tenancy and, as the shape of things to come was growing more apparent, to arrange for some of his furniture and effects to be shipped down to him. Meanwhile much of the surface of Shanghai's foreign community remained undisturbed, but there were strange undercurrents. Ships of the British and Italian navies continued to use the port, and I particularly remember sitting in a cinema with sailors of one nation's navy in the row in front of me and of the other behind me.

Jardine's great office building on the Bund now housed the British Embassy on its top floor, and some of us were by turns on guard duty there in pairs one night a week. Jardine's had long been China agents for the Glen Line, a subsidiary of Alfred Holt's Blue Funnel, and the Glen Line had for some years owned the great office building which stood next door, with only the rather narrow Peking Road joining the Bund in between. But the uncertain situation had reduced the building's investment value to the Glen Line, and they had sold it to Japanese interests not long before. What more natural than that the new owners should have offered their top floor to the German Embassy? When I was on night guard in the British Embassy I often used to look across the narrow Peking Road to where my German opposite number, possibly a man who had been a personal friend two years before, was doing likewise. Another duty involved a rather limited type of watch keeping on British merchant ships at night. I say 'limited' because we could do little more on a strange ship at night than 'be about', but our presence seemed to help to take some of the strain off the ships' officers, who found life at sea sufficiently wearing in war time, without having the further anxiety of continuous watches in a port which was full of enemy nationals. It was little enough that we were thus able to do in the way of personal service to our country in war time, and we were glad of the chance. Beyond the Garden Bridge, which spanned the Soochow Creek at the downriver end of the Bund, the Japanese by this time largely held sway and, though Jardine's had British staff at cotton mills, wharves and a brewery distributed around the districts of Yangtszepoo and Hongkew, the rest of us did not go that way unless we had to. At one time there was a cholera scare and free mass inoculation was carried out by the Shanghai Municipal Council. The Japanese posted sentries on the Garden Bridge and allowed no one to cross into the districts beyond it without an up-to-date certificate of inoculation. It was at this time that a simple coolie decided to make a good thing out of hawking certificates to people who wanted to cross. He got plenty of certificates, but as each required another inoculation every time he came round, he did not survive to enjoy what he had earned. Such a man was quite incapable of appreciating what was being done to him when the needle penetrated his skin. If he could have spoken pidgin English, he would have described it as 'B'long good joss, b'long foreignman joss'—a sort of magic rite.

Although the job I was now doing was in a sense junior to the post I had held in Hongkong, I was in effect manager of my department for north China as well as for Shanghai, and the job carried a car and chauffeur with it. Lee Ah Kong, the chauffeur, had served the department for many years and had started when the mode of transport had been a pony trap. When mechanical horse power had succeeded horse flesh he had been taught how to drive and had become very competent. But George, as he was always called, had no idea what went on under the bonnet or in any other part of the mechanism, and if it failed to do what it should he would jump out with his peaked cap on one side and a knowing look on his piratical-looking features. In one hand was probably a spanner, but the other would certainly be clutching a heavy hammer with which he would produce very satisfying ringing notes from various parts of the metal work. Of course whatever really needed to be done had to await the attention of somebody who knew something about it, but meanwhile face was saved, honour was satisfied. Not long before the time of which I am now writing George had displayed inability to read instructions carefully and clearly written for him in Chinese characters. It had been explained to him that his eyes required testing, and back he came the proud possessor of a pair of glasses, 'all same Master', who was at that time Ken Mason. But Mason's glasses were for general wear, so of course nothing would separate George from his new glasses for one moment. After several near misses of pedestrians and other vehicles in Shanghai's always hectic traffic, Mason intervened firmly and obtained a ruling from the optician. George's glasses were for reading only, and everything that was more than a few feet away had been one large blur to George.

Poor George. When the Japanese seized our cars after Pearl Harbor, and also took control of the firm's bank accounts, there was no way to persuade them to continue to pay him. So he took to smuggling various goods such as rice and eggs in from the countryside, which was an occupation more suited to his brigand-like cast of features, if not to his inwardly kindly disposition. George's heart was of gold and we were all pleased that he was managing to make a living, but alas, later on, in about 1943 or 1944, poor George was caught by the Japanese and shot, as I learnt when the war ended.

But I was very glad of George in the early months of 1941. There was a curious atmosphere of unreality in Shanghai at that time. In the streets I often used to run into Germans whom I had known in earlier days, and although everything seemed then to be going their country's way, they were always friendliness itself in private and as courteous as they dared to be in public. They themselves were not unwatched by rabid Nazis amongst their younger nationals.

That year's annual meeting of ratepayers was held at the grandstand of the Shanghai Race Club, and despite the fact that Japan was largely in control of the China around us, the British still held the majority vote in the International Settlement. As mentioned earlier, Jardine's managing director there, W. J. ('Tony') Keswick, who was also chairman of the Shanghai Municipal Council, was shot at but not seriously wounded by a fanatical little Japanese, at point-blank range. Meanwhile Britain had survived her period of utter isolation in 1940 and had not been invaded, and now Hitler had decided to follow Napoleon's classic example and fling his armies away upon the great wastes of Russia. The tide had temporarily swung against us again in North Africa, but Egypt and the Suez Canal were still held. Despair of our country's survival had now been succeeded, even in the more defeatist amongst us, by a growing certainty that we could still win, and that we therefore would win the ghastly war and that any sacrifices which could be made would not be in vain. The younger men in Shanghai had no British general to stop them leaving, and staffs were rapidly becoming more and more depleted. Agencies for import of mechanical and electrical products from Britain had not enough work to do, but the export of Chinese goods and raw materials was enormous. One reason was the continued depreciation of the Shanghai dollar. Worth about two shillings so few years before, it was now well on the way to the threepence halfpenny-odd value it had reached by the time of Pearl Harbor. The number of, say, eggs that such a dollar would now buy had not greatly diminished, so that part of our cost of living reached an all-time low. Anything imported, however, if available at all, reached an all-time high, so that the art of existence demanded novel skills. Pheasant, for some reason, never appealed as much as chicken to the Chinese, and I found that it became one of the cheapest meats to buy. Beer was brewed locally, and in fact 'Ewo' beer from Jardine's brewery was more readily available in India and the Middle East than any products of breweries at home. That whisky and other spirits were still available in Shanghai a year after Pearl Harbor speaks well for the foresight of importers, but I don't know how they liked the money they were paid in. Insurance companies had to point out to their foreign constituents that to take out a twelve months' policy in Chinese dollars to cover plant or materials which emanated from elsewhere was a waste of time. So they issued policies in English pounds or U.S. dollars, on condition that the premium was paid to them in the like currency in London or New York. This meant a book entry in the local branch of the British or American bank and a corresponding credit in the head office of the bank concerned. But the insurance companies continued to do a lot of business in local dollars, either because the goods or properties concerned were purely local or, in some instances, because the owners thereof had no means of paying premiums in any other currency. Such local currency income was useful for payment of salaries and other purely local expenses.

Meanwhile I had at last got out of the unwieldy house and into new quarters and found myself sharing a third- or fourth-floor flat with two of Jardine's tea specialists. One, the head of the department, was Frank Norton, who is nowadays a tea merchant in his own right in London. The other was poor Ben Stafford, who was to become the partly deaf and weak-sighted substitute for Ian Bruce in Hongkong and to meet death on the beaches there before the year was out.

A large flat immediately below ours was occupied by the head of a big German merchant and shipping firm, Melchers & Company, and the manner of my introduction to him and his wife was very informal. A girl whom I knew well at the British Embassy made me a present of a delightful black kitten whom I called Little Black Sambo in memory of a tale of nursery days. But his donor's name was Janet Momber, so Frank Norton insisted upon calling him Mombo. Mombo used to leap and cavort upon the steel railing of our large sunny veranda, and one day he slipped. In an agony of mind I rushed and looked over, not wanting to, but feeling compelled to do it. As I did so a tremendous hubbub arose in the flat below and I realized that the incredible Mombo had somehow managed to clutch *en passant* and get a grip of the rail of the veranda below ours. But the German and his wife were dog lovers and had three. By the time the couple got to their veranda Mombo was in a corner of it, spitting defiance at three large dogs. More of Mombo later, but when it came to my internment it was Mombo's personality which so appealed to a Swiss acquaintance that he was prepared to give a home to Sally in order to secure Mombo.

Janet Momber, as a British Embassy employee, was repatriated when war broke out and it was with great pleasure that I made her a present of my nearly new portable typewriter, which she accepted without embarrassment, because we both knew that if she didn't have it the Japs would, as they had my Zeiss camera and other such possessions.

But in the meanwhile Shanghai was so accustomed to wars of one kind or another that the global war seemed not to be changing local conditions a great deal. Petrol was in short supply, but I had seen and travelled, in Japan, in cars propelled by gas from charcoal stoves in the boot. Charcoal was not too plentiful in the Shanghai area, so many of us bought bicycles, whilst British-made machines were still available—just in case. How glad we were, a little later, that we had done so. When Ben Stafford left us his place was taken in our flat by Hugh Flint, another Jardine's man, who was to become a director after the war. One of my principal memories of Hugh at that particular juncture arises from the fact that Montgomery was beginning to enter the war news in a big way and that he had been brigade major to Hugh when he was subaltern in Northern Ireland just after World War I. Our flat was very pleasantly situated near Jessfield Park at the western extremity of the more densely built up residential area and, though Shanghai's winters can be just as cold as Essex or east Kent, our veranda faced the morning sun and we often took breakfast upon it that winter.

One of my assistants in the office, Philip Snaith, who, though not particularly robust, was still in his twenties, and another very young youngster, Ronald Burn, were by now clamouring to be allowed to go home and join up, and although they were not overworked, it was quite obvious that I should be if I had to do without them. An elderly representative of a home manufacturer heard of my predicament. His line of goods could no longer be spared from Britain for export and he had a young Russian girl who was his secretary and factotum whom he valued highly but could not afford to keep. So Musa Medvedeff joined us, and in a week she had mastered the job of my trained insurance assistant, Philip Snaith, and was also helping in secretarial and other duties. I already had a secretary, Dorita Breakspeare, who was as nice as she was brainy, but she was very young indeed and lacked experience.

A few weeks later Musa shyly and diffidently approached me. Could she have an extra half-hour for lunch a few days hence? In granting her request, I inquired whether she had a lot of shopping to do and whether the extra half-hour would be enough. 'Oh, thank you,' she said, 'but I don't need any more extra time—really I don't. I am just getting married.' The bridegroom was a formidable-looking young Russian in the Shanghai Municipal Police, and one glimpse of him was adequate to deter any young men who might have sought to 'date' the so pretty new addition to our staff.

At about this time also Japanese control of the lower and middle

Yangtsze basin was becoming such that all British concerns had been gradually closing down and their ships ceasing to ply.

Even in Shanghai the sole representative of British naval power was now the tiny upper river gunboat *Peterel* with a well-known pilot, Captain Polkinghorn, in command.

Several of our river steamers managed to get through to Singapore where their shallow draft made them useful for work in coastal waters within the shelter of outlying islands. One of them, the S.S. *Li Wo*, was to win fame in a gallant action against a Japanese convoy. Her skipper, Captain Wilkinson, realized that his ship had no chance of escape, so decided to do as much damage as he could before she was sunk. He was awarded a posthumous V.C.

At Ichang, at the mouth of the Gorges, the last Britons were Jardine's Leo Frost and his wife Marjorie, who had insisted upon joining him despite very real danger from the hostile Japanese. Before he left Leo was Ichang representative of every British firm, bank, oil company and shipping line in the Far East. Japanese treatment of him appears to have fluctuated between watching him so closely that he was virtually under house arrest; organizing groups of Chinese thugs to launch attacks at night against the Jardine property in which he and his wife lived; trumping up reasons for expelling him; refusing to let him go when he wanted to . . .

I saw Leo on his way through Shanghai, but did not meet him again until the end of 1945 in Hongkong. He was an ex-R.A.F. man and made his way to Australia and did war service there. On his way south he was in Manila when war broke out, and his ship narrowly escaped being sunk in the bombing of the harbour there.

As a youngster Leo had been an outstanding amateur rider on the flat, and had been more than once champion jockey of the year in Hongkong, but in long years as a bachelor he had become a mobile reserve, as I had been, and opportunities for keeping up his riding had been denied him. Some of his experiences had been amusing—it was he whose number one Chinese, in outport, had produced a large magnet for the testing of a tea consignment—some had been exciting, but I did not hear of the majority of them until we met in Hongkong after the war. He had quite a lively time in war service, as he took part in the Australian counter offensive against Japanese-held Pacific Islands between Australia and the Philippines.

Meanwhile it was impossible in Shanghai to doubt the hostility between Japan and the U.S.A. An American newscaster on the local radio made frequent references to the Japanese 'New Order in East Asia', but seemed unable to pronounce the phrase correctly. As the public heard it, it was 'The New Odour in East Asia'. I believe that he left Shanghai at the end of November. He was a very lucky man. Another man lucky enough to get out in time was our old friend Dupree from Hankow, who could not have failed to infuriate the Japanese.

And then it happened.

CHAPTER THIRTEEN

WAR

THE official date of the outbreak of the Pacific war is 8th December 1941, and when I discovered that this had been a Monday I thought that my memory had failed me. But the official date represents the day when the United States declared war upon Japan as a result of the attack on Pearl Harbor on Sunday, 7th December. The Japanese were holding to the assumption of their fellow Axis powers that the Western democracies were too effete to be prepared for war in a week-end—at the expense of their golf and other recreations. How different things would have been if the Pearl Harbor gambit had been a costly failure. I remember hearing the news on the wireless that night, and hastening to get in touch with our then Taipan in Shanghai, Eric Pollock, who had taken command when Tony Keswick went home to England after being shot. Apart from hearing the news, we also heard sounds of gunfire some miles away, but the Japanese were always conducting operations against guerrillas on the outskirts and we thought little of it.

Anyhow, there was nothing we could do that night except try to get a good sleep and be as ready as we could for what the morrow might bring.

When we came down in the morning to our offices on the Bund, it was to the end of it opposite to the Shanghai Club which had the Senior Naval Officer's Buoy lying in mid river about 150 yards away from its doors.

About a mile downriver, at a wharf in the Yangtszepoo district, lay an antiquated Japanese heavy cruiser, the *Idzumo*, which, if stories were true, had been captured from the Russians in the war of 1904–5. I do not know at what time the Japanese got the news of their success at Pearl Harbor, but it was quite late at night when the *Idzumo* suddenly called upon H.M.S. *Peterel* at the S.N.O.'s Buoy to surrender. There was also a comparatively large American gunboat in harbour, fully equipped and manned, which received a like summons and, I understand, surrendered immediately. But Captain Polkinghorn with his scratch crew and his main armament of two tiny six-pounders thought otherwise and the little *Peterel* promptly opened fire upon the aged and formidable *Idzumo* to do whatever damage she could before being sunk. It was only a matter of minutes before *Peterel* went down, but there was little room for doubt about the Japanese view of the affair. Polkinghorn was treated with the honour and respect his courage had earned him while little *Peterel* lay in her last sleep below the S.N.O.'s Buoy.

Some dwellers in the residential quarters of the Shanghai Club had been awakened by the gunfire so close at hand and had had what were probably the closest ringside seats ever held by spectators of any naval engagement in history.

There had long been a British Residents' Association in Shanghai and, in the troublous times which the city had gone through for many years, it had become geared to a very fair efficiency. One of the first things we learned when we reached our offices that morning was that all our consular and diplomatic officialdom had been rounded up and was to be held incommunicado. What they could have done for us if they had remained free I do not know but, as it was, the B.R.A. took over. Japan had a sort of master plan, I believe, for taking over the golden goose that was Shanghai, without impeding her continued production of golden eggs. But my experience of the petty officials to whom fell the actual carrying out of any such plans was that they were insufficiently trained or experienced and were pathetically incompetent: officials of such type tend to seek to hide their own deficiencies by arrogance and brutality. But with the B.R.A. themselves undertaking to organize and control their own nationals, the higher Japanese authorities were relieved of a considerable burden, and we were all spared much unpleasantness from their underlings. Naturally we all had to register our names and particulars and were instructed to surrender to the Japanese any personal possession of the type of binoculars, cameras and the like, as well as our cars. Sports articles, such as golf clubs, later found a ready under-the-counter sale in almost any conditions. Since all our bank accounts were immediately halved and our drawings on the shrunken remains controlled, we were glad enough to raise cash in any way we could. Most of the public services were under British management, although the Power Company was American owned, having been bought from the Shanghai Municipal Council for, if I remember correctly, U.S.$81,000,000 not many years before. Most of us had expected immediate detention of some kind, at the very least, but it was soon apparent that the Japanese had no such ideas. They wanted to take over this entire centre of industry and commerce in good working order and they expected co-operation from us. Our first reaction was instinctive: NO and NO and NO. But we had no means of knowing what our own government desired of us and, when we began to talk things over, even the hotter heads began to cool down. America was now fairly and squarely in the war and, not only did we feel it unlikely that she would take long to acquire the initiative and drive Japan back on her haunches, we felt also that any doubts among the faint-hearted as to the outcome of the war in Europe and Africa and Russia were now resolved. Many millions of friendly Chinese, who were our allies, depended upon the continuance of Shanghai as a living city. The great Western-owned factories, power plants, breweries and the like must be salved against the day when they would be restored to their owners and essential public services must continue. Incidentally one of the first places of manufacture to be liberated by the allied navies in 1945 was Jardine's Ewo Brewery—a very potent source of pleasure to our sailors.

As regards my own line, insurance, the major part of my very substantial branch balances in the local British banks was, as explained earlier, mere book entries of credits in London and New York. The Japanese were welcome to what they might make of that lot, but meanwhile, if they wished to go through the motions of taking over our business, they would authorize continued payment of salaries to my faithful trained staff and, as far as I personally was concerned, I might get a chance to get my invaluable office records into safe keeping.

There were among us a few of the older residents who interpreted all this as meaning that it was another of the phoney wars such as one had become used to in China. Some felt that before long, and in some mysterious oriental fashion, there would be business as usual and who, they inquired, was going to stop them? But although electricity, gas, telephones and waterworks facilities were soon available again, gaps started to appear in our ranks as the Gendarmerie swooped and took people in for questioning. Naturally a lot of questioning of a different kind followed amongst ourselves. What sort of people were they seizing, and why? As the victims, when they returned, were loath to talk, we more fortunate ones remained nervous and mystified. Some, it seems, had been punished for normal patriotic activity on behalf of their respective nations before war broke out. This seemed unfair enough, but when presidents or committee members of clubs or of social and philanthropic societies such as England's St George's, Scotland's St Andrew's, Wales's St David's, etc. were arrested it was at first incomprehensible. It seems that to the Japanese mind any of these organizations were suspect, on the lines of Chinese secret societies or the Mafia. But when the victims were taken in, their quarters were intensively searched and various people, innocent even of the foregoing activities, became involved. A memo on a scrap of paper in the suspect's home; perhaps a telephone number, perhaps a name. All of these were ruthlessly followed up and the persons they led to hauled in as well. The favoured time for such raids was between midnight and 4 a.m., and our sleep tended to be nervous and fitful. How the captives were handled depended partly on luck and partly on psychology. If some other member of the household tried to speak to the prisoner, violence might ensue and the unfortunate victim might go unprovided with the barest necessities of proper clothing on a bitter winter's night. But sometimes skilful intervention by a European friend or by a shrewd boy would lead to the senior visitor being regaled with hot coffee, a cigarette, some beer. Within five minutes the whole party might be sitting down peacefully together.

Catering for ourselves on our tiny budgets was difficult, as we were anxious to continue paying our faithful domestic employees as long as possible. Frank Norton, in our *ménage*, had some expertise in food storage, and we were able to store quite large stocks of flour, for example, in huge tins without their becoming too prolific breeding grounds for weevils and maggots. Some households, I believe, invested in large quantities of dog biscuits, which had obvious food value, but I do not remember that we did so.

Our bicycles were a tremendous boon. Apart from taking us the four-odd miles to our offices and back again, they were invaluable for the limited excursions permitted to us. Our Taipan's country house was another five miles farther out, which involved passing through the Japanese control barriers on the outskirts, but if we showed our passports and explained that we wished to visit a friend there was usually no difficulty. One of the marks of any old resident in Hongkong or China is the 'Hongkong basket' made of a sort of rattan or wicker, and in shape something like a small suitcase. With these on our bicycles' carriers, we would sally forth and the pickets never opened them on our return. In this way, in co-operation with friends, we maintained a constant supply of the fresh eggs which were so plentiful in the surrounding countryside and so lacking in the city.

Had we known what was to happen to poor ex-chauffeur George before long we might have been less enterprising.

The principal concern of the Japanese in Shanghai at this time was with the British, Americans and Dutch, but there were many holders of such passports who were, as far as we were concerned, of dubious loyalties: nationalistic Indians; a variety of Eurasians who sometimes had part Japanese origins; Irish, who might be holders of both British and Irish Free State passports. In the latter category were two couples I knew who were respectively in Hongkong and Manila. Harry and Thea Woulfe-Flanagan, of the Chinese Customs service, I had long known and, when 'Flan' had returned to Hankow from leave with a bride, Thea became known as the girl who cried 'Woulfe' once too often. By the waving of passports and the production of a first-rate line of Irish blarney they evaded internment in Hongkong and did dangerous but effective work in the background for the alleviation of the lot of their British friends in camp.

The young couple in Manila, Paddy and Eileen Shannon, were not so fortunate. Sooner or later the Japanese caught up with them and they disappeared from human ken. As far as I know they were never heard of again. I did not know them well but had met them earlier in Hongkong where Paddy Shannon was employed by the Hongkong and Shanghai Banking Corporation.

Another case was Edmund Francis Ratti who, alas, has lately died in England after a long illness. Ratti, who first came to the Far East as a Merchant Marine officer in a Jardine's ship, was Italian by birth, and in view of his obvious business qualities was soon given a shore job, and became in course of time the displaced Ichang agent for the firm whose paragon of a boy had milked our electric circuit to run himself a lucrative lodging-house in Hankow in 1927. He had long intended to take British nationality, but when war in Europe had broken out between Italy and the Allies all the formalities had not been completed. He was regarded by the British Embassy as a *de facto* British subject, but still held Italian papers. Some silly people did not fully appreciate the difficulties and dangers he encountered in playing his double role. I am sure that many friendly Germans were aware of the position but nobody gave him away.

I believe that British nationals in Shanghai at that time numbered in all some ten thousand, but people such as I have named comprised only one of the strange elements that composed them. Hongkong-born Portuguese Eurasians, for example, might have British passports, but the 'Asian' part of 'Eur-asian' might denote, as may be imagined, almost any Asian racial background, including Japanese. Again, some white Britons had married people of local stock and, however loyal to their spouses the parti-coloured locals might be, there were sometimes means of putting pressure on their families in the background.

The Japanese made great play of being the friends of all Asian people and many, who either accepted their promises at face value or had personal circumstances which left them no alternative, were relatively free of restraint and, when the time came for the rest of us to be locked up, they could claim their freedom.

For many their livelihood had gone and the privations of camp life were likely to be less than those outside, so they were interned with the rest of us.

So the B.R.A. had a Herculean task to perform in administering relief and it made it no easier for them that many of the personnel seconded to them by the big firms were inevitably of the calibre that they could most easily spare. Again, people's ideas of what represented justifiable grounds for relief varied widely. Some who tried to throw their peace-time weight about discovered that the new conditions had abolished that weight; almost as if they were on the moon, they had become weightless. They didn't like it. Nor, if they had been accustomed to their two or three bottles of whisky or gin per week, could they understand the attitude of the B.R.A. in rating the needs of those who lacked clothing, food or living accommodation higher than their own desire to maintain their own luxurious standards of life. But there were not many of these, and there were sufficient men of high standing and influence in the top hierarchies of the B.R.A. to ensure that their blustering threats did not intimidate the underlings at the counters.

The work of the Swiss, who were acting as a sort of protecting power to us, as well as handling the immensely increased International Red Cross responsibilities, led them to call upon a number of Swiss business men whose normal employment had ceased. Amongst these naturally were Jardine's chief silk expert, René Plattner, and some younger men who had been employed in Jardine's engineering interests.

Although our consular and embassy officials were under restraint, their clerical staff were not, and Janet Momber was a regular visitor to see her Mombo as well as us. Another not infrequent visitor was one

Elsa Bergquist of the Swedish Embassy staff, who was quite charming enough to be welcome in her own right, apart from her value as a contact with a neutral embassy.

It was at about this time that I began to feel some eye strain. The glasses prescribed for me nearly four years earlier in Hongkong were intended for all day use and, to avoid the need for superimposition of dark glasses out of doors in summer, were of very slightly tinted glass. I didn't care to wear glasses when riding my bicycle through the traffic, and as spring progressed I found myself suffering from the glare, and developing sore eyes. There were no reputable foreign opticians still functioning, and we were discussing my quandary one day when Elsa was present.

'Ah,' she said, 'I always used to have bad eyesight and my eyes were inordinately sensitive to strong light; but I went through a course of treatment and exercises with a Swedish girl I know—and look at this.'

She whipped out of her bag some snapshots of a winter sports party of which she had been a member in the mountains of Japan. All but Elsa were wearing dark glasses, and there she stood amid the brilliant snow with her big blue eyes wide open and sparkling in the sunlight.

Her girl friend had, it seemed, married a Shanghai Briton who was now, of course, unemployed and Elsa was sure that she would take me on for a modest sum in our rapidly disintegrating currency. Within a few weeks I had abandoned glasses altogether, and as summer came on I found myself riding around for long periods in the tropical sun with no discomfort to my eyes at all. Some of the exercises were muscular and involved swivelling the eyes from side to side and up and down, and required to be performed frequently for short periods of five to ten minutes.

I still retained my own chair at my own desk in my own office at that time, but facing me across the desk sat a little Japanese from the Mitsui Company who had been delegated to liquidate us. I am afraid that I took some pleasure in performing my little eye movements during business hours and in watching the startled reactions of my vis-à-vis. But it was quite important to keep him occupied and keep him guessing. Officially my entire staff were fully occupied in the preparation of sheets and sheets of typewritten statements for the liquidators, but I had early made it clear to them that the longer they took over the work, the longer they would remain in employment. They too had little doubt of the impermanence of the Japanese on their backs and mine. They fully appreciated the value of the duplication of all our most vital records for preservation in a safe place, and this work went on more expeditiously than their work for the liquidators. However, all good things must end, and the time came when the Japanese felt that our commodious office overlooking the river would more appropriately house some of their senior officials. So we began to move into a rear building which faced on to the next road back from the Bund and which had previously been the large office of the Jardine Engineering Corporation, a concern which had no scope in a Shanghai under Japanese rule. My clerical staff were at first embarrassed at the loss of face involved in carting great bundles of files and bound volumes of records. But I was determined that the Japanese should not be put to the bother of finding their own men for the work and took the lead myself. Face was thus satisfied by what they could describe to friends or onlookers as a mad prank of their manager's. Thus it was only too easy to lose some of the carriers *en route*, and if those who were burdened with our own records somehow found their way to a safe storage allotted to us by the Swiss Embassy not far away—well, the poor chaps must have lost their way.

Meanwhile Eric Pollock, as Taipan, had some ideas of his own. He pointed out that the delectable country residence so tastefully developed by his predecessor with charming grassy walks and vistas and tennis courts lay uncomfortably close to guerrilla territory. For the Japanese to inhabit it at that juncture would be certain to inflame the guerrillas to violence, and lives and property might both be endangered. His faithful managers were rapidly completing their conscientious work of liquidation. Let them give up their luxurious separate homes and move into the country mansion as caretakers and watchmen. If he might be permitted to keep there a minimum staff of domestics and gardeners, the whole place could be preserved in perfect condition for its ultimate handover to the honourable Mitsui Company. It would be well worth their paying for its upkeep!

It worked. For the last weeks of my employment I was cycling nine miles to office every morning in the full heat of the Shanghai summer. Hugh Flint was with Frank Norton and me there for a while, and when our need to go to the office ceased we did a lot of work in the gardens and also played a great deal of tennis. Mombo soon took to his new home and followed me about the grounds like a dog. It was a relief to be free of the office at last with the feeling, which I hope was justified, that I had done all I could for employers and employees and country.

I still hold in my files a document which generates a wry grin if I look at it. It is the official letter from the Mitsui Company regretfully terminating my employment and thanking me for my services. There were many of the community who cannot have been so fortunate as we were, but although the Japanese considered it permissible for Jardine employees and friends to visit us, there were limits to their forbearance. We might have made something of a recreational centre of the lovely grounds, but the Japanese might have judged us to be in effect organizing a club, and what was the difference between a club and a secret society in their view? It had only been the key staff in every enterprise that the Japanese had temporarily employed and the number of unemployed was substantial. Relief funds were available through the B.R.A. which were financed, officially, by the Swiss, although I think that sympathizers of other nationalities sometimes dared the displeasure of the Japanese by unobtrusive gifts or loans.

As far as Frank Norton, Hugh Flint and I were concerned, our tenure of the flat in West Park Mansions had been wound up in a monetarily satisfactory manner. Our friendly enemy in the flat below was seeking accommodation for a young married couple on his staff, and we finally negotiated with them the sale for cash of all Ken Mason's remaining furniture. Then we three signed a document agreeing to refund the proceeds to him in sterling after the war at the rate of exchange current at the time of sale. It meant little to him in sterling, but if we had not so sold it the Japanese would undoubtedly have seized it. I suppose that technically this was 'trading with the enemy', but we felt no qualms on that score, and were able to augment our funds very satisfactorily. Personally I felt that if there were any sterling or U.S. dollar notes to be found on the black market they would be a useful standby before the end, and I was lucky enough to be able to get hold of a U.S. $100 bill, of which more later.

In about July 1942 the first negotiated repatriation took place, and it was generally known that another large neutral liner would take another batch about two weeks later, which it did. There was much bitterness and heart-burning over all this, as it was early apparent that the two ships would be able to accommodate far more people than the consular and diplomatic staff and families who had first claim. To anybody who thought for a moment, it must have been apparent that Britain did not want to be cumbered by a lot of civilians who were out of touch with events at home and would be a source of bother, and an additional, if minute, burden upon food supplies. But many who were neither particularly fit nor particularly young were most indignant when they found that their names were not on the list.

If our authorities at home had managed to get word through about anybody whom they particularly wanted for the war effort, it was certain that they would not wish it to be generally known.

It is true that the British in Shanghai had been unfortunate and so had the Dutch. As 1941 progressed the U.S. authorities had made it clear that all non-essential Americans should return home, and many men who remained had at least sent their families to safety.

But Dutch families had nowhere to go, and Britons, already by then affected in their earnings by currency depreciation and exchange control, had only Australia, where they would be unable to support their dependants adequately by remittances and where, if they themselves went, they could not be sure of finding employment suited to their capacities.

I cannot remember exactly when Bunny Bolton, our Formosa agent, first joined us in the house at Hungjao, as that outlying district of managerial residences, golf-course and aerodrome is called. The Japanese were, to some extent, using Shanghai as a concentration point for enemy nationals from a number of outlying places. Bunny Bolton, long, lean and sun-tanned, always seemed to me the picture of the keen enemy agent of fiction. I sometimes feel that he probably longed to be doing something of the kind, and felt that if he had no such official position he would be helping to fuddle his country's enemies if he went round by himself, looking sinister.

After the early July repatriation and another about three weeks later, it gradually became clear that the Japanese were looking forward confidently to the performance being repeated until they were rid of all of us. Many were cheered by this and took it for granted that repatriation would proceed accordingly. But the Swiss knew nothing. All we could ever discover was that 'discussions are going on in Geneva' and 'discussions are continuing' and so forth. In the end it began to occur to some of us that all was not as it seemed. Japan, we gathered, had had many of their best technicians and military or naval espionage men working abroad, especially in America. They obviously expected the inept allied nations to be quite ready to accept two or three elderly business men and their wives and children and a like missionary assortment—say twenty 'bods' in all—in exchange for a like number of their keen young men whom they wanted returned to them. But our governments, with a great show of innocence, went on for months mislaying details and quibbling over trifles. Meanwhile the Japanese at least wished to preserve any potential repatriation candidates in good condition so, next to our being actually repatriated, this rigmarole was the best thing for us.

And then, in November, the Gendarmerie pounced again, this time on a larger scale, and a few hundred selected victims were spirited away to an old U.S. Marine Corps barrack in Haiphong Road. To the best of my recollection, Flint and Bolton were removed, but Norton and I remained; Flint as accountant and Bolton because he was from Formosa—or perhaps because his character acting had been successful. Only two other Jardine's men were taken: Robin Gordon, a director, and Jock McCaig, the shipping accountant.

The Gendarmerie's big game safari was over within a few hours, and thereafter silence.

We had all been given red armbands a few weeks earlier, marked with a large A (American), B (British), N (Netherlands) or X (Greeks, Belgians and others), and a number. I became B 3431. Public appearance without your armband invited the immediate displeasure of the Gendarmerie at the first checkpoint you encountered.

Some days after the Gendarmerie's round-up it leaked out that about 350 men of all ages had been taken. A little later brief messages, limited to requests for necessities, were permitted, and parcels of such things as woollen pullovers, thick socks, toilet necessities, food and smokes were allowed. The Japanese announced that the men so taken were 'political prisoners'. Perhaps they were picked as potential leaders or plotters against the Japanese, but the wildest flights of fancy could not fit some of them to such a part.

Much later indeed we learnt that some half-baked young Eurasian undercover agent (I think that he had been a ship's radio operator and as such might be of value to an 'underground') had secretly approached Eric Pollock for funds to enable him to escape to Free China. Pollock had no more money than the rest of us, but in a good cause was glad to risk his name and Jardine's credit to raise funds from wealthy Chinese. The youngster appears to have been an irresponsible fool, and to have been seen spending money freely in a night haunt. Of course he soon collapsed under questioning and gave poor Eric away. Eric was lucky enough to escape with his life, but though he survived he went through some ordeals which, many months after the war, he was still unwilling to talk about. Of all this we knew nothing at the time, and indeed on Monday, 25th January 1943, Norton and I learnt from the B.R.A. that we were to make ready to be part of an advance party on Friday, 29th, and cross the river to Pootung. The advance party comprised thirteen British and seven Americans, and we were to plan out accommodation, under Japanese direction, in a large block of godowns for some 340 men who were to follow on Sunday, 31st January.

I have told little of the state of my foreign staff, other than British, during 1942, and it must be said that life for them was not easy. The Japanese had not kept them for very long on the pay roll and jobs such as they had been accustomed to did not exist.

In addition to Musa Herman (her married name), I had one Russian male assistant, by name Agafuroff. He had never been a tower of strength, and now went rapidly downhill and I was powerless to help.

But Musa and her husband appeared to be coping with life, and Musa always seemed more concerned about us British than about herself.

As soon as news came that I was to go into camp I got in touch with her and gave her my precious U.S. $100 note to keep and to spend in any way she was able, to send in comforts to me and, if she herself was in difficulties, to use it for her own needs.

If anybody was going to be allowed to send parcels in to us it would be neutrals (as far as the Japanese were concerned) such as the Russians and the Swedes, but especially the Russians, whose continued neutrality the Japanese were counting upon for the moment.

CHAPTER FOURTEEN

THE PRISONERS OF POOTUNG

OUR little group of twenty were men in their thirties to early forties who had all held responsible peace-time posts, but none were quite top executives. Many of the latter were already under restraint in Haiphong Road with the Gendarmerie, but we were destined to have a few with us before long. We had been told to report at a small open yard at the Municipal Buildings and to have our belongings with us. It was a bitterly cold day, with sleet driving down upon us as we arrived and upon a little Japanese in uniform who kept getting submerged amongst us. In the end, to get himself seen and heard, he had to scramble on to the truck which had come to transport our gear and harangue us from there.

Not long before, in December, some strictly controlled and supervised visits had been allowed to the Haiphong Road Camp and, though few had had the chance to go, the information gathered there had gone the rounds and was of the utmost value to us in preparing for our own incarceration. Our financial resources were limited, and it was important not to squander them. Joint ownership of articles such as kettles, saucepans, frying-pans, tin-openers, pliers, helped to overcome the difficulty, but on the other hand even what Haiphong Road had been able to tell us did not necessarily apply to Pootung, as we were to find out.

A launch took us straight across the river to Pootung Point, where we found that our hostelry was to be a big elderly block of empty godowns, with central compound, which belonged to the British American Tobacco Company. The storage compartments varied in size and, whilst some were destined to house about fifty to sixty beds, others took well above a hundred. Our compound gates were not much more than 150 yards from the water-front, and at the back our windows overlooked a desolate waste on the landward side which had once been a populous Chinese workers' living quarter. Sino-Japanese fighting in recent years had left nothing but crumbling remnants of brick walls amidst a sea of craters, made by bombs or shells, and many heaps of rubble.

We were instructed that we pioneers were each to be 'section captains' of numbered groups of our own nationals, about twenty per section, and I found that I was 'captain of B. 6'. My section had been allotted space in a corner of one end of a medium-sized first-floor compartment. My own personal number was P. (presumably standing for Pootung) 158 and I still sometimes find ancient possessions so marked.

A comparatively small single-storeyed block of buildings in the compound housed the kitchen, which had in peace time supplied rice and other meals for Chinese employees, with a wash-house adjoining it. I believe that the large cauldrons in which our food was to be cooked for two and a half years were supplied by the B.R.A. in conjunction with the Swiss; but these were intended, when supplied, as food containers for the twenty pioneers, and it was only the genius for improvisation of some inmates that enabled them to be kept going as cooking utensils for the duration. We had been told to bring our own food for the first two days and these quickly passed; then our 340 men were upon us. We had thought ourselves well acquainted with the composition of Shanghai's Anglo-American community of the time, but were astonished at the variety that faced us. My own section included the secretary-general-manager of the Shanghai Waterworks; an Irishman who seemed to have a finger in a lot of pies; two Eurasians, one with a British and one with a German name; a Burmese; an asthmatic little Welsh engineer with a knowledge of radar; a Clydeside Scot from a local shipyard; another Scot who had been superintendent engineer of the Power Company in Hankow; and a very large and rather brash young member of the Shanghai Municipal Police. But the Japanese net had spread far throughout China. Another new arrival was a wealthy elderly American who had been caught in Shanghai on, of all things, a holiday cruise; there were also a number of British and Americans, mostly missionaries, who had been swept up from various remote parts of the interior. It was not altogether surprising that the holidaying American had only a suitcase, but many from upcountry arrived with little more than they stood up in. Apparently they had been bustled off protesting and had been told that they were being moved to Shanghai just to facilitate their repatriation. About two weeks later another batch of 'assemblees' arrived, and so it continued until, by 15th March, we were over a thousand strong.

As we began to sort ourselves out, it was hard to imagine more unpromising human material for the great social experiment in communal living which was before us. There was no dearth of sound people —it is rather their diversity which must be emphasized. Any big city in England is, of course, made up of many elements: its artisan labour of the unskilled sort, its skilled technicians and factory workers, its commercial and professional white collar class, its civic administrators and police, its sprinkling of religious workers and those who live on past earnings of themselves or others, including the indigents. Artisans form a solid foundation to the social structure in England, but Shanghai had no such class. We had instead a disproportionate abundance of the others. All foreign workers in Shanghai were executives in greater or less degree. The factory workers were foremen; the engineers superintendents; the policemen sergeants or inspectors; all were in authority over Chinese or other oriental subordinates. Many, whose upbringing had been largely in the narrow confines of a specialized trade, came from their home countries to wield authority in Shanghai over a class of workers whose living scale was much below their own. Many had fought hard in earlier life for the chance of this comparatively exalted position, and it is not surprising that such found it hard to adjust themselves to camp life, to give up their hard-won positions of small authority, and to subordinate themselves without cavil to the administration of leaders who were not, in the first place, of their own choosing. It was the same with the white collar class. There were no clerks amongst Shanghai's foreign employees of banks or merchant firms. The cost of importing labour from Europe or the United States prohibited its employment in subordinate jobs. The small nucleus of foreigners thus formed the greater part of what might perhaps be termed the *élite* class of a great city of, at that time, about four million inhabitants. Consider also how individual were the specialized experts in the different manufactures: tobacco—Southern States, Lancashire or Bristol; wool—Yorkshire; cotton—Lancashire or Southern States, and so on. Many of these had their own clubs and recreation grounds. All of us, I suppose, had our own little worlds which we had created for ourselves in ordinary life and in which we could put up a brave enough show. How woefully exposed we were in our petty weaknesses when it came to communal existence! Pootung started as a tough camp for men only, but after a few months we were to have a considerable influx of women and children. These were largely British owing to the fact, mentioned earlier, that it had been easier for America to bring out women and children from the danger area than for the British who could send them only to Australia.

Another unexpected ingredient in our community, and this was with us from early days, was a batch of sailors from an American merchant ship which had been captured by a Japanese armed merchantman. American friends in the camp told me that the United States had been having difficulty in manning their merchant ships in Far Eastern waters. Sailors' unions insisted upon danger money for entering, for example, the Formosa Channel, that fairly wide stretch of water between the Island of Formosa and the Chinese mainland. This had led, during the year so so before the outbreak of the Pacific war, to the big President Line ships sailing outside Formosa and rounding its southernmost tip to set an almost due westerly course to reach Hongkong. Even at that time and in their best ships, the crews were not always all that their captains could have desired, and when on one occasion one of their biggest ships had misjudged the course and run on to the rocks of the headland in bad weather, many of the crew had virtually run amok and started looting. In the end it was the intervention of armed Japanese from the shore that had protected passengers from crew and restored order. Years later I was to meet in England after the war a married couple who had been on that ill-fated voyage, and it seemed that what I had heard had been no exaggeration.

To return to Pootung, we soon heard that the ship in which our sailor friends were serving had been challenged by a fast Japanese armed merchantman and that their captain had elected to run for it. But his crew, which had been recruited with difficulty on the San Francisco water-front, would have none of that. They mutinied, hauled down their flag and proceeded to beach the vessel very gently in a sheltered cove where they could clamber ashore, almost without getting their feet wet.

I should add that recruiting on the San Francisco water-front included the acceptance of gentlemen released from jail sentences on condition of helping their country by going to sea.

Such then was this addition to our numbers, but it also included a number of Negroes, most of whom were of West Indian origin and were far more adaptable to our community life than their shipmates.

One early recruit came in alone and nobody seemed to know much about him. He was a timid, unobtrusive little man of middle age who passed largely unnoticed, but whose mild eyes glowed with pleasure whenever anybody was nice to him. It was perhaps unfortunate that the space allotted to him was in a section of men who were very rough indeed, but the section captain of such a lot had naturally been carefully picked. The captain, whom I will call Mack, swiftly took the little man under his wing, and although he had to know his full names and particulars, agreed to keep all but his first name to himself. Wilfred, as I shall call him, was so pitifully inadequate that the rough-necks had soon taken him to their hairy bosoms and looked after him like a child. For a few days all went well. His companions hardly noticed Wilfred except when he needed something, and continued life as usual. But their conversation was of the sort which, mainly from lack of wider vocabulary, contained a number of 'fill-in' words which were of the type which used to be called army language. In the evening of Wilfred's first Saturday the conversation became lively and general, and blasphemy succeeded obscenity which succeeded blasphemy, etc. Such was the hubbub that they hardly noticed little Wilfred rush madly to his bed and leap upon it in a state of highly charged emotion. 'Stop! Stop! Stop!' he screamed and, as they suddenly became aware of him and fell silent, he burst into an impassioned rendering of their entire repertoire. 'There now,' he went on, his voice breaking into a sob, 'you've even got me doing it now. Oh, oh, what will happen tomorrow?' he ended in a high-pitched wail. In the hush that followed, there was a purposeful cough from Mack. 'Gentlemen,' he remarked, 'I think that it is time that our Wilfred's incognito was broken. Allow me to present to you the Right Reverend Wilfred Whipple, Bishop of X-Tung Province, who is to preach a sermon at our camp service tomorrow.'

But Wilfred was not the only one who encountered difficulties of adjustment with his stable companions. One young American tobacco expert who, as might be expected, hailed from the Deep South, found that his fellow Americans who were to occupy the beds on each side of him, less than two feet away, were Negroes.

One mishap which occurred in the earliest days arose from, of all things, a desire for cleanliness. By the time that a host of rain-drenched new arrivals had trampled in with muddy boots and muddy luggage, the timber floor of one upper storey dormitory was so begrimed that the newcomers could not tell what the previous colour of it had been. This, felt one man, was no way to start life in what was to be his home for some time. So he got a bucket of water and started to wash the boards immediately around his bed. Within seconds a bellow of rage from the compartment below could be clearly heard, and it was rapidly followed by a huge, irate Negro who came bounding up the stairs to discover what some Goddarned Limey thought he was doing, pouring coffee through the spaces between the floorboards. His newly made bed had been soused by streams of what appeared to be black coffee. Mercifully he was successfully pacified and the whole matter investigated. Many years of the storage of thousands of bales of tobacco leaf had thoroughly impregnated all the floors of our new home, and a glass of clean water spilled upon them at once penetrated the cracks between boards and emerged below as a very dark stain. Nobody ever made that mistake again.

One other personality stands out in memories of those early days. Joe was a tough, honest, Shanghai municipal policeman, but he was a man of fixed ideas or, as some called him, a rugged individualist. In Joe's view the Japanese had put us in there; they must look after us. Joe did not propose to do a hand's turn and lost no opportunity of saying so. Someone quickly came up with a story of a member of some other such community who had adopted such an attitude. All the food was prepared and cooked by inmates and carted and served by others. If he didn't want to participate in camp life he would be issued with his unprepared and uncooked rations and left to his own devices. Such heating as we had for the first winter, until coal ran out, depended on men shovelling and carrying coal and stoking fires. Surely Joe did not expect to sit by a stove serviced by others? He soon came to heel, and afterwards did his very fair share of the work of the camp.

One of the first duties of a section captain was to investigate the capacities of all members of his section so that all that was necessary to keep the camp running smoothly could be done with the minimum of unnecessary effort. Although we hoped that we would soon be allowed to send messages and receive parcels we were for some weeks isolated, as Haiphong Road had been, and our camp was controlled by the Japanese Consular Police instead of the Gendarmerie, and we could not be sure that we would get any parcels to augment our very sparse diet. Energy must be conserved and utilized to best advantage. The beginnings of organization were speedy and one of the first things discovered was the value of the tobacco men's knowledge of the property in which we were living. A common precaution against fire in large blocks or mercantile or industrial buildings is a sprinkler system. Highly sensitized valves in each compartment respond to any undue heat and release an effective spray of water which often controls a fire outbreak before it can take hold. The system involves literally miles of mild steel piping on such large premises, and one of its essentials is a very large fresh water storage tank so highly placed that gravity will produce adequate pressure to enable the sprinklers to be effective even if the mains fail. We had plenty of engineers of all kinds, and before long four old steel drums had been thoroughly cleansed and sterilized and adapted on the geyser principle to provide boiling water to meet all needs. Wide-mouthed locally made thermos flasks with split cane casings could receive the small-sized egg which most Chinese hens lay. Leave it there for a reasonable time and it was the same as if it had been lightly boiled—if you had an egg. To the best of my recollection this invaluable plant was called the Varspal, a name made up from the group that installed it, each letter representing an initial of one of the group. This party of seven men included a policeman, an auctioneer and a tobacco expert, besides the engineers. Indeed the camp's Public Works Department was very ably run by Frank Norton who, whilst he was professionally a tea buyer, was also a do-it-yourself man *par excellence*. Apart from the callings above mentioned, his department included shipbuilding company and tobacco factory engineers, cable company men, general merchants, accountants. And so it was with every camp need. Canteen? Who better to run it than the managing partner of a large Shanghai provision store? Haircut? A Protestant missionary would oblige, whether you were a Roman Catholic priest, a Jew or a Parsee. I had a splendid job made of a nasty dental filling by an oil company's installation engineer and was proud to be able to show it to the admiring gaze of a top-grade practitioner in Upper Wimpole Street after the war. I believe that it is still in place and in good order. The secretary of the Shanghai Gas Company was Alec Davies, a nephew of the famous musician Sir Walford Davies, and it may have been his influence that had got a job with his company for an ex-army bandmaster who had married a Chinese. Who better than these two to organize our music? Another high-class musician was an American life insurance salesman, and there was also Henry Nathan, violinist and leader of the orchestra at the plush Cathay Hotel. We had a number of Negroes other than merchant seamen, and most of them were providers of music in the Shanghai night spots. Saxophonists were in the majority, and it might be thought that it would be difficult for them to produce classical music; but the tireless efforts of Alec and his bandmaster friend, whose name, I think, was Eason, specially orchestrated a number of difficult pieces of music to suit the instruments available, and one violin concerto, with Henry Nathan as the virtuoso, remains a memory to this day. Negro night club musicians did not at first take to the idea of being drilled by a British army bandmaster; but when they found that, as part of his training, he had learnt to play any instrument at sight, they respected him and submitted gracefully.

The overloading of the pitifully inadequate sanitation system with its paltry two dozen flushes was another problem to be coped with. Alec Mackenzie, power station engineer and old artilleryman of World War I, took charge of this and, with an indefatigable gang of stalwarts, was kept busy almost daily flushing the drains by main force of water pressure from fire hoses. When the mains supply failed, as it often did, a complete alternative system, constructed from sprinkler pipes, ensured a supply of water to lavatories from the great reserve tanks.

Another splendid improvisation was the Community Grill. Much of such food as came in in parcels, when they started to be permitted, required heating or cooking and, as the small room stoves were removed after the first winter, it became impossible for the main kitchen, preoccupied as they were with preparing the two regular meals a day, to allow for individual enterprise.

Fire bricks were quickly sorted from the rubble heaps of our playing-field-to-be and a large open-air hotplate and oven was soon designed and built which functioned from 6.00 a.m. to 9.00 p.m. on as many days as coal supplies permitted. Fortunately amongst Pootung's facilities for shipping in normal times had been vast coal dumps and, whilst the living quarters had no heating after the first winter, we had enough coal for the main kitchen and the hot water throughout our stay.

There was soon another need for fire heat and boiling water. All the tubular metal beds which came to us after use in refugee camps were riddled with bed bugs and, though we fortunately had missionary doctors among us who had experience in dealing with them, we never managed to eradicate them utterly. Pouring boiling water through the tubes of the bed frames was one method, and another was to roast the bed frame on an open fire. But you could never be sure that one of your neighbours, even if he had been debugged the day before, might not have acquired one or two of your population overnight. Then, when your once overcrowded bed came back all clean and uncrowded, it must have been an obvious lure to prodigals to return. It will be seen that we became as watchful of our neighbours' beds and floor space as we were of our own. Bed bugs are nasty things when they bite you at night, but even their pungent smell is sufficiently off-putting. Enough of bed bugs. For those who wanted to occupy themselves there were inumerable occupations, both in the way of 'further education' and in camp work for the general weal. Apart from a multiplicity of professors of subjects such as economics, psychology, languages, biochemistry, we had also an experienced deep-sea diver, an American thoracic surgeon, who was in China on an officially sponsored mission to study diseases of the chest there, a young Australian, Arthur Lindsay, of the well-known Australian family of writers and artists, an English one-time concert singer, my little Irishman who, besides being a flautist, claimed some knowledge of osteopathy (or it may have been chiropractics). Also a St John Ambulance gold medallist who gave first-aid training. Before long, as I shall tell later, I myself was to be roped in by the camp's eye doctor to run an eye therapy clinic.

Despite all this opportunity for sensible ways of spending one's time, there was a considerable number of malcontents. In many ways our equality was not what it seemed. Plenty had entered with inadequate clothing. Some of us could spare the odd pullover for such and did so. Some of us could, but did not. Again, those who were in the later batches had had, if they were based in Shanghai, better opportunity to equip themselves with tinned foods, reserves of clothing and cash or credit arrangements. On the other hand, we pioneers had certainly been able to pick what we deemed to be the best sites for our sections. Being near a window was a great boon, unless some fitness-fetish young he-man in an inner bed space insisted upon opening the window wide, whatever the weather, even if it meant clambering over you in the middle of the night and then retreating hurriedly from the succeeding blast of rain or sleet that would rapidly affect all the nearer beds. My waterworks tycoon was always adjuring me to be more positive and dogmatic: 'Don't discuss things with us. Just give orders.' But this was not as practical as he thought with such a community in such bewildering conditions and with no real authority to support one.

There was, I think, only one suicide in the whole two and a half years and it occurred in these early days, with a throat decently cut over a lavatory. Many had left relatives outside, for the Japanese made great play of not interning persons of oriental racial origins unless they wished to be included. Hence a number of Japanese and Chinese wives and other such people stayed outside, and provided useful contacts for their imprisoned menfolk. Many ladies also, who enjoyed the status of what would ordinarily be known in England as mistresses, now came into the picture. In some cases the attachment was genuine and of long standing, and men were anxious to afford their women whatever help they could in the way of living allowances from the Swiss Consul. But since such women had no legal standing as allied nationals, the Swiss Consul had no authority to support them, and there was much anxiety and despondency for a time. Then was heard, by many of us for the first time, the term 'Common-Law Wife'. It appeared that the British Navy recognized as a 'Common-Law Wife' for the purpose of allowance payments a woman who had lived for a number of years with a man as his wife and was known as such to neighbours, even if no legal marriage had been performed. Many couples who were in such case put in a plea for recognition by the Swiss Consul, but so also did a number of partners in stray pick-ups and liaisons. So too did some eminently respectable friends between whom no sex relationship had ever arisen, but who hoped thereby to get money for sending in parcels and perhaps to be permitted to visit the camp, if or when visits by relatives were allowed.

On the other hand, there was a sprinkling of persons who elected to be interned despite obvious oriental blood ties which might be Japanese. Were they sent in to spy on us? There was also one alleged doctor of Middle European origin of whom we all had the greatest suspicions. How genuine were his protestations of sympathy with the Allies? How genuine were his papers?

It was at about this time that I again encountered the Italian name that I had met in Kobe some three years earlier. When I met its owner I mentioned idly the Italian of the same name whom I had met in Kobe. At once he exploded. 'My —— Fascist brother!'

'But', I said, 'he was full of anti-Mussolini talk and expressed a lot of pro-French and pro-British sentiments.'

'I'll bet he did,' was the reply. 'You were a British shipping agent. Did you not know that he was specially decorated by Mussolini not long afterwards?'

As far as I know, our Pootung inmate was the genuine article and his British papers were authentic. But even white Britons or Americans could, if they had left oriental dependants outside, be influenced by pressures which the Japanese might exert upon such dependants. All these little details are not intended to invoke sympathy or to suggest that we Pootungites suffered any serious hardships by comparison with hardships and dangers endured by allied civilians and service people elsewhere. They are rather intended as a report of the complications of a unique experiment in integration of unlike elements into a community, and on the whole it was a successful experiment.

There was no doubt that the Japanese sometimes had an unhealthy knowledge of undercurrents of feeling in the camp. All reports emanating from Haiphong Road had told us that at first the Japanese had been repressive and unco-operative, but that, by dint of constant complaints from the inmates' elected representative, many abuses had been stopped and extra amenities granted. So the British representative in Pootung, as spokesman for the majority of 'assemblees', was for ever demanding many things. Our Japanese consular guardians, without doubt, had little power of getting things done, if it were a question of competing with requisitions from their service-run camps. Still less against the all-powerful Gendarmerie of Haiphong Road. Later, when even they had to acknowledge the need for supplies which they could not get, assemblees would come forward and offer to obtain them if they could be allowed out under guard to make certain personal calls.

Thus we had many basic needs fulfilled, as the Japanese commandant preferred the embarrassment of such an admission of failure within the camp to having the Swiss making derogatory comparisons between his administration and that of other camps. The perpetual nagging of the British representative of the time, W. W. Mackenzie, who pressed our just claims with courage and determination, got under the skin of the commandant. From the first it had been clear that the Japanese consular underlings in charge of our camp were terrified of us. They forbade at first any 'meetings' of assemblees and thereby prevented the representative from meeting the captains of sections in committee. This made the organization of the life of the camp very difficult, and the coherent dissemination of information or instructions almost impossible. Captains were under constant fire from their section members, some of whom would do almost nothing they were asked without wanting to know details of who said so and why. The consular police were, fairly obviously, rejects from more strenuous forms of war service and, without the internal police force which we had soon organized amongst ourselves, there would have been chaos. The loud voices of some malcontents led the Japanese to believe that poor Mackenzie was disliked by his own nationals. The commandant actually said so. What easier therefore than to remove this agitator and hand him over to the dread Gendarmerie for correction? When the Japanese announced this intention, the true underlying feelings of the camp emerged in a display of ugly temper which threw the little Japanese into a panic. There was a demonstration as Mackenzie and another man, Forsyth, were led away by gendarmes, and it was probably only the growing certainty that the more we demonstrated the worse the gendarmes would make matters for their captives which avoided serious trouble.

The real agitators? Well, there was a small minority who hailed Mackenzie's removal with glee, because they hoped thereby to gain power and were so ill-advised as to say so. Soon afterwards, in September 1943, a sudden repatriation of a large number of Americans and Canadians from Shanghai took 150 of our number, and another 200 were transferred to other camps. Our new representative, in succession to Mackenzie, was John Gadsby, the reason for whose presence in Shanghai at that time I do not know. John Gadsby, former legal adviser to the British Embassy in Tokyo, was, by his training and life's work, more than a match for any foes, whether Japanese or British, and those who had been concerned in fomenting ill feeling against Mackenzie found themselves sent separately to different other camps with our commandant's tip that they were potential trouble-makers. I am afraid that two of my section were in this category, but I lost a number of other transferees and my old B. 6 section virtually ceased to exist.

The next news, which we received with some trepidation, was that a camp at Yangchow, some miles away in the interior, was to be liquidated and its inhabitants distributed between ourselves and the other camps which had by now been long established in Shanghai. Yangchow, we all knew, was a mixed camp and we would have a proportion of women and children in our replacement intake. To some of us the implications of this were terrifying. We knew that we were a tough camp. We accepted it. But it was commonly said, with what truth I do not know, that at least one of our Sing Sing graduates was a convicted murderer, and we none of us knew of what crimes the others might have been found guilty. How could we allow women and children to be exposed to such men, but on the other hand how could we prevent it? We need not have worried. I have never seen a greater transformation than took place throughout the camp when the new arrivals were installed. If any of the tough elements now wanted to show off their toughness, it was to gain the admiration of all females from six years to sixty. The only danger of squabbling was in competition between various tough gentlemen as to who should be this or that particular female's protector. Doyenne perhaps of the ladies was Lorna Dean, wife of the Shanghai head of Butterfield & Swire, Far Eastern general agents for the Blue Funnel Line interests. I had known him well in his bachelor days, but had never met her till now and she soon earned my respect and that of many others. There were also women of various accomplishments, including one who had had pictures hung in the Royal Academy, and many who took upon themselves much of the help necessary for the doctors and a great deal of invaluable repair of clothing. There were also leading ladies of the Shanghai Amateur Dramatic Society of which I need say no more than that, as Mary Hayley Bell, Hayley Mills's mother had not long before been also one of its stars. But it all led to many difficulties in the running of the Community Grill. How could women repay their menfolk or, if they had none of their own, their protectors better than by transforming dull stuff out of tins and packets into tempting delicacies? In season peaches were cheap in Shanghai and some came in in parcels. What man would have thought of salving well-sucked peach stones from the refuse, drying and cracking them and using the kernels for almonds?

During the rush hours around meal times the grill was too small to accommodate everybody who wanted to use it. As with a Japanese soldier's devotion to his God-Emperor, so some women deemed no holds barred when it came to titillating their menfolk's palates with the meagre materials available. The harassed unattached male was apt to find it difficult to get cooking space in the limited time to spare from camp fatigues, washing his clothes, debugging his bed and so on. It was certainly annoying for a mere man to have to push for space for his occasional half-rasher of bacon amongst enormous pots which had been put on to steam for hours to produce a pudding for a family group. So supervisors had to be appointed. Many were the brave if foolhardy volunteers for the job who retired after a brief spell of hazardous duty, some bearing outward scars, others wounded in spirit. A handful of coloured lads were the only ones who, with imperturbable good humour, survived two years at the hazardous grill. Once only in all that time was a knife drawn, and then bloodshed was averted.

In our purely masculine days, before the departure of the Americans and Canadians, one little American had insisted that an effort should be made to put on Shakespeare in the camp's big dining and assembly hall. Shakespeare? It was true that there were likely to be more copies of Shakespeare's plays available than of any other playwright, but we

British were very dubious of the reception it would be accorded by our Sing Sing graduates and such. However, we succumbed to pressure and put on certain parts of *Julius Caesar* in which no female characters were involved. Indeed that play was picked because its women's parts are relatively unimportant. So *Julius Caeser* it was, and for some reason I was asked to play the name part and, as the production was without benefit of costume, I wore a fairly clean pair of white shorts to distinguish me from the others, who were mostly in khaki ones. All the from rows were filled by the roughest of the American element, and our reception was almost rapturous.

But I think that the main task performed before the ladies joined us was the creation of recreation space in the open. All able-bodied men willing to volunteer to clear a central space as a games field became thereby eligible to participate in a draw for allotments—which of course they had to clear for themselves. My fellow landowners were the two B. 6 Scots; Alec Mackenzie, one time Power Station engineer and now in charge of the sanitation squad, and George Mitchell, ex-shipbuilding foreman and now a general mechanic of the Public Works Department. Two finer partners I could never wish for. Mac, although he must have had a reasonable vocabulary, never bothered to use it, but was instead an expert in foul language that I have never heard beaten. I think I told him once that he had the foulest mouth and purest heart of anyone I ever met. Mitch too was a splendid friend, and the two of them looked upon me, a mere white collar type, as someone to be looked after and shielded from the rougher elements. I remember Mitch going for a big Yank who, he thought, was being nasty to me. He was twice the size of Mitch, but retreated in haste from his ferocity.

It must have been at about this time that Mac, who wore glasses, began to complain about his sight. There was little doubt that our diet was deficient in vitamins and this could hardly help our eyes, but although Godfrey Gale, a British doctor, was a qualified ear, eye, nose and throat man, there was no way for him to get glasses for people who broke theirs or needed a change. So I started to tell Mac of my own experience with the Swedish girl, and suggested to him some of the simpler exercises which she had taught me. 'Try anything once,' said Mac, and in a very short while his eyes were feeling better. The news soon spread and it was not long before I was belligerently buttonholed in the compound by Godfrey Gale. 'Weren't you a business man in ordinary life?' he asked, and when I admitted it he asked me what I thought I was doing, messing around with people's eyes—which were his responsibility; so we repaired to the tiny cubby-hole which served him as office and consulting-room and talked for nearly an hour. At the end of it Gale remarked that in present conditions my exercises could do no harm and might do good; but he pointed out that our community included all sorts, such as might have backgrounds of venereal disease or hidden injuries from brawls in bars or other such medical histories. He therefore insisted that for my own protection I was to accept nobody that had not first been vetted and had a vision test by him. He would send them on to me and they would report to him for further checks and vision tests once a month. So I found myself running an eye therapy clinic and continued to do so until the camp ended. Never, in a fairly long life, have I had such a rewarding experience. I was soon joined by Ada Welch, elderly American widow of a British financier in Shanghai, and we had our classes every morning in a corner of the dining-hall which was discreetly screened for the purpose by means of sheets, blankets, matting or anything else available. I was particularly pleased with Dr Gale's report, after two months, on three young teenage brothers who all came to me wearing glasses. The report stated that vision was now almost perfect, and that he could see no reason why they should ever have to wear glasses again. Another case, a devout elderly missionary lady, who used to read a Chinese Bible with the book almost touching her nose, was the most sensational. At first a face across a table was no more than a pale blur to her, but within two months she was able to count the white insulators on the far-away telephone poles beyond our barbed wire. It is true that whilst we lacked vitamins we had plenty of time for therapy—more of it than is available to most of us in everyday life. But these facts suggest that much could be done for eyesight in general by such methods. I have also found, in teaching, that the techniques practised in stimulating the response of the brain to images projected through the lens, which is the eye, are most helpful to children in memorizing. Many of my present day school-pupils would testify to this.

In our two and a half years of camp life we had no milk, other than in powder or liquid form in tins, and these came in solely on the occasions when we got gift parcels through the Red Cross. By arrangement amongst the Allies, these were entirely the responsibility of the United States in the Pacific theatre of war, and when they first came some of the rougher and less responsible elements amongst our Yanks clamoured that American parcels were for Americans only. Many of this type of inmate were more interested in Camels, Chesterfields, Lucky

Strikes and other well-known brands of American cigarettes than in the food. This was a good thing, as judicious bargaining made it possible to increase greatly the amount of important foods available for the very young and for the sick. Parcels when issued took no account of age or of tastes and the tinies got parcels with cigarettes in them and so did confirmed non-smokers and men who, like myself, stuck to a pipe. So much tobacco is grown in China that local food parcels could usually produce tobacco and cigarettes of a sort. With B.A.T. Company staff amongst us, it was also not long before secret access was somehow found to stocks of tobacco, in its leaf form, in adjacent godowns. This became a minor racket, as there were amongst us not only tobacco men but also old seafarers who were expert in twisting and compressing the leaf into a sort of pigtail, for which sailors have another name, too rude for publication. Some cigarette smokers were glad to roll any tobacco they could get in almost any sort of paper. This led to certain industrious gentry spending long hours hunting down and salvaging fag ends so that they could market the contents. Another discovered skill was in the making of wooden clogs. Shoe leather soon wore out and was irreplaceable, and whilst in warm weather the obvious course was to wear the skin of one's feet, as it would go on repairing itself, it was another matter in winter. We soon discovered that thick wood between sole and soil was far better for keeping one's feet warm than fancy footwear which climbed half way up one's calf but had only a thin underside.

One little creeping plant which the British looked upon as weed was recognized by our Dutch friends as being of a genus cultivated in Holland in a small way and valued for its Vitamin C content. Potato peelings from the kitchen, when planted, sometimes struck roots. Red peppers were also easy to grow in our allotments as well as tomatoes and lettuce. But the latter could be dangerous in such surroundings, so close to Chinese dwellings, unless very well washed. I remember Herbert Hodgkin, a Quaker missionary doctor, of whom more later, publicly pointing out in the dining-hall that gentle rinsing in a solution of permanganate of potash 'b'long velly good joss', but that a strong jet of clean water from a tap would do more to remove potential sources of dysentery. Our one loaf of bread per head per day did not always arrive and, as it was made from a blend of flour which contained soya-bean and other vegetable products, quickly acquired a type of mould, which our doctors pronounced dangerous if kept more than a day, so it was sliced thin and rusked in the hot sunshine. Then, it could be crushed small, enabling a large quantity to be stored in a tin and eaten, in emergency, rather like a sort of Grape Nuts.

Another great source of food was American 'Cracked Wheat' of which the Red Cross had had many tons in store for several years for famine relief. This was cooked like porridge and made our first meal of the day, giving us three meals in all. Unfortunately protracted storage had led to its infestation by weevils and maggots, and many of us, especially the women, could not face it, and a special camp version soon appeared of an old saying, 'Hear no weevil, see no weevil, speak no weevil', as, to many, they were unmentionable without inducing nausea. Herbert Hodgkin did all he could in his own way. He used to sit at a table picking out and eating the maggots with chopsticks and smacking his lips as he did so—an act of great courage. He pointed out that all the meat we eat in normal life is vegetable—and often cereal—fed. We were lucky to be getting an addition to our meat ration which had been raised on the best American wheat, he would say. There was some point to his remarks, as our official meat supply, especially in warm weather, was apt to be heralded by its aroma as it entered the compound—not quite a stench, but nasty enough. But not even my Mac and Mitch could quite see it that way. We three would retire into a dark corner and gulp down the stuff after flavouring it liberally with home-grown red peppers—to kill the taste of mildew which was often present. Another and more juicy memory of maggots relates to bacon. One of my messmates—it may have been Mac—had somehow acquired about a pound of bacon and decided, as the weather was then warm and such precious food would be more valuable in cold weather, to store it. Lacking the expertise of Frank Norton in such matters, he placed it in a tin which would just accommodate it. When, many weeks later, he decided to fry some for himself, Mitch and me, the tin, on being opened, revealed a number of maggots who were thoroughly enjoying their luxurious home. When he came to cut the bacon it was interesting to note that the parts chiefly affected were those in contact with the metal of the container. I do not know the reason for this, but perhaps if he had first wrapped the bacon in paper he would have lost less bacon. However, when the bacon was placed in a frying-pan, the maggots quickly jumped out as the heat increased and were disposed of. After all, these maggots, unlike those in the wheat, were carnivores. Probably the principal predators of the community's food were rats of the two-legged variety. Some people on the kitchen detail were not above cutting off a good chunk of meat from camp supplies when it was worth pinching and selling it to even more despicable persons who had money and were willing to bribe them. There were also rats of the four-legged kind, but the camp had two or three dogs and the buildings harboured a type of small snake, presumably of the python family, which a young expert told us were called rat snakes, and we did not see many rats.

There was no serious beri-beri in the camp, and the only people to develop even mild symptoms were one or two ladies who could not overcome their squeamishness at the wheat. However, another fortunate factor also helped in this respect. Just as many British people insist on white flour, so any Chinese who could afford to insisted upon very white rice. This involved polishing the grain and thus, so our experts told us, removing the Vitamin B element which is such a staunch defence against beri-beri. Naturally our captors supplied only the cheapest rice available, scathingly described as 'red rice' by the Chinese, but valuable for its Vitamin B content. With our lack of milk, calcium deficiency was very real, but I was lucky in that my dear Musa never failed to send me one parcel per month and each one contained calcium tablets. To the Hongkong Red Cross dentist, who drew out several rotting stumps from my mouth in 1946, it was not unlike drawing corks from miniature cesspools. What would my teeth have been like without Musa?

Camp life, simple enough in some ways, was in others so complex that one is in danger of wandering over such a wide field of interrelated events and circumstances as to confuse the reader. I will now therefore touch more particularly upon one or two aspects worthy of special mention.

I believe the name of the head of our camp's medical department was Dr Graham but, perhaps because I had much to do with Dr Gale, was a dormitory neighbour of Dr Hodgkin and had known the American chest expert, Dr Thorngate, in the Shanghai Short Story Club before we were interned, I have little memory of personal dealings with him. One of his great bugbears was the lack of proper facilities for emergency treatment, such as operations, but of this good was to come. It was brought home to our little hosts that the Swiss would take a poor view of any deaths occurring in Pootung in consequence of inadequate facilities and, if their service personnel were still rather cock-a-hoop, the consular Japanese were already having grave doubts as to how the war would end. Finally, it was agreed that we would train stretcher bearers and would take emergency cases across the river under guard to the Shanghai International Hospital which lay not far from the Garden Bridge across the Soochow Creek. The commandant was delighted and so, very soon, were we. I quickly enlisted for the stretcher gang, and after a high-pressure first-aid course from our St John Ambulance gold medallist, learnt the basic skills of stretcher work. We stretcher bearers had a duty roster, and it was accepted that if any emergency suddenly arose others would take over any current tasks from a stretcher man called out for duty. Not only was it a worth-while job, but it enabled one to get out of the Pootung compound and cross the water, even if only for an hour or two. These trips also had other advantages. The International Hospital, as it implies, was staffed by international medical personnel and, with a little care and discretion, it was possible to pick up interesting items of news there: news of the other Shanghai camps and their inmates; news of the state of the war; contacts perhaps with old friends or friends of old friends. There was also the possibility of small-scale smuggling into the camp. The party was always accompanied by one consular police guard and one assemblee capable of interpreting. The system was quickly exploited, and those in camp who had cash at their disposal began to be of use to the community at large. Lavish cash hand-outs to the interpreters enabled them, with a little tact and skill, to point out to the guard that, once the party was safely in the hopsital, he was virtually relieved of responsibility until the time came for them to return. There were plenty of quiet little bars around this or that corner. What about a quick one? This *modus operandi* was very successful for a long time, and we stretcher bearers could wander uninhibited around the spacious corridors with at least as much sense of freedom as small schoolboys on a trip to, say, the British Museum in term time. The star interpreter at this game was a young girl of twenty or so who had been brought up in Japan and who, I suspect, may have had traces of Japanese blood in her veins. But, finally, she went too far. It was not a trip in which I personally was involved, and I happened to be in the open compound near the gateway as the party returned rather behind schedule. When the guard on duty opened the gate two stretchers came in in single file. Upon one, in complete disarray and with her skirts decently masking her face, lay our little lady interpreter, a most unwell martyr to her sense of duty. Upon the second sprawled the unconscious body of the Japanese guard and, behind, the reserve stretcher bearers that made up the rest of the party were busy picking up things that fell off the stretchers. Alas, though neither the sergeant of the guard nor the commandant witnessed this distressing incident, the sentry at the gate reported it and there was much closer—I nearly said 'tighter'—control of subsequent expeditions. However, this did not happen until 1945, so the consequences were not serious.

One evening in, I think, 1944 I was suddenly called upon to help to carry an emergency case across at once. The International Hospital, contacted on the phone, could do nothing that night and recommended that the party should go the rounds of various downtown Japanese-controlled hospitals until we found one that could help. The patient was a huge ex-policeman who was suffering from a duodenal ulcer, and our doctors felt that he must be operated upon before next morning. As it was obviously liable to be a very long trek and the patient was large and heavy, six stretcher bearers were authorized so that we could each do short spells with plenty of reliefs. Round we trudged and it must have been past midnight before we found what we wanted. The trouble was that acceptance of the patient was useless unless a competent surgeon was on hand to operate at once. Even then there remained the language difficulty. Dr Hodgkin was with us but, via the interpreter, seemed unable to explain what was needed. Then he tried various ways of saying the actual technical terms in English, which, in medical circles, is of course Latin. A gleam appeared in the eye of the Japanese surgeon, and sufficient understanding was quickly reached. The operation was successfully performed and the patient returned to camp a few days later. I often tell this tale to little boys who ask me what use Latin can possibly be in after life. But my own strongest memory of that night is of the patient's breath. Foul breath is an inevitable consequence of duodenal ulcer and if, breathing deeply, with your head slightly bowed over the stretcher, you trudge for a mile or two carrying such a heavy patient, it is not easily forgotten.

Whilst on the subject of our medical men, I must mention that the only qualified dentists we ever had in the camp were two Americans who were repatriated with the party that left us within the first seven months. But, as they had been unwilling to do anything without payment, either in cash or in U.S. dollar IOUs for collection after the war, we were glad to see the back of them. Black, the oil installation engineer, who did such good work for me, was entirely trained by our own doctors. The advent of women, many of them with nursing experience, was of great assistance to our medical men, but they also brought problems. Within a year a number of babies were born to various of the till then unattached females, and space had to be provided for a crèche where the mothers could live with their babies and take care of them. One English girl, quite young and very proper, volunteered to help in the clinic. One night, when she was on duty, she awoke to discover a large increase in the number of occupants of the crèche, and her embarrassment was extreme when she realized that several of the mothers had been joined in bed by the fathers and that there was considerable activity.

Apart from the transporting across the river of hospital cases, we of the stretcher squad used to be called upon to move around the camp anybody who was temporarily not self-propelled, such as people injured at games or ill. I remember one lordly young man who was confined to his bed, but had the doctor's permission to attend one of our theatrical shows if he could be transported there and back. He had been in charge of the local office of a fairly substantial firm, and in camp found it difficult to forget the fact. Two stretcher men, who happened to be on duty, were asked to carry the young man down to the show, but when they arrived the young man chose to act the temperamental big shot. He wasn't ready—they must wait for ten or more minutes. The stretcher men were not amused: camp shows were something of a high light in the lives of many and, whilst they were willing enough to miss a few minutes of theatre-going to transport the young man, even that would not have been necessary if he had been ready when they had come. I happened to know the young man's chairman rather well and knew what he would think of such attitudes, so I took the place of one stretcher bearer and announced the fact to the young man, adding that I was not prepared to wait all night, and that if he wanted to see the show it was now or never. He replied with a very rude four-letter word, but I did not mind. His bluff had been called, and after his one little explosion he came like a lamb. I am happy to say that he and one or two of his kidney appeared to hate me. My friendship with his chairman was one of the legacies left me by my father. When, very young, I had arrived friendless in Shanghai, a very senior tycoon in the club turned his head at the sound of my unusual name. 'Any relation of the Hongkong judge?' he asked, and when I replied that I was his youngest son, he said: 'Never will I forget his kindness to me as a youngster, when I first came out east. If ever I can help you in any way at all, nothing—repeat nothing—will ever be too much trouble.' My father was not a rich man, but was not such a legacy—for I found this attitude among many of the older men—worth more to me than thousands of pounds? It never had any direct financial value, but it was a great inspiration.

The hazards undergone by food servers and checkers were greater than might be supposed. One early discovery when the camp got under way had been several thousand round brass discs about the size of five-shilling pieces and bearing a number in Western characters as well as a Chinese inscription. These had been used in peace time as tally checks for the coolies carrying cargo, and now they were issued to assemblees, each of whom had his or her own number. The great pots of food, when ready, were carried some twenty or thirty yards between kitchen and hall, slung on Chinese coolies' carrying poles between the shoulders of two servers. These men needed to be strong and to know the methods of stretcher bearers whereby, by keeping out of step with each other, they prevented their burden from getting into a rhythmical swing and slopping over. Not only was food too precious to be spilt—it could also scald very badly. Then they stood at one end of the hall and queues were formed to each pot server. The pots were on a bench and checkers stood beside to ensure that nobody got served without handing in his meal ticket. With over a thousand meals to serve, very nice judgment had to be used in size of portions. The last fifty would be unamused if food ran out before their turn. There was also some luck in whether your half ladle full contained naught but fat, gristle and gravy. Another difficulty was that the recipient was sometimes dissatisfied with the nature of the rations, and some of the rougher elements tended to become enraged and fling their enamel plate full into the face of the unlucky server without pausing to think that it was not his fault. However, our own camp police force were soon in control of such incidents. As time went on our insides became quite unable to digest the more greasy foods, and this was another reason to be grateful for any food parcels. Rice was cooked, by men who knew how, in large cauldrons, and when it was ready to serve it was barely moist, with a thin crust covering the entire inner surface of the container. To those who wanted it rice crust was served at the end of the meal. My Mac and Mitch soon discovered that, boiled up again and flavoured with one or two sardines between about six people, or even with red peppers, it could make a good extra meal. In early days we used to chew the hard crusts, but I soon found that these bruised and cut my gums badly. Infection set in and I then discovered the therapeutic value of milkless, unsweetened tea as a mouthwash. By dint of massaging and squeezing the gums and rinsing with warm tea I successfully doctored myself. A tip worth knowing.

Camp entertainments fall easily into three main categories: outdoor games; shows in the hall; self-entertainment in small groups, whether in chess challenges between one dormitory and another, dancing instruction, bridge or poker. There was also the spinning of yarns in the evenings. It was not long before American aircraft were in the vicinity and black-out precautions were rigorous. Pootung Point was at a major curve of Shanghai's Whangpoo River and as such was, we were told, a navigational check point for aircraft. A result of this was that the little promontory surrounding our camp was well filled with anti-aircraft guns. This meant that it was an area where the Japanese were especially vigilant at night and, as it was impossible to black out the huge expanse of windows, our lights were limited to tiny dark blue bulbs with a small paler spot on the end. Talking was therefore the most practical occupation in dormitories at night.

Shows in the hall, now that we had women among us, became far more enterprising. Home-made revues, Shakespeare, Oscar Wilde, A. A. Milne, orchestral concerts, vocal concerts—all these were produced on our stage built up by tables put together. I myself remember playing the butler in Milne's *The Dover Road* and Wilde's *The Importance of being Ernest*, Sebastian in *The Tempest*, the Duke of Cornwall in *King Lear*. The name part in the last play was grandly played by Herbert Hodgkin and, of his daughters, the part of Goneril was played by a young English girl. The latter, in the opinion of many males, found her main occupation in camp in luring simple-minded young men and, pretty though she was, the majority, including Hodgkin, did not love her. I have a vivid memory of the dress rehearsal of the poignant scene in which Lear, half demented by the calculating treachery of his elder daughters Regan and Goneril, turns upon Goneril who is present, with a stream of very real curses upon her womanhood. I was in the wings a few moments later when Hodgkin, rubbing his hands together and grinning all over his face, stalked off.

'Never enjoyed myself so much in all my life,' he remarked quietly to me; a harsh indictment from such a kindly man.

To be fair to the young girl, rumour had it that she had lost a boy friend killed in the fighting in Europe and was going through a difficult time. In the roles of Sebastian and the Duke of Cornwall I was sketched in full rig by young Arthur Lindsay, who gave me the pictures. Looking at them again recently, I was reminded of one particular item of my attire as the duke. He was not only a duke but a church prelate, and as such fittingly wore a red hat of suitable shape. The ladies were for a while floored by the problem of this headgear until one of them had an inspiration. One not young missionary lady had been seen to possess a fine pair of red woollen bloomers. By artistic and skilful use of a pin here and a stitch there they were transformed—and that was the hat I wore.

One of our orchestral concerts took place upon some national anniversary. I do not remember whether it was the King's birthday, or perhaps St George's Day; but a whisper, very secret in case there were informers among us, warned us all to pay special attention to one particular item. This was either an arrangement or an original composition at the hands of Bandmaster Eason, and all ears, except those of our camp commandant and many Japanese guards in the front rows, were specially cocked for it. We all held our breath as the unmistakable strains of *God Save the King* penetrated the outward pattern of the music. Eason got away with it, but it was a brave thing to do.

The most amusing role that fell to my lot was as a turn in a music hall show. At rather short notice I was rehearsed in gym shoes, long winter underwear, a mask over my upper face and a large blond moustache. My equipment was two suitably metal-coloured, large, round toy balloons which were joined together in dumb-bell fashion by a wooden bar. I was Eugene Sandow restored to life—Eugene Sandow, the most famous strong man of the early part of the century. I think it was the fact that I have very muscular calves that gave someone the idea, but my bicep muscles were quite inadequate, so the upper part of my arms was quite ludicrously padded under the long-sleeved vest. My entry on stage was preceded by an immense fanfare, and as I approached the pseudo dumb-bell lying in the centre there was a roll of drums. I was no expert, but the musicians were and their accompaniment magnificently over-dramatized my every movement. In the front row sat our Japanese hosts, goggle-eyed and mouths agape, as I laboured and struggled to raise the great weights and hoist them above my head. When I had finally got them down again to the floor I made my bows amidst tumultuous applause, and marched off in a manner in which I tried to combine immense conceit with nonchalance. As I disappeared into the wings a very small Indian boy ran on from the other side and, tucking the dumb-bells under one arm, scampered off again while a deep breathed 'Ah' came from the Japanese in front. I really believe that they had been taken in. Incidentally the little Indian boy was amongst our better chess players.

Outdoor games? Well, most of us had plenty to do in our gardens whenever we could find the time, but the Americans challenged the

British at cricket and, though we had not the necessary equipment for baseball, the British in return played its soft ball substitute, which is somewhat like rounders. Unfortunately for the *amour propre* of the Britons, several of the American Negroes were of West Indian origin and their cricket was as good as their baseball—'plenty good'. I have vague memories also of a little football, and perhaps some hockey, but Mac and Mitch kept my head well down in our garden for most of my spare time.

Now back to some generalities of camp life. Mention of Mac brings to my mind the one occasion when he felt defeated by his drains job and was tempted to give up. The various appurtenances of female hygiene added greatly to the already excessive burden upon the capacity of the flush system. When a long queue of women at a flush have each certain toilet articles to dispose of, the chain gets pulled more rapidly and often than it can possibly function and an accumulation finally choked the exit pipe. This happened so often that even Mac's noble team grew rebellious, and upon such a scene came suddenly Lorna Dean. As she saw what the trouble was, she pushed everybody aside and, rolling up her right sleeve to the shoulder, thrust her arm far into the waste pipe and cleared the stoppage handful by handful. 'Rather her than me', remarked someone, but her courageous act so shamed the women standing round, some of whom had presumably contributed to the stoppage, that Mac and his lads never had any more trouble. There was little doubt that there was nothing that our strange collection of human beings could not cope with in one way or another. For many months there was a 19,000-ton Lloyd Triestino passenger liner, the *Conte Verde*, lying off Pootung Point, and for a long time there had been stirrings of hope of another repatriation, but they faded; and then the standard camp joke was to suggest asking the Japanese to let us man her and sail her home. Every necessary element of a crew for such a ship was present among us. 'Yes,' said some wag, 'we've even got first-class passengers.'

I have sometimes been asked, in later years, whether there were any escape attempts made from Pootung Camp and, if not, why not. In considering this matter, certain circumstances need to be taken into account.

Firstly, it is the duty of any prisoner of war to attempt to escape, but Pootung was a civilian camp and any preventive measure taken by the Japanese against assemblees would have fallen equally upon women and children.

Secondly, as mentioned earlier, there was some indication that we were pawns in the repatriation lark which our Government seemed to be carrying on with the Japanese. We did not ever really know how serious these were.

Thirdly, many felt that untrained civilians, mostly between their forties and early sixties, would be of no particular value at that stage. On the other hand, we had a sense of obligation to stick to our jobs and our loyal staffs so as to be on hand when the end came. I remember feeling uncertain, when the first repatriations occurred, whether I would be right to take the chance of wangling a passage if it came my way. I was never sure.

We did have one escape from the camp in 1945, though I cannot remember whether it was before or after V.E. Day, and it was successful. I believe that the man was a qualified radio operator and he may have been a Eurasian. At all events he had a wife of oriental blood still living free in Shanghai, and the first result of his escape was a pounce by the Gendarmerie upon his home. They seized his wife and took her away for 'questioning' in their own inimitable way. What was his value to the war effort at that time if he did succeed in getting through to the Allies before the end? If there was any such value, did it justify the inevitable consequences to his wife? These are hard questions to answer.

As time went on allied air raids became a very real threat, although we were mercifully spared knowledge of the bombing which inadvertently killed a number of men and women at Stanley Internment Camp in Hongkong. There were no very great concentrations of Japanese armaments or troops in Shanghai, and I do not think that any really large-scale bombing was contemplated; but we were unfortunately placed at Pootung Point, so near to anti-aircraft guns, and our buildings were old and contained many thousands of square feet of windows. Short of a direct hit by misadventure, our greatest danger was broken glass. I remember watching one small bomb come down and trying to judge, from its angle of flight, whether it was going to hit us. It didn't, and though it fell close by it was not large enough to cause any appreciable loss of glass.

It must have been some time in 1944 that an incident occurred which brought home to us very sharply the advantages of having consular hosts rather than Gendarmerie, even if they were less efficient. Some idea has been given of the wide variety of technical abilities to be found amongst us. Two young Americans were expert radio technicians and, by dint of patient smuggling of small and innocent-looking bits and pieces over a period of months, had succeeded in assembling a reasonably efficient short-wave receiver. When I had lived in West Park Mansions, one young British neighbour, Roger Gaine, had managed something of the sort. His punishment, if the Gendarmerie had caught him, would probably have been a hideous death, but he at least had better opportunity to install the equipment in secrecy. In Pootung there was no privacy, and it is remarkable that the young men managed to install it, and listening in, even under bedclothes, must have been very hazardous. But when they were finally caught our Japanese commandant was terrified. If the Gendarmerie were to hear of it, he himself would be in grave jeopardy; so the two young men were quietly slipped away into the Shanghai jail on an imaginary charge and that was that. It had been nice to get authentic news from home, but most of us had by now learned to interpret Japanese news. The Japanese had continued to produce a former Shanghai daily—the *Shanghai Times*—in English, and their official communiqués were singularly naïve. The paper often quite legitimately found its way into the camp and, whilst the Japanese were not much concerned to rebut allied reports of successes in North Africa, and later in Europe, the alleged doings of that reprehensible American admiral, Nimitz, in the Pacific theatre of war were another matter.

We had little means of knowing that Nimitz claimed a victory until the Japanese called him a liar in the *Shanghai Times*. Then we drew our own satisfying conclusions. During the daylight air raids of the last few months of war we would watch great Flying Fortresses sailing serenely over at what were in those days immense heights, and the rather futile efforts of little Japanese fighters to harm them. The only planes I ever saw damaged on these occasions were the fighters. At night too there were raids, but these seemed mostly to be carried out by no more than one or two bombers. One night there was an eye-searing flash and a bigger than usual explosion, and it was said that an American plane had been brought down and that the Japanese were looking for the crew, who had escaped. Eric Pollock, who had survived his time of punishment, was by this time in the jail several miles away, and he told me afterwards that they used there to listen and watch for the night raids of a bomber which they nicknamed 'One-Bomb Willie' as that seemed to be all it ever dropped. I do not think that the Americans were attempting more than to keep the Japanese jittery. My eye clinic was continuing to function with the help of Ada Welch, and one day she mentioned that before marriage she had been an official court stenographer in America and that she would be happy to teach me shorthand. I wish that she had been successful but, alas, her only other pupil was a young Texan and, as she herself was a proper eastern Yankee and I was a Limey, the complications of reproducing three different sets of vowel sounds were too much for her.

And then came Hiroshima and Nagasaki, and we knew that all was almost over. But there was still no certainty for some days as to how the local Japanese garrison would react. Some people thought that they would massacre all prisoners, whether civilians or not. But the changed attitudes of our camp guards were soon unmistakable. We had acquired a new sergeant of consular police in those last few months and he was always a puzzle to us. He was a man of some education and, apart from being very efficient in his duties, he was quite chatty in English with many of us. After V.E. Day he had often been heard to say that he hoped to meet us again when it was all over. How had such a man come to be posted to us at such a time?

Then one day a twin-engined plane, which may have been a Dakota, flew low over the camp and parachutes floated down supporting great crates of supplies. It was all over.

Of course we felt emotion, but perhaps it would be easier to write about if one had not oneself felt it.

It was by no means the end of Pootung Camp, as the great majority of the inhabitants—I think that we can now gladly drop the word 'assemblees'—had no homes to go to. However, there was no limit to visits by friends and relations, nor to commuting to Shanghai itself. I was very soon visited by a number of my staff, including Musa Herman, and many little luxuries of life were also quickly available. I had entered camp with an old whisky bottle full of high-grade spirit. In many places outside Britain it is not illegal to distil spirits from grain as well as the cruder spirits permitted under the label 'surgical spirit', without paying duty. Janet Momber's father, a chartered accountant with many connections, had given me the bottle of grain alcohol to take with me into camp, and it was great joy to be able to offer one tot each to two or three friends each Christmas and New Year. I do not know of anybody else who possessed any hard liquor in camp. One unobtrusive little man comes especially to memory in connection with our first day of liberation. For the first few weeks of internment he had kept very much to himself, gloomy and reserved. But this state of mind had gradually ameliorated and, though always unobtrusive, he developed into one of the best workers on any job, however unpleasant. Within a few hours of our being able to go outside the camp he was found face down in a ditch, fortunately a dry one. He was carried back to the camp unconscious, and when he came to had the father and mother of all hangovers. The poor little chap had been an alcoholic, but in time forced abstinence in the camp had made a new man of him. Once free, the temptation had been too strong and he had gone straight out and drunk himself stupid on the very lowest kind of liquor—the first he could lay hands on.

What a pity, for him, that internment could not have continued.

CHAPTER FIFTEEN

LAST DAYS IN CHINA

WHILE we remained in Pootung there was adequate transport across the river. Chinese organizations ran a frequent free service of launches, but, although they operated them with much zeal and enthusiasm, they were so anxious to accommodate all comers that shipping and insurance men among the passengers were often terrified and would shut their eyes and pray for safe arrival of the top-heavy craft. However, there were no accidents and those of us who had work to do in the city soon got temporary quarters on the Shanghai side. Somewhat prophetically, I was a guest of the schoolmaster brother-in-law of a wealthy Chinese merchant and was most royally pampered for a week or two. The merchant himself also took in several of us and put on tremendous parties for our benefit, complete with cabaret shows of jugglers, acrobats and other entertainers.

His great house was filled with objects of value, but I think that his most treasured possession was a large glass-fronted cabinet full of innumerable tiny bottles. Ranged in rows, with special lights shining upon them, stood shelf upon shelf of miniature bottles. They were samples of every kind of whisky, gin, brandy and rum that I had ever heard of and many that I had not.

The massive Jardine building was in tolerably good order after its Japanese occupation, but all the central heating had been ripped out for scrap metal, and we had to make do with makeshift paraffin heaters of primitive type.

The excellence of parcels I had received from Musa Herman had worried me a little, as I felt sure that she had spent more over the two and a half years than the U.S. $100 I had left with her. When I asked her about it she burst into tears. Amidst sobs it finally came out. The U.S. $100 had been lost or stolen within a few weeks of the beginning of my internment, and she had continued to support me for all that time out of her own pitifully small and precarious earnings under Japanese rule. If I had been royalty I could have awarded a medal, but I did manage later to bring her a present of some antique English jewellery from home. She had had another problem. Whatever his reasons, her husband had decided to become a Communist Russian subject and their marriage had broken up. I was glad to be able to arrange for her transfer to the Hongkong office of Jardine's, and from there she ultimately managed to get the necessary papers to enable her to emigrate to Australia. I have lost touch with her now, but I believe that she married again and found a new life in her new country. I hope that she may read these lines. God bless her.

By November I felt that I had done all that could be done for the moment, and as my second in command, Jake Kendrew, had had leave in 1939 or 1940, I felt that the fact that my last home leave had been in 1934 entitled me to the first chance of repatriation, despite the fact that Jake was married, with children. So in November I set sail in a large repatriation liner with all my remaining possessions safely stowed in her deep hold. Just before I went on board I learnt that the one man of my department, Mason, who had escaped internment, was still unable to get air passage from England, and that I must therefore go to Hongkong and get things moving there. So I disembarked again two or three days later in Hongkong.

The Shanghai I had left had been found comparatively unspoiled, and the full extent of the impending rivalry between Chiang Kai Shek and Mao Tse Tung had scarcely begun to be felt. But Hongkong had been a scene of battle followed by Japanese military government. The main city of Victoria on the island was not much damaged, but many of the European dwellings on the Peak had been wrecked beyond repair, and the moment that Japanese control had weakened many thousands of half-starved and jobless Chinese were prowling the outlying districts. One of their means of livelihood was a wholesale slaughter of trees, and if it had gone on for long the careful afforestation of about a hundred years would have been ruined. When I brought a bride out eighteen months later, she still had to be warned not to go out wearing rings or wrist-watch. If a ring was hard to shift a sharp slash with a knife would remove the finger quickly enough to enable the thief to make his getaway. Even a wrist could be severed if it facilitated removal of a wrist-watch or bracelet.

The largest population of Jardine's great office building was of rats.

The newly arrived health authorities were anxious to catch them alive for examination for plague, and issued us with wire cage traps for the purpose. But though the drawers of my desk were alive with rats, they none of them deigned to notice the supposedly alluring baits in the traps. Then I observed something. I had been issued with multi-vitamin pills, to which I had become accustomed despite their rather strong smell, which I did not like. But the rats did and the packets in my drawer were constantly being torn and devoured. There was only one answer. Bait the traps with multi-vitamin pills. So we did, and the rats were soon caught.

Most of the survivors of my British civilian friends in Hongkong had long been repatriated, but I had many good friends amongst the Chinese and amongst my own former Portuguese staff, especially Claudio Lisio Rocha, one time head clerk and today in well-earned retirement in Hongkong. It was good to see them all, not too seriously damaged by their war experiences.

It was about three months before Ken Mason arrived, and by this time all organized large-scale repatriation was over.

In the end I went by R.A.F. Transport Command, whose Dakotas and Yorks were by now feeling very tired and looking it. There had been some forced landings in rice fields and forests, and one or two crashed; but I escaped all these and, after a delay of three weeks in Calcutta, where I was lucky enough to find hospitality with my cousin Denis Campbell, got home in about six weeks to England, which I had left in January 1935, after a long leave.

Unfortunately, before I had been home more than a few weeks, poor Jake Kendrew, in Shanghai, began to feel the strain and needed relief. So I flew back and was able to make my little present to Musa Herman before she left Shanghai for good.

But my stint in Shanghai was only about eight months long this time, and although it was apparent that there was still too much administrative chaos to allow of proper use being made of the United States' lavish aid of all kinds to China, there was still no real certainty that Mao was going to oust Chiang.

Unfortunately there was no middle-class cadre of integrity to support anything that the more honest members of Chiang's Government might wish to do. Precious relief supplies were often squandered, left to rot or 'flogged' on the black market.

The real problems of life for the remaining white men in Shanghai were to begin a year or so later, with the advent to power of Mao Tse

Tung, and of this period I have no personal knowledge. I only know that it broke the health of many, including my old friend Robbie.

In October 1947 I got married in England, and from that time my personal and family affairs altogether excluded other considerations and I reluctantly resigned my job in the Far East in May of 1948.

As I write these concluding lines, I find it hard to look back upon these past days without repining. But there is also a feeling somewhat akin, I imagine, to that of servicemen who have been through a long war. Those years, with all their ups and downs, did something for, as well as to, one, and if one is of little account now one could have been less than nothing without them. I am sure that they have also helped me in my present calling of schoolmaster.

Our Far Eastern communities were a great training ground, and we shall be lesser people until we can find some comparable challenge in our future and meet it in a like spirit.

INDEX